Less is More

Less is More

The Art of
Voluntary Poverty

An Anthology of Ancient and
Modern Voices Raised in
Praise of Simplicity

Selected and Edited by Goldian VandenBroeck
with a Foreword by E. F. Schumacher

Inner Traditions
Rochester, Vermont

Inner Traditions International
One Park Street
Rochester, Vermont 05767
Web Site: http://www.gotoit.com

First Inner Traditions edition 1991

ISBN 0-89281-431-4

For permissions to incorporate selections from the works indicated below, grateful acknowledgment is extended to the following publishers, translators, and copyright proprietors:

Doubleday and Company, Inc., New York. From the *Where the Wasteland Ends,* copyright © 1972 by Theodore Roszak. Reprinted by permission of Doubleday & Co., Inc. and Faber and Faber, Ltd.

Harcourt Brace Jovanovich, Inc., New York. Excerpted from the *The Acquisitive Society* by R. H. Tawney, copyright © 1920, by Harcourt Brace Jovanovich, Inc.: renewed 1948, by R. H. Tawney. Reprinted by permission of Harcourt Brace Jovanovich, Inc. and G. Bell and Sons, Ltd.

Harold Arnold Hedges, trans. *Georgic III* by Vergil.

Harper & Row, Publishers, Inc., New York. E. F. Shumacher, *Small Is Beautiful: Economics as if People Mattered* (New York: Harper & Row; London: Blond & Briggs, 1973). Copyright © 1973 by E. F. Schumacher. Reprinted by permission of the publishers; Ivan Illich, *Tools for Conviviality,* New York: Harper & Row; London: Calder and Boyers, Ltd.

Lama Foundation Publications, New Mexico. *The Yellow Book: The Sayinggs of Baba Hari Dass,* 1973.

The Loeb Classical Library, Harvard University Press; William Heinemann, London. From the *Moral Epistles* of Seneca, trans. Richard M. Gummere, 1916, and the *Moral Essays* of Seneca, trans. John W. Basore, 1931.

Macmillian Publishing Company, New York. "Effron Siminsky's Afterdinner Speech" in *Medusa in Gramercy Park* by Horace Gregory. © Horace Gregory 1961.

Pendle Hill Publications, Pendle Hill, Wallingford, Pa. *Functional Poverty* by Mildred Binns Young, Pendle Hill Pamphlet 6, 1939; *Insured By Hope* by Mildred Binns Young, Pendle Hill Pamphlet 90, 1956.

Hilda Neihardt Petri, Missouri. *Black Elk Speaks* by John G. Neihardt, copyright John G. Neihardt 1932 and 1959.

Princeton University Press. *The Romance of the Rose (Roman de la Rose)* by Guillaume de Lorris and Jean de Meun, trans. from the French by Charles Dahlberg (copyright © 1971 by Princeton University Press).

Rainbow Bridge Publications, San Francisco. *The Smiling Forehead* by Hazrat Inayat Khan, 1973.

Library of Congress Cataloging-in-Publication Data

Less is more : the art of voluntary poverty : an anthology of ancient and modern voices raised in praise of simplicity / selected and edited by Goldian VandenBroeck ; with a foreword by E. F. Schumacher.
    p. cm.
Includes index.
ISBN 0-89281-554-X
    1. Poverty—Religious aspects—Christianity—Quotations, maxims, etc.
I. VandenBroeck, Goldian.
BV4647.P6L47 1995
179'.9—dc20

94-44249
CIP

Printed and bound in the United States

10 9 8 7 6 5 4 3 2 1

Distributed to the book trade in Canada by Publishers Group West (PGW), Toronto, Ontario
Distributed to the book trade in the United Kingdom by Deep Books, London
Distributed to the book trade in Australia by Millennium Books, Newtown, N. S. W.
Distributed to the book trade in New Zealand by Tandem Press, Auckland
Distributed to the book trade in South Africa by Alternative Books, Randburg

To My Affluent America

CONTENTS

CONTENTS

Throughout this anthology, a single asterisk at the end of a fragment indicates abridgment of the text. Two asterisks indicate slight rearrangement of the quoted material.

FOREWORD

LESS IS MORE? What is this? Is it the mathematics of *Alice in Wonderland?*

"Take some more tea," the March Hare said to Alice earnestly.
"I've had nothing yet," Alice replied in an offended tone, "so I can't take more."
"You mean, you can't take *less,*" said the Hatter; "it's very easy to take *more* than nothing."

Or is it the logic of the Witches?

"Fair is foul, and foul is fair. . . ."

In terms of straight-line logic or mathematics, it is quite simple: nonsense. But *life,* disconcertingly and reassuringly, is bigger than straight-line logic; it conforms with a kind of *curved* logic which turns things around and often, before you become aware of it, turns them into their opposites.

Pacifists become militants.
Freedom fighters become tyrants.
Blessings become curses.
Labor-saving devices become intolerable burdens.
Help becomes hindrance.
More becomes less.

As an economist, I was lucky enough to learn this many years ago. (It did not seem luck at the time, as most people thought I had gone crazy!) I learned this:

Impermanent are all created things, but some are less impermanent than others. Any system of thought *that recognizes no limits* can manifest itself only in extremely impermanent creations. This is the great

xi

charge to be laid against Materialism and its offspring, modern economics, that they *recognize no limits* and, in addition, would be incapable of observing them if they did. This is the terror of the situation.

Self-imposed limits, voluntary restraint, conscious limitation—these are life-giving and life-preserving forces. The *New Economics* of which we stand in need would be based on the recognition.

> —that economic progress is healthy only "up to a point";
> —that the complication of life is permissible only "up to a point";
> —that the pursuit of efficiency or productivity is good only "up to a point";
> —that the use of nonrenewable resources is wise only "up to a point";
> —that specialization is compatible with human integrity only "up to a point";
> —that the substitution of "scientific method" for common sense is bearable only "up to a point";

and so on and so forth, never forgetting that all these "points" lie far lower on the scale than most people dare to think.

Yes, indeed, the New Economics would be a veritable "Statute of Limitation"—and that means a "Statute of Liberation."

At that time—it was February 1955—I concluded my remarks with the Buddhist formula: "May All Beings Be Happy." How unhappy they have become since those "hard times," more than twenty years ago!

Straight-line logic is easy; computers are very good at it. In humanity, the most logical creatures are small children: They ae wonderfully, almost infallibly *logical.* "More is more, and less is less"—no doubt about it. As we grow older, into maturity (not all of us do so!), we are able to *transcend* straight-line logic, which does not mean losing it but keeping it in its own very modest place. And then (unless there is a case of *arrested development*) we are able to see that *less may be more*—indeed, that less is more when you are already, as an average American, consuming fifty times as much as an average Indian.

Why are we talking about these materialistic trivialities? Only because straight-line logic tends to get in the way of *Truth.* Our lives are made or marred primarily by our personal and suprapersonal relations. "Personal" means our relations with husband, wife, children, relatives, friends, colleagues, etc. "Suprapersonal" means our relations with Purposes, Aims, Aspirations, Ideals, "Powers," "Principalities"—*God.*

Logic does not do much for our personal and suprapersonal relations. But it is, all the same, an indispensable tool for our *material* relations—how to keep the wolf from the door and how to gain a modicum of material security in this uncertain world.

So there is, inquestionable, *straight-line* logic, which we need for living. But there is also a kind of *curved* logic—whereby things require "measure," or they turn into their opposites—to make the living worthwhile.

And the, suddenly, it becomes possible that less is more.

There is no greater joy in life than the discovery of (what in this context I call) *curved logic.* Less is more has the power of *liberating you.* The less you need, the less you need to worry; and the less worry there is, the better are likely to be your personal and suprapersonal relations. You don't *have* to join the rat race; you don't *have* to be a great financial success. If they raise the tax on tobacco, and you don't need tobacco—what is there to worry about?

Life on this earth is not about *consuming as much as we can afford,* but about some very simple things, which can be expressed in very simple words like:

> Do for others what you want others to do for you;
> —Love your neighbor as you love yourself;
> —Prove all things; hold fast that which is good.

Why beat about the bush? *This* is what life is about. *More is more* stands in the way of it. *Less is more,* even though it sounds absurd can show the way. For what we really need is so little that any system of good will can provide it. It follows that it is not so much a matter of "system" but of good will—and this depends on our own inner understanding.

FOREWORD

The VandenBroecks have done a great job for all of us. This anthology, at the very least, shows that we are in the best possible company when we order our lives in accordance with the principle of *voluntary simplicity.*

E. F. Schumacher
1978

1

VOLUNTARY POVERTY
AND
THE MONOPOLY OF VALUES

Fortune is conceivable today only in terms of economic value. The striving of nations and individuals is overwhelmingly geared to the attainment of wealth, regardless of the effect on natural resources and personal integrity. Wealth has become the only means of possession, and man's faculties are increasingly directed toward its accretion, rather than toward the development of these faculties for the sake of creativity. Artistic and philosophic endeavors, until recently, still furnished grounds for the exercise of creative faculties in their own right; these disciplines now stand co-opted into the general economic body: Philosophy and art are academic careers in connection with powerful private interests and institutions.

Only a very small percentage of the wealthy escape the considerable suffering which this Monopoly of Values has infused into civilization. Nor is there any hope for relief through condescending welfare, as the problem is much more a moral than a physical starvation. Poverty is inescapable as long as wealth exists, but there is undoubtedly a natural richness to be achieved by every human individual in his course through life. The striving along an imposed scale of values, the struggle up a narrow ladder of financial ascent jutting out into a void to be filled with the wealthy's retirement problems, this is the structure which begs for alternatives. Yet, as long as money is everything (and this it has become in the bridled popular mind), all faculties will have to remain geared to its attainment, and the steadily increasing demand of the consumer can be filled only by the Treasury printing presses with the disastrous, already strongly felt results.

Among the most regrettable casualties of the competition for the necessarily restricted positions of financial power is the free access to human relations. These deteriorate as intercourse with fellow humans becomes calculated in order to bring adequate return. Contacts are limited to the sphere best thought to further financial rather than cultural, let alone spiritual, advantages, so that the Monopoly of Values held by the mirage of wealth atrophies spontaneous discovery in self and in others until a monolithic structure is achieved where the spirit of man barely manifests itself in stunted outcroppings.

To underline these existing conditions is admittedly easier than to remedy them. The powerful cartel based on the hunger for mostly useless goods can be busted only by the cultivation of alternative values. While the shallowness of received ideas is seen with increasing clarity by younger generations, a dearth of positive replacements is evident. The refusal to participate in the struggle for goods and position tends to lead to strained conditions which become acceptable only by a thorough understanding of Voluntary Poverty. In *The Other America,* Michael Harrington speaks of the intellectual poor, "those of talent and insight who are driven to prefer poverty, to choose it, rather than to submit to the desolation of empty abundance." Yet he points out that in this segment of our society, people have chosen their lot only on a temporary basis, to afford time for their creative aspirations, until they have gained a measure of recognition, or merely to take time off before returning to their place in the society of their fathers. They do not truly choose poverty as the end in itself, as the creative activity per se.

Thus it is by no means an abolition of possession as such that is desirable, but merely a redefinition of the notion of fortune in men's lives. That the time is ripe for such a reevaluation can be seen in the increasing scarcity of those aspects which money *cannot* buy: fresh air, clean water, silence, peace of mind, health, and, above all, freedom in the largest sense of the word. Wealth as a rule is tied to cities, and the pursuit and maintenance of wealth entails participation in their condition. Wealth creates dependency and preoccupation with the fluctuations of markets and currencies, factors beyond any one man's control, and sources of worry concerning loss. Disease trails in the wake of opulent living, of overeating and self-indulgence. Such miseries are known only to the wealthy, and they are relatively absent from the life of good fortune. For this wealth, which we could qualify as inconscient, refers to the possession of goods, property, and money; fortune, to those uncertain benefits of human life which money alone is incapable of insuring. A fortunate man need not be burdened by wealth, and the wealthy are more often than not seen to lead unfortunate lives.

Solutions to the problem of wealth are to be found in the refining of the values which motivate the striving rather than in attempts to abolish possession; it is an effort to infuse consciousness into wealth. Of increasing concern to youth is the structuring of new scales of values, or the reviving of traditional values forgotten in the mad scramble for wealth, and the affirmation of individual values in the face of the herd instinct. Unfortunately, these pursuits must often be relegated to the background of after-hours and "free" time, while the principal efforts go toward survival within the wealth-oriented society. This survival work then has the effect of strengthening the very values which need to be replaced. It must be fully understood that the only attitude insufferable to the inconscient wealth of the Monopoly is the withdrawal from it: The first step toward the eventual dissolution of its acquisitive selfishness is Voluntary Poverty.

The concept of poverty is not immediately attractive in a culture which strives after wealth for its ease, security, ready pleasure of senses and comfort of bones, and considers such striving a valid expression of an ethical life-style. Materialism of all persuasions eventually comes to hail the safety of a status quo in disregard of all requirements of consciousness-in-evolution. Against such received and prefabricated existence, consciousness wills its negation. To this agent, cosmos is a voluntarism of the "no" rather than a creation out of nothing by the "yes." The gods above create by affirmation, as does the beast below; man, being neither and yet partly both, mediates the two. His con-

3

sciousness sports this unique reflexivity spurned by both god and dog as they create their universe directly and immediately by unexamined affirmation, the first as spiritual intuition, the other in the sensed substance of materiality which the lower brain experiences, and which we may experience, if we choose, as our basic contact with existence. Only the exercise of the cerebral cortex, however, can consciously refuse, examine, and mediate, and, in these articulations, human conduct finds its true worth.

The wealthy bungle their lives when they miss the bid of Voluntary Poverty to achieve the ultimate refinement their privileged status allows: to choose their *own* experience within the values that money can command, and not to remain fettered by the monopolistic dictate. With freedom at hand, why should they choose slavery? Given to them is *choice divorced from need,* a most exquisite species. It is the option of Voluntary Poverty to operate within a realm of freedom prone to breed heroic decisions. Is it possible that wealth could be inconscient to the point of squandering such opportunity? This exalted level of choice is within reach of a minority only, and a small minority at that. Yet this minority commands an inordinate share of wealth, and any inroads into this domain would mean a powerful release, and the liberation of important means.

For the general public, such unconditional choice is inconceivable, yet this disfranchisement need not exclude it from the benefits bestowed by our discipline. It merely makes a righteous choice especially meritorious and more rewarding. For Voluntary Poverty could spring into action at the slightest evidence of excess, as soon as basic needs are fulfilled and the unnecessary begins littering our lives. Now, this condition surely is abroad among most households, including a good part of the "American poor." Like the starving woman in India, stretching out an idle, begging hand while her feet smother a tuft of highly nutritious herbs, so our "poor" with their TVs and snowmobiles are often poor only in knowledge and ingenuity, bearing witness to an ignorance imposed once again by the Monopoly of Values. We have become accustomed to pay for our food and not to bypass its industry merely by stooping to pick berries and edible roots. Here is a poverty which no voluntarism can alleviate. It can only point an accusing finger to its cause, the inconscient wealth of civilization, indicted by its lowest and most pitiful effect. But though it cannot be determined where Voluntary Poverty is able first to step forth, still a general region can be recognized where choice becomes possible between the increased burden of ownership and the realization, at the first sign of excess, that a primary objective has been met and that time and opportunity are at hand for exploring some of life's further facets. Only at the very bottom of the spectrum of possession, at the opposite pole of choice without need, is there a minority of the desperately poor in need without choice, where the only possible concern can be for day-to-day survival. Here the time is lacking for reflection, and the space to withdraw, and Voluntary Poverty cannot possibly address itself to this destitution either. Here there can only be a waiting and hoping for an evolving consciousness among more fortunate brothers, a process Voluntary Poverty is certain to accelerate.

Those who will profit most from what this anthology advocates undoubtedly are those who, as the saying goes, have everything; for with their well-cushioned peace of mind, they are at leisure to explore the freedom of simplicity, knowing fully well that if need be, or if will and nerve should fail, the means are in the background for an instant rescue. Commitment to Voluntary Poverty need never be irrevocable or irreversible; it needn't be the total renunciation of a St. Francis, and could today simply take its model from Seneca, who spoke of it as an exercise.

What should be evident by now is that the conscious stand against monopolistic wealth is no destructive opposition, but, if anything, a gentle reeducation. An individualistic point of view which craves no dominion save over itself, this withdrawal from the power of wealth cannot be subverted by political organization. Stepping aside from the striving mass, Voluntary Poverty gains its strength in a privacy filled with Self. It is private to the point of anarchy, which it alone can justify. Indeed, legal and gubernatorial oversight is needed in a milieu of greed, desire, and undue expansion for personal advantage: Voluntary Poverty resides beyond such motives. Yet far from wanting an abolition of wealth, this passive resistance acts as its guardian. Wealth is needed for the exercise of Voluntary Poverty, which thus becomes an extension of wealth and a path to its ultimate understanding. Wherefore Voluntary Poverty feels its calling in a world where wealth is endangered by its own arrogance, and in turn will endanger the world by increasing oppression in order to guarantee its own survival, unless Voluntary Poverty grants it a gentler stay. Shameful indeed would be a bounteous planet which has ceased to yield the concept of plenty!

This, then, is primarily a discipline for the needy rich, among whom a near future shall count all those who have more than enough. Shrinking space and resources on tomorrow's globe, coupled with the growing impatience of groups and nations forced into institutionalized poverty, will make sure that the adventurers of an expansive free enterprise be duly contained. A defense of conscious wealth, of creative and unselfish capital, will be needed, and Voluntary Poverty alone can settle the conflict without upset to the basic rights of freedom. Therefore it is important that the thoughts be presented of individuals who found in this conduct the object so rare and, ironically, so frequently elusive to the rich: satisfaction in their lives.

André VandenBroeck

2

IN PRAISE OF POVERTY

Among us English-speaking peoples especially do the praises of poverty need once more to be boldly sung. We have grown literally afraid to be poor. We despise any one who elects to be poor in order to simplify and save his inner life. If he does not join the general scramble and pant with the money-making street, we deem him spiritless and lacking in ambition. We have lost the power even of imagining what the ancient idealization of poverty could have meant: the liberation from material attachments, the unbribed soul, the manlier indifference, the paying our way by what we are or do and not by what we have, the right to fling away our life at any moment irresponsibly—the more athletic trim, in short, the moral fighting shape.

It is true that so far as wealth gives time for ideal ends and exercise to ideal energies, wealth is better than poverty and ought to be chosen. But wealth does this in only a portion of the actual cases. Elsewhere the desire to gain wealth and the fear to lose it are our chief breeders of cowardice and propagators of corruption. There are thousands of conjunctures in which a wealth-bound man must be a slave, whilst a man for whom poverty has no terrors becomes a freeman. Think of the strength which personal indifference to poverty would give us if we were devoted to unpopular causes. We need no longer hold our tongues or fear to vote the revolutionary or reformatory ticket. Our stocks might fall, our hopes of promotion vanish, our salaries stop, our club doors close in our faces; yet, while we lived, we would imperturbably bear witness to the spirit, and our example would help to set free our generation. The cause would need its funds, but we its servants would be potent in proportion as we personally were contented with our poverty.

I recommend this matter to your serious pondering, for it is certain that the prevalent fear of poverty among the educated classes is the worst moral disease from which our civilization suffers.*

William James, 1842–1910

□

GETTING THE WORD

In the excitement over the unfolding of his scientific and technical powers, modern man has built a system of production that ravishes nature and a type of society that mutilates man. If only there were more and more wealth, everything else, it is thought, would fall into place. Money is considered to be all-powerful; if it could not actually buy non-material values, such as justice, harmony, beauty, or even health, it could circumvent the need for them or compensate for their loss. The development of production and the acquisition of wealth have thus become the highest goals of the modern world in relation to which all other goals, no matter how much lip-service may still be paid to them, have come to take second place.

This is the philosophy of materialism, and it is this philosophy —or metaphysic—which is now being challenged by events. There has never been a time, in any society in any part of the world, without its sages and teachers to challenge materialism and plead for a different order of priorities. The languages have differed, the symbols have varied, yet the message has always been the same: "Seek ye *first* the kingdom of God, and all these things [the material things which you also need] shall be *added* unto you." They shall be added, we are told, here on earth where we need them, not simply in an after-life beyond our imagination. Today, however, this message reaches us not solely from the sages and saints but from the actual course of physical events. It speaks to us in the language of terrorism, genocide, breakdown, pollu-

8

tion, exhaustion. We live, it seems, in a unique period of convergence.

Everywhere people ask: "What can I actually *do?*" The answer is as simple as it is disconcerting: we can, each of us, work to put our own inner house in order. The guidance we need for this work cannot be found in science or technology, the value of which utterly depends on the ends they serve; but it can still be found in the traditional wisdom of mankind.*

E. F. Schumacher, 1973

☐

The present world is divided into those who do not have enough and those who have more than enough, those who are pushed off the road by cars and those who drive them. The have-nots are miserable and the rich anxious to get more. A society whose members know what is enough might be poor, but its members would be equally free. Men with industrially distorted minds cannot grasp the rich texture of personal accomplishments within the range of modern though limited tools. There is no room in their imaginations for the qualitative change that the acceptance of a stable-state industry would mean; a society in which members are free from most of the multiple restraints of schedules and therapies now imposed for the sake of growing tools. Much less do most of our contemporaries experience the sober joy of life in this voluntary though relative poverty which lies within our grasp.

Ivan Illich, 1973

☐

A gentle wind fans the calm night:
A bright moon shines on the high tower.
A voice whispers, but no one answers when I call;
A shadow stirs, but no one comes when I beckon.
A kitchen man brings a dish of lentils:
Wine is there, but I do not fill my cup.
Contentment with poverty is Fortune's best gift:
Riches and Honor are the handmaids of Disaster.

9

LESS IS MORE

Though gold and gems by the world are sought and prized,
To me they seem no more than weeds or chaff.

Fu Hsüan, 3d cent.

□

The cultivation and expansion of needs is the antithesis of wisdom. It is also the antithesis of freedom and peace. Every increase of needs tends to increase one's dependence on outside forces over which one cannot have control, and therefore increases existential fear.

E. F. Schumacher, 1973

□

When a Man from the greatness of his Soul (or an obstinate Vanity, which will do as well), resolving to subdue his Appetites in good earnest, refuses all the Offers of East and Luxury that can be made to him, and embracing a voluntary Poverty with Chearfulness, rejects whatever may gratify the Senses and actually sacrifices all his Passions to his pride in acting this Part, the Vulgar, far from contemning him, will be ready to deify and adore him. How famous have the *Cynick* Philosophers made themselves only by refusing to dissimulate and make use of Superfluities? Did not the most Ambitious Monarch the World ever bore, condescend to visit *Diogenes* in his tub, and return to a study'd Incivility, the highest Compliment a Man of his Pride was able to make?

Bernard Mandeville, 1670?–1733

□

Legend has it Diogenes (412?–323 B.C.) was sunning himself in front of his tub when Alexander, on a visit to Corinth, sought him out. When the philosopher saw so much company approaching, he bestirred himself slightly and vouchsafed to look at the famous general. The Macedonian told him to utter a wish and it would be granted. "Stand out of my light" was the reply. So impressed was the young world-conqueror by this man who took so little notice of him, that as he departed he said to his followers, "Were I not Alexander, I would choose to be Diogenes."

☐

Would you like to know what a truly poor man is? That man is truly poor of spirit who can do without everything that is not necessary. Hence the man who sat naked in a large barrel spoke to the great Alexander, who had the entire world under him: "I am," he said, "much greater than you, for I have despised more things than you have possessed. What you consider great to possess is too small for me to despise." He is much happier who can do without everything and does not need anything, than the one who has possessed all things and needs them. That man is the best who can do without that which he does not need.

Meister Eckhart, 1260?–1327

☐

Aspire to simple living? That means, aspire to fulfill the highest human destiny. All of men's agitations for greater justice and more light have been also movements toward a simpler life; the simplicity of olden times, in manners, art and ideas, still keeps its incomparable value, only because it achieved the setting forth in high relief of certain essential sentiments and certain permanent truths. If it is impossible for us to be simple in the forms our fathers used, we may remain simple, or return to simplicity, in their spirit. Our ways are not their ways, but the journey's end remains in truth the same.

Too many hampering futilities separate us from that ideal of the true, the just, and the good, that should warm and animate our hearts. All this brushwood, under the pretext of sheltering us and our happiness, has ended by shutting out our sun. When shall we have the courage to meet the delusive temptations of our complex and unprofitable life with the sage's challenge: "Out of my light"?*

Charles Wagner, 1895

□

As the merchant gladly takes money from his income to add to his capital, so is the great man very willing to lose particular powers and talents so that he can gain in the elevation of his life. The opening of the spiritual senses disposes men ever to greater sacrifices, to leave their signal talents, their best means and skills of procuring a present success, their power and their fame, to cast all things behind, in the insatiable thirst for divine communications. Diogenes, Socrates, and Epaminondas, are gentlemen of the best blood, who have chosen the condition of poverty, when that of wealth was equally open to them.*

Ralph Waldo Emerson, 1803–1882

□

Savage man and civilized man differ so much at bottom in point of inclinations and passions, that what constitutes the supreme happiness of the one would reduce the other to despair. The first sighs for nothing but repose and liberty. On the contrary, the citizen always in motion is perpetually sweating and toiling, and racking his brains to find out occupations still more laborious. . . . In fact, the real source of all those differences, is that the savage lives within himself, whereas the citizen, constantly beside himself, knows only how to live in the opinion of others; insomuch that it is, if I may say so, merely from their judgment that he derives the consciousness of his own existence. . . . In short, ever inquiring of others what we are, and never daring to question ourselves on so delicate a point, we have nothing to show for ourselves but a deceitful and frivolous exterior, honor without virtue, reason without wisdom, and pleasure without happiness. It is sufficient that I have proved that this is not the original condition of man, and that it is merely the spirit of society, since it is evidently against the law of nature that infancy should command old age, folly conduct wisdom, and a handful of men should be ready to choke with superfluities, while the famished multitude want the commonest necessaries of life.*

Jean Jacques Rousseau, 1712–1778

□

Most of the luxuries, and many of the so called comforts of life, are not only not indispensable, but positive hindrances to the elevation of mankind. With respect to luxuries and comforts, the wisest have even lived a more simple and meagre life than the poor. The ancient philosophers, Chinese, Hindoo, Persian, and Greek, were a class than which none has been poorer in outward riches, none so rich in inward. None can be an impartial or wise observer of human life but from the vantage ground of what *we* should call voluntary poverty.

Henry David Thoreau, 1817–1862

□

It is well for a man to be frugal, to abstain from luxury, to possess no treasure, nor to covet this world's goods. Since olden times there has rarely been a sage who was wealthy.

Yoshida Kenkō, 1283–1350

□

Though there have been previous ages as lustful for wealth and ostentation as our own, there have also been ages when money-getting and millionaire-envying were not the sole preoccupations of the average man. And such an age will undoubtedly succeed to ours. Few things would surprise me less, in social life, than the upspringing of some anti-luxury movement, the formation of some league or guild among the middling classes (where alone intellect is to be found in quantity), the members of which would bind themselves to stand aloof from all the great, silly, banal, ugly, and tedious *luxe*-activities of the time, and not to spend more than a certain sum per annum on eating, drinking, covering their bodies, and being moved about like parcels from one spot of the earth's surface to another. Such a movement would, and will, help towards the formation of an opinion which would condemn lavish expenditure on personal satisfactions as bad form. However, the shareholders of grand hotels, restaurants and racecourses of all sorts, together with popular singers and barristers, etc., need feel no immediate alarm. The movement is not yet.

Arnold Bennett, 1867–1931

☐

As long as the consumer could afford to buy only the necessary food, clothing, and shelter and had little left over for "discretionary spending"—purchases of nonessentials—only a decrease in his income could cause him to curtail his rate of spending. Today there is no reason why consumers should behave mechanistically in response to changes in income; they may themselves initiate changes. Consumers might decide that they wished to delay their purchases.

There is a second possibility, which has been very little discussed. The desire of the consumer for additional goods and a higher standard of living might decline. People would then come to spend less time and effort augmenting their incomes. Many commentators claim that the contempt for material goods is already more widely spread than is generally realized and that a real revolution in this field can be expected within a relatively limited time.

Robert Theobald, 1961

☐

POVERTY: WHAT IT IS, WHAT IT IS NOT

"Just give me a chance," I hear people say. "Just let me get my debts paid. Just let me get a few of the things I need and then

14

I'll begin to think of poverty and its rewards. Meanwhile, I've had nothing but." But these people do not understand the difference between inflicted poverty and voluntary poverty; between being the victims and the champions of poverty. I prefer to call the one kind *destitution,* reserving the word *poverty* for what Saint Francis called "Lady Poverty."

Dorothy Day, 1963

□

We make the word poverty a synonym for calamity, but it is in truth a source of happiness, and however much we may regard it as a calamity, it remains a source of happiness still.

Count Leo Tolstoy, 1828–1910

□

All plenty which is not my God is poverty to me.

St. Augustine, 354–430

□

Poverty is your treasure. Never exchange it for an easy life.

Zengetzu, T'ang Dynasty

□

It was asked of Syncletica of blessed memory if to have nothing is a perfect good. And she said, "It is a great good for those who are able. . . . Even as stout garments trodden underfoot and turned over in the washing are made clean and white, so is a strong soul made steadfast by voluntary poverty."*

Sayings of the Fathers

□

LESS IS MORE

For poverty's a splendor from within....

Rainer Maria Rilke, 1875–1926

□

Give me the poverty that enjoys true wealth.

Thoreau, 1817–1862

□

As touching the effect of money on the efficient ordering of the human machine, there is happily no necessity to inform those who have begun to interest themselves in the conduct of their own brains that money counts for very little in that paramount affair. Nothing that really helps towards perfection costs more than is within the means of every person who reads these pages. The expenses connected with daily meditation, with the building up of mental habits, with the practice of self-control and of cheerfulness, with the enthronement of reason over the rabble of primeval instincts—these expenses are really, you know, trifling. . . . All that is required is ingenuity in one's expenditure. And much ingenuity with a little money is vastly more profitable and amusing than much money without ingenuity.*

Arnold Bennett, 1867–1931

□

Our arms are holy poverty, which was so greatly esteemed and so strictly observed by our holy fathers at the beginning of the foundation of our Order. (Someone who knows about this told me that they never kept anything from one day to the next.) . . .

These arms must appear on our banners and at all costs we must keep this rule—as regards our house, our clothes, our speech, and (which is much more important) our thoughts. So long as this is done, there need be no fear, with the help of God, that religious observances in this house will decline, for, as Saint Clare

16

said, the walls of poverty are very strong. It was with these walls, she said, and with those of humility, that she wished to surround her convents.*

St. Teresa of Avila, 1515–1582

☐

Poverty is my pride.

Muhammad, 570–632

☐

Destitution is almost always confused with poverty; this mistake comes from the fact that destitution and poverty are neighbors. No doubt they are neighbors, but situated on either side of a boundary. All is misery within the boundary; misery of uncertainty or misery of certain destitution. The first zone beyond the boundary is that of poverty. After which rise, tier upon tier, the successive zones of riches.

Many economic, moral, social, or even political problems could be clarified in advance if the consideration of this boundary were introduced—or rather, if this consideration were recognized as a duty.

Destitution is the entire domain within this boundary. Poverty begins beyond it and ends early. Thus destitution and poverty are neighbors. They are closer neighbors in quantity than certain riches are neighbors of poverty. If one evaluates according to quantity alone, a rich man is much farther removed from a poor man than a poor man is removed from a destitute man. But between destitution and poverty a boundary arises. And the poor man is separated from the destitute man by a difference of quality, of nature.

Charles Péguy, 1873–1913

☐

There is a genuine poor man and also a spurious and falsely named poor man, the one poor in spirit, the inner personal poverty, and the other poor in worldly goods, the outward alien poverty.

Clement of Alexandria, 150?–220?

☐

For us, Poverty does not mean scorn for goods and property. It means the strict limitation of goods that are for personal use. It means the opposite of the reckless abuse and misuse of property that leaves our country spotted with the graveyards of broken and abandoned machinery. It means a horror of war, first because it ruins human life and health and the beauty of the earth, but second because it destroys goods that could be used to relieve misery and hardship and to give joy. It means a distaste even for the small carelessnesses that we see prevalent, so that beautiful and useful things are allowed to become dirty and battered through lack of respect for them. We have in America in this day the strange spectacle of many comely and well-equipped small homes kept in a state of neglect and disorder that would shock peasants anywhere.

For a long time I have preferred the word "poverty" to "simplicity" because I have felt it was less ambiguous. Simplicity does not define itself as to degree. It seems to define the manner in which possessions are used and the kind of possessions they are, rather than the scale of possessions. One can have large possessions and still be simple in the use of them; in poverty the possessions themselves have been let go, or never accumulated.

But "poverty" too can be an ambiguous word. First of all, let us not confuse it with "destitution." It is not possible to idealize destitution. The persistence of destitution anywhere in the world is what most strongly challenges a high standard of living anywhere else.

Let us grant that multitudes spend their lives in poverty, or with moderate possessions, without ever receiving the gift of simplicity, which is the beatitude reserved for the poor in spirit. Nevertheless, poverty freely accepted does release people from some of the worst strains of our civilization, with the complicated forms of unhappiness that these bring with them.*

Mildred Binns Young, 1956

IN PRAISE OF POVERTY

☐

Assuredly he who possesses great store of riches is no nearer happiness than he who has what suffices for his daily needs, unless luck attend upon him, and so he continues in the enjoyment of all his good things to the end of his life. For many of the wealthiest men have been unfavored of fortune, and many whose means were moderate, have had excellent luck.

Solon to Croesus, 6th cent. B.C.

☐

Do not only look at the much-vaunted splendor of the men you envy and admire, but open and draw, as it were, the gaudy curtain of their pomp and show, and step inside. You will see that they have much to vex and distress them.

Plutarch, 46? B.C.–A.D. 120

☐

Poverty, when measured by the natural purpose of life, is great wealth, but unlimited wealth is great poverty.

Epicurus, 342?–270 B.C.

☐

We were not poor, we just didn't have any money.

Bruce Barton, 1886–1967

☐

Before considering the question of a practical return to the simplicity of which we dream, it will be necessary to define simplicity in its very essence.

We are tempted to believe that simplicity presents certain external characteristics by which it may be recognized, and in which it really consists. Simplicity and lowly station, plain dress, a modest dwelling, slender means, poverty—these things seem to go together. Nevertheless, this is not the case.

Need we say that one does not rise to this point of view without a struggle? The spirit of simplicity is not an inherited gift, but the result of a laborious conquest. Plain living, like high thinking, is simplification.

No class has the prerogative of simplicity; no dress, however humble in appearance, is its unfailing badge. Its dwelling need not be a garret, a hut, the cell of the ascetic, nor the lowliest fisherman's bark. Under all the forms in which life vests itself, in all social positions, at the top as at the bottom of the ladder, there are people who live simply, and others who do not. We do not mean by this that simplicity betrays itself in no visible signs, has not its own habits, its distinguishing tastes and ways; but this outward show, which may now and then be counterfeited, must not be confounded with its essence and its deep and wholly inward source. *Simplicity is a state of mind.**

Charles Wagner, 1895

□

We can have a society of abundance in the rich countries before the end of the twentieth century. But abundance is not a specific quantity of goods; it is a state of mind, a set of attitudes. Man could *never* produce *all* he could use; abundance depends on the *acceptance* of a reasonable standard of living.*

Robert Theobald, 1961

□

In present parlance, a society is civilized when it is affluent enough to move its outhouses indoors, to do away with physical effort, to heat and cool its homes with electric power, and to own more automobiles, freezers, telephones, and gadgets for leisure time than it really needs or can enjoy. Gentle behavior, humane laws, limitations on war, a high level of purpose and conduct have disappeared from the concept.*

René Dubos, 1972

□

Civilization is a limitless multiplication of unnecessary necessaries.

Mark Twain, 1835–1910

□

The essence of civilization consists not in the multiplication of wants but in their deliberate and voluntary renunciation.

Mohandas K. Gandhi, 1869–1948

□

True affluence is not *needing* anything.

Keith Murray, 1970

□

Said the abbot Hyperichius, "The treasure house of the monk is voluntary poverty. Wherefore, my brother, lay up thy treasure in heaven."

Sayings of the Fathers

□

Our Lord Jesus Christ begins His Sermon on the Mount with the words, *Blessed are the poor in spirit.* That is, Blessed are not only those who, by embracing voluntary poverty, have left all to follow Jesus . . . but also those whose hearts are detached from earthly goods, who, being poor, bear their poverty without murmuring or impatience, or who, being rich, have no *spirit* of *riches*, no haughtiness, no pride, none of that insatiable, devouring self-love which is ever seeking its own. To such as are thus truly poor in spirit belongs the right to eternal happiness.*

Jacques Bénigne Bossuet, 1627–1704

□

"Blessed are the poor in spirit," our Lord says so remarkably. Poor is he who has nothing. "Poor in spirit" means: As the eye is poor and devoid of color but receptive of all colors, so he who is poor in spirit is receptive of all spirit. Now God is the Spirit of spirits. The fruit of the spirit is love, joy and peace. To be stripped, poor, to have nothing, to be empty—this transforms nature; the void causes water to climb mountains and performs many other marvels of which we would not now speak.

Eckhart, 1260?–1327

□

What right have you to take the word "wealth" which originally meant "well-being" and degrade and narrow it by confining it to certain sorts of material objects measured by money?

John Ruskin, 1819–1900

□

VOLUNTARY: THE IMPERATIVE OF CHOICE

In the end excesses will be self-defeating. In view of this do we have to wait till defeat is imposed upon us? It would be wiser to come to terms while we still have some choice.

We do have the choice, at least to some extent. We can set limits, if we can control ourselves, to the quantity of humanity so that a margin is left on the earth for something besides bread and human beings. We can decide whether the margin for life and beauty other than our own shall be large or small. We can choose between quality and quantity in all things. The choice is ours and so in the course of time, if we look beyond our own individual life time, will be the consequences.*

N. J. Berrill, 1955

□

IN PRAISE OF POVERTY

From having come this far into the twentieth century with economists interpreting the alleged increase in our real income as "enrichment" or, more sagaciously, as "an extension of the area of choice," and then to be told almost daily that we have no choice; that if we are to pay our way in the world we must work harder than ever . . . this is enough surely to tax the credulity of any being whose judgment has not yet been swept away by torrents of economic exhortation.

But of course we have a choice, a wide range of choice!*

E. J. Mishan, 1970

☐

When I don suitable attire, or walk as I should, or dine as I ought to dine, it is not my dinner or my walk or my dress that are goods, but the deliberate choice which I show in regard to them, as I observe, in each thing I do, a mean that conforms with reason.

Lucius Annaeus Seneca, 4 B.C.?–A.D. 65
Epistle XCII

☐

I believe that this experience of freedom to choose is one of the deepest elements underlying change. . . . It is the burden of being responsible for the self who chooses to be. It is the recognition of a person that he is an emerging process, not a static end product.*

Carl A. Rogers, 1964

☐

Neither a fixed abode nor a form that is thine alone nor any function peculiar to thyself have we given thee, Adam, to the end that according to thy longing and according to thy judgment thou mayest have and possess what abode, what form, and what functions thou thyself shalt desire. The nature of all other beings is limited and constrained within the bounds of laws pre-

23

scribed by Us. Thou constrained by no limits, in accordance with thine own free will, in whose hand We have placed thee, shalt ordain for thyself the limits of thy nature. . . . With freedom of choice and with honor, as though the maker and molder of thyself, thou mayest fashion thyself in whatever shape thou shalt prefer. Thou shalt have the power to degenerate into the lower forms of life, which are brutish. Thou shalt have the power, out of thy soul's judgment, to be reborn into the higher forms, which are divine.

Pico della Mirandola, 1463–1494

☐

When I came into the country, and being seated among silent trees, and meads and hills, had all my time in mine own hands, I resolved to spend it all, whatever it cost me, in the search of happiness, and to satiate that burning thirst which Nature had enkindled in me from my youth. In which I was so resolute, that I chose rather to live upon ten pounds a year, and to go in leather clothes, and feed upon bread and water, so that I might have all my time clearly to myself, than to keep many thousands per annum in an estate of life where my time would be devoured in care and labor. And God was so pleased to accept of that desire, that from that time to this, I have had all things plentifully provided for me, without any care at all, my very study of Felicity making me more to prosper, than all the care in the whole world. So that through His blessing I live a free and a kingly life as if the world were turned again into Eden, or much more, as it is at this day.

Thomas Traherne, 1637?–1674

☐

Mankind has indeed a certain freedom of choice: it is not bound by trends, by the "logic of production," or by any other fragmentary logic. But it is bound by truth. Only in the service of truth is perfect freedom, and even those who today ask us "to free our imagination from bondage to the existing system" fail to point the way to the recognition of truth.

E. F. Schumacher, 1973

□

Truth alone is the austerity of the *Kali Yuga*.

Sri Ramakrishna, 1836–1886

□

One not only chooses poverty, one loves it.

Martha Shaw, 1976

□

As the hawk becomes unhappy if the food is taken away from him and happy if he gives it up himself, so the man who gives up everything voluntarily is happy.

Kapila, 8th cent. B.C.

□

Any attempt at poverty which is not voluntary defeats the end which is freedom—freedom from the slavery of matter.

Swāmī Vivekānanda, 1863–1902

□

Less is more.

Ludwig Mies van der Rohe, 1886–1969

□

More! More! is the cry of a mistaken soul.

William Blake, 1757–1827

LESS IS MORE

□

It is vain to do with more what can be done with less.

William of Occam, 1300?–1350?
"Occam's Razor"

□

The more we have the less we own.

Eckhart, 1260?–1327

□

Let your soul turn always
Not to desire the more, but the less.

St. John of the Cross, 1542–1591

□

One gains by losing and loses by gaining.

Tao Te Ching

□

Carry *"Nothing"* in the heart. It is *"Everything."*

The Ten Virtues in Japanese
Flower Arrangement

□

Amazingly small means lead to extraordinarily satisfactory results.

E. F. Schumacher, 1973

□

26

IN PRAISE OF POVERTY

Much can be done with little.
The exclusion of the trivial must be effected.

Robert Henri, 1923

☐

Always bear this in mind, that very little indeed is necessary for living a happy life.

Marcus Aurelius, 121–180

☐

The love of poverty makes us kings.

St. Bernard of Clairvaux, 1091–1153

☐

THE DIRECT WAY

This way of poverty is a way in which you attain all your desires. Whatsoever thing you have longed for will certainly come to you on this way, whether it be the shattering of armies, victory over the enemy, capturing kingdoms, reducing people to subjection, excelling your contemporaries, elegance of speech, and all that is like to this. When you have chosen the way of poverty, all these things come to you. No man has ever traveled on this way and had cause to complain, contrary to other ways.

When, however, you have entered the world of poverty and practiced it, God most High bestows upon you kingdoms and worlds that you never imagined; and you become quite ashamed of what you longed for and desired at first. "Ah," you cry. "With such a thing in existence, how could I seek after such mean things?"*

Jālāl al-Dīn Rūmī, 1207–1273

27

3

LADY POVERTY:
THE TRADITION

Since Hindu fakirs, Buddhist monks, and Mohammedan dervishes unite with Jesuits and Franciscans in idealizing poverty as
the loftiest individual state, it is worthwhile to examine into the
spiritual grounds for such a seemingly unnatural opinion.

William James, 1842–1910

□

"He who is willingly poor is free, and without the cares of this
world's goods," says Ruysbroeck, going straight to the heart of
all that has ever been written about poverty.

In search of such liberation, men have always abandoned home
and wealth either with the inner renunciation of detachment or
in holy vagabondage: The bravest voyages in the world have
been made for Poverty.

Ancient indeed is the belief that a man must disencumber his
life of all belongings and minimize his needs in order to tap the
treasures of self. The idea comes down the ages of spiritual break-
through speeded by this deliberate dispossession. It is the lineage
of wisdom designed to release spirit from matter's dominance.

From Tibetan snows to Egyptian sands, from the Cynic's tub to
Walden, men and women alike have elaborated the high-vibrat-
ing tradition of Voluntary Poverty, the ultimate wish-fulfilling
jewel.

Arrayed in a gamut of skins and togas, saffron robes, burlap
tunics, esoteric patches, djellabas, dhotis, Gandhi homespun,

dungarees, or in the full sun of the naked *sannyasin,* their ranks include those whose common dress conceals a Franciscan cord, or its mental equivalent.

Binding these motley, far-flung seekers is their aim of simplicity, the better to live an essential life near the bone, where it is sweetest, and where most meaning might be found in the round of daily existence. Not theirs the extremes of mortifying austerities, but the Middle Way's easy restraint which enjoys a frugal plenty, pruning all superfluous interests and property which dissipate the precious creative energies. Thus has been perfected the art of refusing.

Simultaneously coined with its reverse affirmation of life, the *via negativa* abstains from the luxury of ego and its self-detracting sense of ownership. In passive resistance to a mercantile technocracy which consumes its consumers, it is the dread adversary of Mammon.

The essence of this poverty is a state of mind on which neither rich nor poor have the monopoly.

Every movement that humanity has made toward enlightenment and justice is in reality a movement toward simplicity of life. Many of these movements inflamed whole populations, for the powerful acquisitive instinct is checked not only by precept but impressive example, and their names illuminate the mists of history: Orphics, forest-dwellers, Pythagoreans, Stoics, Spartans, Essenes, Therapeutae, Gymnosophists, bhikkus, Sufis, Gnostic Illuminati, Poor Men of Lyons, Humble Men of Lombardy, Poor Clares, Béguines, Albigensians, the Perfect among the Cathares, Dominicans, Carmelites, Carthusians, Hospitalers, Teutonic Knights, Capuchins, and those warrior-banker-monks, the Knights Templar; mystical hermits of all ages and holy men of the inner city—the worker pauper-priests; Quakers, Shakers, and Amish, and all their guiding lights; God's fools and athletes, known and unknown; the Prince Siddhartha, Muhammad, Apollonius of Tyana, John Golden-Mouth Chrysostom, Arnold of Brescia, Joachim of Flora, Origen, Alcuin, the all-giving Elizabeth of Hungary, Peter Waldo, Philip Neri, Ramon Lull, Charles de Foucauld, George Fox, the gallant Bapu, Peter Maurin, and today's Danilo Dolci, Lanza del Vasto, Dorothy

Day . . . divine *ad infinitum* of Poverty's lovers, still alive and recognizable in the style of their descendants.

□

The voluntary embracing of poverty, therefore, by no means originated with Saint Francis of Assisi, but the idealized love of the *Lady* dovetailed monk, troubadour, and knight, and Francis embodied all three of these great medieval types, which makes for his indelible afterimage, his lingering overtones.

"Glowing as the light bearer and as the morning star, was Francis seen to arise." Thus begins an early account of the holy poet who in his twenty-fourth year, at the thirteenth century's dawning, began to woo that most difficult of brides, the Lady Poverty.

As the son of a prosperous merchant, Francesco da Bernardone seemed born to be a worldly favorite. Carefree, artistic, fond of gleaming armor and fine horses, he was the admiration of all, unsurpassed in wit and song, and in softly flowing attire, for he was very rich.

By his mother he was early versed in the repertoire of heroic ballads—*chansons de geste,* bestiaries and chivalric fairy-tales that filled the medieval ear. For she hailed from Provence, home of the troubadours, where the very idea of "Lady" first flowered in Europe, hothouse that it was of the Courts of Love whose specific function was Love's definition and its rules, the dialectic of *ars amandi,* elevating love to the heights of a rite and code of life.

Like a boon brought back by returning crusaders was Islam's imago of woman as idol and muse. Enshrined on a Moorish pedestal of chaste admiration, the *Dame* inspired outrageous acts of prowess in jousting and verse. Gentlemen vied in composing subtly erotic praises of the lady to whom the ascetic knight swore fealty.

This rare rose of an ideal, once transplanted in France, took, spreading like a blush over Europe, proliferating in all shades of Gothic genius, each designed to fire such an imagination as possessed Francis. Thus instilled with his mother's memorized dowry of Provençal music and myth, the talented youth was finely tuned to his time. But intimations of his destiny strangely interrupted his role as the popular Master of Revels.

Once, as if sunstruck, he seemed immobilized, and his friends mockingly inquired if he were lovesick. "Truly have ye spoken," he responded, "for I thought of taking unto me a bride nobler and richer and fairer than ever ye have seen." His companions jeered but remembered his reply when the bride turned out to be Ma-Donna Poverty.

A business trip to Rome found him exchanging clothes with a beggar, and then one day, encountering a leper on the road and reacting with his customary revulsion, he prepared to throw a coin when compassion overwhelmed him and he dismounted, handed the man the money and embraced him. "And when I left, what had seemed to me nauseous was changed into sweetness of body and soul," he relates in his Testament.

From then on, he frequented the destitute and initiated the scandal of his lavish alms-giving. Eventually his father complained, "He cannot refuse a poor man. He sells my silks and distributes the money." And when the outraged merchant brought his prodigal son before the Bishop of Assisi to compel him to renounce his patrimony, Francis showed himself willing to do so.

"My lord, I will not only give him his money, but the clothes he provided me as well," and before the spiritual court, proceeded to disrobe, disclosing beneath his costly garments a hard hair shirt. It was as if he were defrocking himself of the world, and the Bishop wept at this unprecedented renunciation, wrapping Francis in the folds of his mantle until a workman's tunic could be found.

Thus shedding family, fortune, and ambition, outwardly becoming his own man, Francis was now the captive of his ideal. In truth it was his marriage day, that April of 1207. At last, in high mysterious espousals, he could publicly wed the poverty he coveted. For, devoutly enamoured, he had long been drawn to the untouchable beloved who made all other women his sisters. But his surrender came into focus when he disinherited himself, and in this freedom found his deepest yearning.

Well might Francis desire that enchantress who gives back manyfold all she takes away. Unknown and fecund treasure, she had revealed herself to him as the one sure condition of liberty. Bhakti that he was, a natural practitioner of the yoga of Love, he knew pious rapture in allegiance to the image whose severe beauty was his greatest poetry. His inborn romanticism richly adorned the stark idea, thus awakening an antique goddess.

"I am not new, but ancient and full of days," she tells us herself in the *Sacrum Commercium,* that supernatural scenario of the Holy Marriage between Francis and Madonna Poverty. "In Paradise I was in Man, and of his Essence when he was naked. Very joyful was I, entertaining him at all times, for possessing nothing he belonged wholly to God." When Adam, evicted to live by the sweat of his brow, gives himself up to multiplying his labors whereby he might become rich, Lady Poverty leaves him. As Penia, she gives herself to Poros, the Plenty who sires her own son, Eros. But as Christ's widow, until this wedding, she found no faithful mate. Such lovers as Francis are rare in any age.

What was revolutionary about his concept was how literally he interpreted the Sermon on the Mount. From the day its phrases struck home as a command, he abandoned all but breeches and the tunic which he girded with a cord, thrice-knotted in honor of the Trinity, and as a sign that his body, like a beast—Brother Ass, he called it—required to be led by a halter. In fashioning this habit, he metamorphosed the dashing cavalier into the barefoot, empty-handed "Poverello," henceforth leading an almost extravagantly simple life. His purpose was nothing less than imitation of the daring peripatetic of the Gospels, and its ritual was poverty: the sacrament of liberation.

"Beloved Lady Poverty!" he vowed, "however low in the judgment of men may be thine extraction, I esteem thee, since my Master wed thee." How could he better have revealed his vision? For to found an Order was not his intent. Rather was it to inspire a wandering spiritual knighthood to champion his Lady, a new league of paupers who would protect and glorify the universally most despised of human conditions. Willing to take their chances—at feasting on kitchen crusts, at sleeping under a hedge, uncomplaining of hardship—they formed an army of Gothic yogis: the *Friars Minor,* so called by their inventor to ensure they might never consider themselves more than *that.* They were soon seen everywhere, earning their food by the work of their hands, accepting nothing more than they needed, and never touching money, which Francis called "a venomous serpent." He taught a new attitude toward manual labor, recognizing its relationship with prayer and fellowship.

Released from the shackles of providing for superfluous needs, untrammeled by property, the brethren were made free of the world and the world, in turn, became their spacious monastery. The Franciscan demonstrated that such a state may furnish dignity and happiness. Indeed, the sign of true vocation in the company of Francis was *joie de vivre.*

The inner joy he radiated, together with the power of his idea and the taste of *la libertà francischina,* drew multitudes to this pied piper of a saint. Whereas Plato never found fifty families to realize his ideal Republic, the charismatic Francis, at the end of eleven years, numbered a following of fifty thousand men and women.

Many were those he deterred from actually joining him. Conceiving the ideal of a spiritual elite united by a Rule of Moderation, for them he created the Third Order. Designed to assist ordinary people to be ordinary with an extraordinary exultation, to share in the Franciscan movement without leaving home, it still remains a dynamic attempt of ascetic penetration into everyday life.

Many were aristocrats, the flower of chivalry, surfeited with wealth and hot for certainties, ready to enter the lists for Lady Poverty—for the true knight abandons the world. Scattered abroad to raise her standard, they went honeycombing Europe, seeking to ensure that anyone who met them by chance should have a spiritual adventure.

The twentieth century finds Francis nominated as the patron saint of ecology, for it was no accident that he sang his "Canticle to the Sun" under open skies, and preached his overflowing love for all life to the creatures of field and forest. The wild wolf

of Gubbio, the ungovernable ass of Trevi, birds, squirrels, and
foxes all seemed to understand him, and now, in the unrenew-
able resource of our day, so must we.

☐

... Between Tupino and the stream that drops from the hill chosen by
the blessed Ubaldo, a fertile slope hangs down from a lofty
mount ...

From this slope, where most it breaks the steepness of decline, was born
into the world a sun, even as ours doth at times rise from the
Ganges ...

Not yet was he far distant from his rising when he began to make the
earth to feel from his great power, a certain strengthening:

for in his youth for such a lady did he rush into war against his father,
to whom, as unto death, no one unbars the gate of his good
pleasure;

and in the spiritual court that had rule over him, and in his father's
presence he was united to her, and then from day to day loved her
more strongly.

She, reft of her first husband, a thousand and a hundred years and more,
despised, obscure, even till he stood before her without invita-
tion ...

and naught availed her to have been so constant and undaunted, that
she, when Mary stayed below, mounted the Cross with Christ.

But, lest I should proceed too covertly, Francis and Poverty as these
two lovers do thou now accept in speech made plain.

Their harmony and joyous semblance made love and wonder and tender
looks the cause of sacred thoughts. . . .*

Dante, 1265–1321

☐

Breaking barriers by means of renouncing wealth suggests a mere
negation which was foreign to his nature. Francis' strength lay
in staunch affirmation. So, troubadour that he was, he created a
noble lady to whom he could swear allegiance. This lady, feared
and despised by all, he would make his wife and serve with courage and fidelity—the Lady Poverty.

LADY POVERTY: THE TRADITION

All the imagery of chivalry and courtly love was then evoked to give this allegorical lady reality for Francis and his friars. No service was too servile to perform at her injunction; indeed, service to her was an honored privilege. Did not the great ladies presiding over tournaments throw to their knights their scarves and the sleeves of their fine garments to wear in jousting? So with an equal loyalty would the friars wear ragged, patched habits in their knightly enterprises for Lady Poverty's sake. Was she homeless and a beggar? So would they be in order to be worthy of her company. By their very squalor, then, they were knighted and in her presence ennobled.

Joan Mowat Erikson, 1970

☐

When a man, adapted like St. Francis to the age in which he lived, adapted (I mean) by birth and position, resolves to find his pleasure in poverty and all that poverty means and entails, do we not feel that his must be a soul filled with contempt for all that we think most desirable and most worthy of appreciation? Look at the picture which has been drawn for us from the life. Here is Francis, the rich merchant of Assisi, who has been sent by his father to Rome to negotiate matters of business, standing in the open street engaged in conversation with a poor man! What can the young merchant have in common with people of this sort? What kind of business could he possibly transact with such an individual? What bargain can he be thinking of driving with a beggar? What bargain? Why, the best in the world! He wants the beggar's coat in exchange for his own, rags instead of a sound substantial garment; and see his smiling face, his air of satisfaction, almost of triumph, as he parts with kindly words from the poor man, who goes on his way in bewilderment and scarcely knows himself in this elegant dress. . . .

But before passing on to consider his other actions, we must try to disabuse ourselves of that foolish admiration of riches in which we have been brought up. . . .

Bossuet, 1627–1704

LESS IS MORE

☐

If we had any possessions, we should need weapons and laws to defend them.

St. Francis of Assisi, 1182–1226

☐

Placed in the vale of tears, that blessed father set at naught the common paltry wealth of the sons of men, and in his ambition to attain a more exalted height longed after Poverty with all his heart. Considering that she was the familiar friend of the Son of God, he strove in perpetual charity to espouse her, now that she was cast off by all the world. Therefore having become a lover of her beauty, in order that he might cleave yet closer to her as his wife, and that they two might be united in one spirit, not only did he leave his father and his mother, but even put all things from him. Therefore, he clasped her with chaste embraces, nor for an hour did he endure not to be her husband.

No one was so greedy of gold as he of Poverty, no one more careful in guarding a treasure than he in guarding this pearl of the Gospel. Deriving hence gladness, confidence and freedom to run his course, he rejoiced in having exchanged perishable treasures for one a hundredfold greater.

Thomas of Celano, 1200?–1255

☐

To the passionate lover that was St. Francis the object of his adoration must be always present, and he saw to it that at no time in his life, and at no place in his journeyings, she should be slighted by the least inattention. He made ready for her with scarcity as other men make ready with rich offerings, and he was rewarded by her freedom and her strength as other men have seldom been. He wooed her in hunger and cold, and won her in want; and if at the present day it should seem that different methods are demanded, it is possible at least to render the honor that is due to so wholehearted and impassioned a seeker.

D. H. S. Nicholson

☐

O my most sweet Lord Jesus Christ, have pity on me and on my Lady Poverty, for I burn with love of her, and without her I cannot rest. O my Lord, who did cause me to be enamoured of her, You know that she is sitting in sadness, rejected by all.

Behold, O Lord Jesus, how truly Poverty is the queen of virtues; for, leaving the abode of angels, You did come down to earth that You might espouse her to Yourself with constant love, and produce from her, in her, and by her the children of perfection. At Your birth, she received You in a stable, and during Your life she stripped You of all things.

As a most faithful consort she accompanied You, and in the conflict of Your passion she alone stood by as Your armor-bearer. On account of the height of Your cross, even Your Mother could not reach You; but Your Lady Poverty embraced You more closely than ever.

And now You have given to Your Lady Poverty the seal of Your kingdom, that she may sign the elect who walk in the way of perfection. O who would not love the Lady Poverty above all! I beseech You to grant me this privilege: I beg to be enriched with this much-desired treasure.

Prayer of St. Francis of Assisi
to Obtain the Grace of Poverty, 1305

☐

Many followed in the footsteps of Francis, despising all the vanities of the world, so that the number of his followers, marvelously increasing from day to day, soon reached the utmost limits of the world: for holy poverty, which they took with them as their only procuratrix, made them prompt in obedience, strong to labor, and swift of foot. And because they possessed nothing earthly, loved nothing earthly, and feared to lose nothing earthly, they were secure in all places; troubled by no fears, distracted by no cares, they lived without trouble of mind, waited without solicitude for the coming day, or the night's lodging. And from this their penury they reaped exceeding abundance, according to the counsel of the wise man, who chose less rather than more.

St. Bonaventura, 1221–1274

4

LADY PECUNIA

THE PRAYSE OF LADY PECUNIA

I SING not of *Angellica* the faire,
(For whom the Palladine of *Fraunce* fell mad)
Nor of sweet *Rosamond,* olde *Cliffords* heire,
(Whose death did make the second *Henry* sad)
   But of the fairest Faire *Pecunia,*
   The famous Queene of rich *America.*

Goddesse of Golde, great Empresse of the Earth,
O thou that canst doe all Things vnder Heauen:
That doost conuert the saddest minde to Mirth;
(Of whom the elder Age was quite bereauen)
   Of thee Ile sing, and in thy Prayse Ile write;
   You *golden Angels* helpe me to indite.

. . .

But now vnto her Praise I will proceede,
Which is as ample, as the Worlde is wide:
What great Contentment doth her Pressence breede
In him, that can his wealth with Wysdome guide?
   She is the Soueraigne Queene, of all Delights:
   For her the Lawyer pleades; the Souldier fights.

For her, the Gentlemen doeth raise his rents:
For her, the Seruingman attends his maister:
For her, the curious head new toyes inuents:
For her, to Sores, the Surgeon layes his plaister.
   In fine for her, each man in his Vocation.
   Applies himselfe, in euerie sev'rall Nation.

. . .

Then how can I, sufficiently commend,
Her Beauties worth, which makes the World to wonder?
Or end her prayse, whose prayses haue no End?
Whose absence brings the stoutest stomack vnder:
    Let it suffice, *Pecunia* hath no peere;
    No Wight, no Beauty held; more faire, more deere.*

Richard Barnfield, 1574–1627

□

MONEY AS AN ENTITY

I have given *Pecunia* the title of a Woman, both for the termination of the Word, and because (as Women are) she is lov'd of men. The bravest voyages in the World have been made for Gold.

Barnfield

□

A simple invention it was in the old-world Grazier—sick of lugging his slow Ox about the country till he got it bartered for corn or oil—to take a piece of Leather, and thereon scratch or stamp the mere Figure of an Ox (or *Pecus*); put it in his pocket, and call it *Pecunia*, Money. Yet hereby did Barter grow Sale, the Leather Money is now Golden and Paper, and all miracles have been out-miracled. . . .

Thomas Carlyle, 1795–1881

□

In all ages man has made coins of gold, and there man proves again his soul's longing for light, for gold is the color of light, and among metals gold reflects the light most.

Hazrat Inayat Khan, 1882–1927

□

LADY PECUNIA

So easily might men get their living, if that same worthy princess, lady money, did not alone stop up the way between us and our living, which a God's name was very excellently devised and invented, that by her the way thereto should be opened. I am sure the rich men perceive this, nor they be not ignorant how much better it were to lack no necessary thing, than to abound with overmuch superfluity; to be rid out of innumerable cares and troubles, than to be besieged with great riches. This hell-hound creepeth into men's hearts, and plucketh them back from entering the right path of life, and is so deeply rooted in men's breasts, that she cannot be plucked out.*

Sir Thomas More, 1478–1535

☐

These individuals have riches just as we say that we "have a fever," when really the fever has *us*. Conversely, we are accustomed to say: "A fever grips him." And in the same way we should say: "Riches grip him."

Seneca, 4 B.C.?–A.D. 65
Ep. CXIX

☐

Lately in the wreck of a California ship, one of the passengers fastened a belt about him with two hundred pounds of gold in it. with which he was afterward found at the bottom. Now, as he was sinking—had he the gold? Or had the gold him?

Ruskin, 1819–1900

☐

As far back as there is history, men have dreamed of wealth: to what heights have they not reached—and to what depths have they not sunk—in quest of those golden dreams! High treason and low trickery, great affairs of state and petty squabbles over an inheritance, marriages and murder: What aspect of the tragi-

41

comedy of man has not been touched by the love of gain? Truly the drive for riches must be adjudged as powerful and protean a stimulus as any to which the human mechanism responds.

Robert L. Heilbroner, 1956

☐

CREON (King of Thebes):
  No thing in use by man, for power of ill,
Can equal money. This lays cities low,
This drives men forth from quiet dwelling-place,
This warps and changes minds of worthiest stamp,
To turn to deeds of baseness, teaching men
All shifts of cunning, and to know the guilt
Of every impious deed.

Sophocles, 496?–406 B.C.

☐

In wealth no limit is set up within man's view; those of us who now have the largest fortune are doubling our efforts; what amount would satisfy the greed of all? Gain is granted to mankind by the immortals; but from it arises disastrous folly, and when Zeus sends her to exact retribution, she comes now to this man, now to that.

Solon, 638?–559? B.C.

☐

Note that money, which ever since it began to be regarded with respect, has caused the ruin of the true honor of things; we become alternately merchants and merchandise, and we ask, not what a thing truly is, but what it costs.

Seneca, 4 B.C.?–A.D. 65
Ep. CXV

☐

LADY PECUNIA

It is not gold that complicates, corrupts, and debases life; it is our mercenary spirit.

The mercenary spirit resolves everything into a single question: *How much is that going to bring me?* and sums up everything in a single axiom: *With money you can procure anything.* Following these two principles of conduct, a society may descend to a degree of infamy impossible to describe or to imagine.

Charles Wagner, 1895

☐

It is not money, but power that lives in money
That heats the blood and turns the soul to ashes,
Freezes the heart, and changes life to clay,
Invisible spirit against the human spirit.

Horace Gregory, 1961

☐

Imagine some savage who, in his ignorance, thinks that it is the paper of the banknote that has the magic, by virtue of which the possessor of it gets all he wants. He piles up the papers, hides them, handles them in all sorts of absurd ways, and then at last, wearied by his efforts, comes to the sad conclusion that they are absolutely worthless, only fit to be thrown into the fire. But the wise man knows that the paper of the banknote is all *māyā*, and until it is given up to the bank it is futile. It is only *avidyā*, our ignorance, that makes us believe that the separateness of our self like the paper of the banknote is precious in itself, and by acting on this belief our self is rendered valueless. It is only when the *avidyā* is removed that this very self comes to us with a wealth which is priceless.

Sir Rabindranath Tagore, 1861–1941

☐

LESS IS MORE

Beside the burning ghats of India,
A naked yogi stands:
Freshly minted rupees
Keep pouring from his hands

Sofya, 1966

☐

For money is *invisible*. Certainly paper or gold is visible; but the *power* of money is invisible and with the growth of commerce and development of banking, money always tends to grow more invisible, more abstract, and to correspond less and less to any tangible reality.

Rodney Collin, 1954

☐

. . . Blest paper-credit! last and best supply!
That lends Corruption lighter wings to fly!
Gold imp'd by thee, can compass hardest things,
Can pocket States, can fetch or carry Kings;
A single leaf shall waft an Army o'er,
Or ship off Senates to a distant Shore;
A leaf, like Sibyl's, scatter to and fro
Our fates and fortunes, as the winds shall blow:
Pregnant with thousands flits the Scrap unseen,
And silent sells a King, or buys a Queen.
    Since then, my Lord, on such a World we fall,
What say you? "Say? Why take it, Gold and all."
    What Riches give us let us then enquire,
Meat, Fire, and Cloaths. What more? Meat, Cloaths, and Fire.
Is this too little? Would you more than live? . . .

Alexander Pope, 1688–1744

☐

Covetousness is the most fantastical and contradictory disease in the whole world. It increases the appetite, and will not con-

44

tent it. It swells the *principal* to no purpose, and lessens the *use* to all purposes; making *money* not to be the instrument of exchange or charity, nor corn to feed himself or the poor, nor wool to clothe himself or his brother, nor wine to refresh the sadness of the afflicted, nor his oil to make his own countenance cheerful; but all these to look upon and tell over, and to take accounts by, and make himself considerable and wondered at by fools; that while he lives he may be called rich. If the man can be content to feed hardly, and labor extremely, and watch carefully, and suffer affronts and disgrace, that he may get money more than he uses in his temperance and just needs, [he] might better be content with a virtuous and quiet poverty than with one artificial, troublesome and vicious. The same diet and a less labor would at first make him happy, and forever after rewardable.*

Jeremy Taylor, 1840

☐

"Daddy, what is money?"

"Well you dig gold out of the ground and everybody recognizes that it is valuable, but because the gold is so heavy and wears out, you give out paper money to represent what the gold is worth and then you put away the gold in the Federal Bank and use the paper money."

"It sounds foolish to me to take a lot of time digging a lot of gold out of the ground and then hiding it somewhere else. Why do they do it that way, Daddy?"

"Son, don't bother me about questions like that. You'll learn all about it at High School and College."

MANAS, 7–7–48

☐

[Gold and silver, whereof money is made, they do so use, as none of them doth more esteem it, than the very nature of the thing deserveth.] Whereas they eat and drink in earthen and glass vessels, which indeed be curiously and properly made, and yet be of very small value: of gold and silver they make commonly chamber pots, and other like vessels, that serve for most vile uses, not only in their common halls, but in every man's private house.

And therefore these metals, which other nations do as grievously and sorrowfully forgo, as in a manner from their own lives: If they should altogether at once be taken from the Utopians, no man there would think that he had lost the worth of one farthing.*

Sir Thomas More, 1478–1535

☐

HIS PRAYER TO PECUNIA

GREAT Lady, sith I haue complyde thy Prayse,
(According to my skill and not thy merit:)
And sought thy Fame aboue the starrs to rayse;
(Had I sweete *Ovids* vaine, or *Virgils* spirit)
 I craue no more but this, for my good will,
 That in my Want, thou wilt supplye me still.

Richard Barnfield, 1574–1627

☐

The gods only laugh when men pray to them for wealth.

Japanese proverb

☐

When I was older, I learned what the fighting was about that winter and the next summer. Up on the Madison Fork the Wasichus [white men] had found much of the yellow metal that they worship and that makes them crazy, and they wanted to have a road up through our country to the place where the yellow metal was; but my people did not want the road. It would scare the bison and make them go away, and also it would let the

46

other Wasichus come in like a river. They told us that they wanted only to use a little land, as much as a wagon would take between the wheels; but our people knew better. And when you look about you now, you can see what it was they wanted.

Black Elk, ca. 1880

☐

Not only did men demand of the bounteous fields the crops and sustenance they owed, but they delved as well into the very bowels of the earth; and the wealth which the creator had hidden away and buried amidst the very Stygian shades, was brought now to light, wealth that pricks men on to crime.

Ovid, 43 B.C.–A.D. 18

☐

I might make complaint against Nature because she did not hide gold and silver more deeply, because she did not lay a weight upon them too heavy to be removed. . . .

Seneca, 4 B.C.?–A.D. 65

☐

For the love of money is the root of all evil. . . .

I Timothy 6:10

☐

It is not "money" that is the "root of all evil," as we often misquote, but "*the love* of money."

Bruce Barton, 1886–1967

☐

Consider whether it may be that it is not the peace of this world of ours that corrupts great natures, but much rather this endless

47

war which holds our desires in its grasp, yes, and further still the passions that garrison our lives nowadays and utterly devastate them. For the love of money, that insatiable craving from which we all now suffer, and the love of pleasure make us their slaves, or rather, one might say, sink our lives (body and soul) into the depths, the love of money being a disease that makes us petty-minded, and the love of pleasure an utterly ignoble attribute.

On further reflection, indeed, I do not see how, if we value the possession of unlimited wealth, or, to give the truth of the matter, make a god of it, we can avoid allowing the evils that naturally attend its entry into our souls. For vast and unlimited wealth is closely followed—step by step, as they say—by extravagance, and no sooner has the one opened the gates of cities and houses than the other comes in and joins it in setting up house there. . . .

This will inevitably happen, and then men will no longer lift up their eyes nor take any further thought for their good name; the ruin of their lives will gradually be completed as their grandeur of soul withers and fades until it sinks into contempt, when they become lost in admiration of their mortal capabilities and neglect to develop the immortal.*

Longinus, 213?–273

□

For the prosperity of fools shall destroy them.

Proverbs 1:32

□

[It] seems clearer every day that the moral problem of our age is concerned with the love of money, with the habitual appeal to the money motive in nine-tenths of the activities of life, with the universal striving after individual economic security as the prime object of endeavor, with the social approbation of money as the measure of constructive success.

A revolution in our ways of thinking and feeling about money may become the growing purpose of contemporary embodiments of the ideal.

48

LADY PECUNIA

There are valuable human activities which require the motive of money-making and the environment of private wealth-ownership for their full fruition. Moreover, dangerous human proclivities can be canalized into comparatively harmless channels by the existence of opportunities for money-making and private wealth, which, if they cannot be satisfied in this way, may find their outlet in cruelty, the reckless pursuit of personal power and authority, and other forms of self-aggrandizement.

But it is not necessary for the stimulation of these activities and the satisfaction of these proclivities that the game should be played for such high stakes as at present. Much lower stakes will serve the purpose equally well, as soon as the players are accustomed to them.*

J. M. Keynes, 1883–1946

□

Beware lest you think that anything could be more true than the words, "The root of all evil is avarice." Don't will to have more than is sufficient, and "sufficient" means the amount that a nature needs to maintain itself in its own kind. For avarice, which the Greeks call *philargyria* [love of money]—the word is probably derived from the fact that the ancients used coins made of silver and alloys of silver—is to be understood not only as love of money or coins, but also as any sort of love in which one has immoderate desire and wants more than is enough.

St. Augustine, 354–430

□

Nothing is real to us but hunger, nothing sacred except our own desires. Shrine after shrine has crumbled before our eyes; but one altar forever is preserved, that whereon we burn incense to the supreme idol—ourselves. Our god is great, and money is his Prophet! We devastate nature in order to make sacrifice to him. We boast that we have conquered Matter and forget that it is Matter that has enslaved us.*

Okakura Kakuzo, 1904

49

LESS IS MORE

☐

Although we may have conquered matter with money, we have not won it over to our side.

André VandenBroeck, 1969

☐

I do declare that unless we can remove the Western ideal of "prosperity" our civilization is doomed and damned. But even now no one seems to think of it. No statesman is great enough to say the desire for national wealth is a hellish will-o'-the-wisp. No one has yet put into practice the knowledge that every one in the country may be "well off" and yet every life be parasitic and verminous . . . things must be said clearly and unequivocally. Men must be told they're either to live for ideal and immaterial ends or be slaves to matter whose slavery becomes crueler every day we serve it.*

Max Plowman, 1915

☐

Prepare for a conscious domination of man over matter.

Simone Weil, 1909–1943

☐

It has been the historic function of the United States to evolve the Western technical and scientific heritage into a system and society where material survival has ceased to be a problem and where material security, comfort, and even luxury seem like a birthright of the great majority of citizens. As a result, the more conscious segment of the population has the leisure to refine tastes and habits, and to create a harmonious style of living representing a high level of human conduct.

For the less conscious and unfortunately much larger segment, the ideal of harmonious humanity is inaccessible, and although material aims have been fulfilled, these people continue to belabor matter and to use the abstract representation of material power, *money*, in order to produce more useless money and more superfluous goods.

Both of these groups have their function in the cosmic play, at a moment when the curtain rises for the opening scene of a new act: a new age. In the first group will be found those few who are ready to go beyond the acquisitive self, to contribute more directly to the commonwealth of consciousness. Willing to make material achievement subservient to the arid challenge of spirit, they will sacrifice the ornamental ballast of their lives, in order to participate in the processes by which matter is spiritualized.

Nor will the second segment be able to escape the unrelenting evolutionary pressure. It will dawn upon them that the senseless multiplication of material goods is a cancerous process and the resulting glut a deadly disease. They will recognize that the point has been reached where matter can no longer be violated for the selfish sake of man, but that it must be understood as an expression of spirit, and that its manipulation must be an offering to spirit. Money, the abstract entity extracted from matter, turns upon itself like a caged beast. It clamors for redemption by spirit.

André VandenBroeck, 1965

5

THE RIGHT THING

RIGHTEOUS WEALTH

Great parts of the world are free from the necessities of labor and employments, and have their time and fortune at their own disposal. But as no one is to live in his employment according to his own humor, or for such ends as please his own fancy, but is to do all his business in such a manner as to make it a service unto God; so those who have no particular employment are so far from being left at greater liberty to live to themselves, to pursue their own humor, and spend their time and fortunes as they please, that they are under greater obligations of living wholly unto God in all their actions.

The freedom of their state lays them under a greater necessity of always choosing, and doing, the best things. They are those of whom much will be required, because much is given unto them.

William Law, 1686–1761

□

The true Use of Riches is known to few,
most fall into one of the extremes,
Avarice or Profusion.

Alexander Pope, 1688–1744

□

THE RIGHT THING

An instrument, if you use it with artistic skill, is a thing of art; but if you are lacking in skill, it reaps the benefit of your unmusical nature, though not itself responsible. Wealth too is an instrument of the same kind.

The man who is truly and nobly rich, then, is he who is rich in virtues and able to use every fortune in a holy and faithful manner; but the spurious rich man is he who is rich according to the flesh, and has changed his life into outward possessions which are passing away and perishing, belonging now to one, now to another, and in the end to no one at all.

Clement of Alexandria, 150?–220?

☐

There will always be a number of men who would fain set themselves to the accumulation of wealth as the sole object of their lives. Necessarily, that class of men is an uneducated class, inferior in intellect, and more or less cowardly. It is physically impossible for a well-educated, intellectual, or brave man to make money the chief object of his thoughts; as physically impossible as it is for him to make his dinner the principal object of them. All healthy people like their dinners, but their dinner is not the main object of their lives. So all healthily-minded people like making money—ought to like it, and to enjoy the sensation of winning it; but the main object of their life is not money; it is something better than money. . . .

Ruskin, 1819–1900

☐

The use of money is all the advantage there is in having money.

Benjamin Franklin, 1706–1790

☐

LESS IS MORE

Silly people think that money commands the bodily goods most worth having.

St. Thomas Aquinas, 1225?–1274

☐

Power (and money, power's master key) is a means at its purest. For that very reason it is the supreme end for all those who have not understood.

Simone Weil, 1909–1943

☐

Toward a Functional Poverty

Some people are content with the outward pattern of their lives; their material surroundings seem to them the soil in which their personalities and special gifts can appropriately flower. They feel that their part in life is best fulfilled through arrangements of beauty, amenity, or comfort. Others feel limited and blocked, weighed down by the conditions of their outwardly fortunate lives, their strength and purpose frittered away in uncongenial activity and care, their souls dwarfed in a hostile and infertile soil. They long to set themselves free. What I have to say is intended for people in whom this longing has got past denying.

My thesis is that some of the means for freeing our lives lie in drastic limiting of material possessions and processes, in a discipline which paradoxically has its reward in extension of our strength and insight to use them to the full. But we cannot grasp these means for freeing our lives until the necessity is made plain in our own hearts and we want it completely.

When the necessity becomes plain, when the longing to set ourselves free is past denying, we begin to open into a realization of personal responsibility, of the oneness of human life, of what has been called *unlimited liability*. We feel the obligation and the privilege to live as if we each had many lives to live and could afford to hold loosely our little footholds in this one. This opening out is the great release.

Now, frankly, most of us have our hands so full of baubles that we haven't even a finger free with which to reach out and satisfy the claim of *unlimited liability*. Poverty, or some approximation to it, willingly assumed, would set us free both for finding our responsibility and for fulfilling it when found. That is why I have called it *functional* poverty. It is to be embraced not as an ideal of beauty, our Lady Poverty of the Middle Ages, though it may wear her features. It is to be embraced not as a penance for the benefit we have long had from a society that starves our brothers, though it may be partly that. It is to be taken up not as a shirking of the responsibility of wealth or privilege, but as acceptance of wider responsibility. It is to be taken up as a way to freedom, and as a practical method for finding the time and strength to answer one's deepest need to be serviceable for a new world.

Functional poverty means an adjustment of the mechanics of living by clearing off the rubble. This is a clearing off that opens the way for new growth in wisdom, love, and function. It means a discipline that tempers the tools by which we work, and scours clean the glass of self through which we see at best but darkly.*

Mildred Binns Young, 1939

□

I do not mean to prescribe rules to strong and valiant natures who will mind their own affairs whether in heaven or hell, but mainly to the mass of men who are discontented. I also have in mind that seemingly wealthy, but most terribly impoverished class of all, who have accumulated dross, but know not how to use it, or get rid of it, and thus have forged their own golden or silver fetters.*

Thoreau, 1817–1862

□

55

LESS IS MORE

The poor rich: all they have is money.

Tom Moore, 1976
Bowery & Great Jones St.
New York City

□

A great fortune is a great bondage.

Seneca, 4 B.C.?–A.D. 65
Ep. XXVI

□

His master or his slave is each man's hoard,
And ought to follow, not to pull, the cord.

Horace, 65–8 B.C.

□

Wealth is the diploma of slavery.

Seneca, 4 B.C.?–A.D. 65
Ep. CIV

□

There is no wealth but life.

Ruskin, 1819–1900

□

As there is an apprenticeship, often very difficult to serve, for the exercise of every social office, so this profession we call wealth demands an apprenticeship. To know how to be rich is an art, and one of the least easy of arts to master. Most people, rich and poor alike, imagine that in opulence one has nothing to do but to take life easy. That is why so few men know how to be rich.

In the hands of too many, wealth, according to the genial and redoubtable comparison of Luther, is like a harp in the hoofs of an ass. They have no idea of the manner of its use.

So when we encounter a man at once rich and simple, that is to say, who considers his wealth as a means of fulfilling his mission in the world, we should offer him our homage, for he is surely markworthy.

Charles Wagner, 1895

Passion for gold can never be right;
the pursuit of money leads a man astray.
Many a man has come to ruin for the sake of gold
and found disaster staring him in the face.
Gold is a pitfall to those who are infatuated with it,
and every fool is caught by it.
Happy the rich man who has remained free of its taint
and has not made gold his aim!
Show us that man, and we will congratulate him;
he has performed a miracle among his people.
Has anyone come through this test unscathed?
Then he has good cause to be proud.

Ecclesiasticus 31:1–10

What several in all ages have made pretense to, the Contempt of Riches, is more scarce than is commonly imagin'd. To see a Man of a very good Estate, in Health and Strength of Body and Mind, one that has no reason to complain of the World or Fortune, actually despise both, and embrace a voluntary Poverty for a laudable Purpose, is a great rarity.

Bernard Mandeville, 1670?–1733

LESS IS MORE

In the courtyard of Great Bliss,
I was gathering the Dharma wealth;
I had no time to make money in this world.

Milarepa 1052?–1135

☐

The masses are lazy and unintelligent; they have no love for instinctual renunciation and they are not to be convinced by the argument of its inevitability; and the individuals composing them support one another in giving free rein to their indiscipline. It is only through the influence of individuals who can set an example and whom the masses recognize as their leaders that they can be induced to perform the work and undergo the renunciations on which the existence of civilization depends.

Sigmund Freud, 1856–1939

☐

Limitation must be carried out in the right way if it is to be effective. If we seek to impose restrictions on others only, while evading them ourselves, these restrictions will always be resented and will provoke resistance. If, however, a man in a leading position applies the limitation first to himself, demanding little from those associated with him, and with modest means manages to achieve something, good fortune is the result. Where such an example occurs, it meets with emulation, so that whatever is undertaken must succeed.

I Ching

☐

I am firmly convinced that all the riches in the world would not further humanity, even in the hands of some as devoted as possible to progress. Only the example of great and pure personalities can inspire noble conceptions and noble actions. Money attracts egotism and irresistibly leads to its misuse. Can one imagine Moses, Jesus, or Gandhi equipped with Carnegie's wallet?

> Albert Einstein, 1879–1955, who was known to use his uncashed Princeton University paycheck as a bookmark

□

This, then, is held to be the duty of the man of wealth: to set an example of modest, unostentatious living, shunning display or extravagance; to provide moderately for the legitimate wants of those dependent upon him; and, after doing so, to consider all surplus revenues which come to him simply as trust funds, which he is called to administer for his poorer brethren, bringing to their service his superior wisdom, experience, and ability to administer, doing for them better than they would or could do for themselves.

> Andrew Carnegie, 1835–1919

□

THEORY OF TRUSTEESHIP

Those who own money now are asked to behave like trustees holding their riches on behalf of the poor. You may say that trusteeship is a legal fiction. But if people meditate over it constantly and try to act up to it, then life on earth would be governed far more by love than it is at present. Absolute trusteeship is an abstraction like Euclid's definition of a point, and is equally unattainable. But if we strive for it, we shall be able to go further in realizing a state of equality on earth than by any other method.

> Gandhi, 1869–1948

□

LESS IS MORE

Let the amelioration in our laws of property proceed from the concession of the rich, not from the grasping of the poor. Let us begin by habitual imparting. Let us understand that the equitable rule is, that no one should take more than his share, let him be ever so rich.

Emerson, 1803–1882

☐

The rich have a superfluous store of things which they do not need, and which are therefore neglected and wasted; while millions are starved to death for want of sustenance. If each retained possession only of what he needed, no one would be in want, and all would live in contentment. As it is, the rich are discontented no less than the poor. The poor man would fain become a millionaire, and the millionaire a multimillionaire. The rich should take the initiative in dispossession with a view to a universal diffusion of the spirit of contentment. If only they keep their own property within moderate limits, the starving will be easily fed, and will learn the lesson of contentment along with the rich. Perfect fulfillment of the ideal of nonpossession requires, that man should, like the birds, have no roof over his head, no clothing, and no stock of food for the morrow. He will indeed need his daily bread, but it will be God's business, and not his, to provide it. Only the fewest possible, if any at all, can reach this ideal. We ordinary seekers may not be repelled by the seeming impossibility. But we must keep the ideal constantly in view, and in the light thereof, critically examine our possessions, and try to reduce them. Civilization, in the real sense of the term, consists not in the multiplication, but in the deliberate and voluntary reduction of wants. This alone promotes real happiness and contentment. . . .

Gandhi, 1869–1948

☐

THE RIGHT THING

Once we begin not to worry about what kind of house we are living in, what kind of clothes we are wearing; once we give up the stupid recreation of this world, we have time, which is priceless, to remember that we are our brother's keeper and that we must not only care for his needs as far as we are able immediately but we must try to build a better world.

Dorothy Day, 1973

□

To live with some rigor of temperance . . . seems to be an asceticism which common good nature would appoint to those who are at ease and in plenty, in sign that they feel a brotherhood with the great multitude of suffering men.*

Emerson, 1803–1882

□

For my own part, I feel the force of mechanism and the fury of avaricious commerce to be at present so irresistible, that I have seceded from the study not only of architecture, but nearly of all art; and have given myself, as I would in a besieged city, to seek the best modes of getting bread and butter for the inhabitants.

Ruskin, 1819–1900

□

I say to you, O rich men of this age, that you do wrong to treat the poor with such unmerited disdain; and to prove to you that this is so, if we go back to the origin of property we shall perhaps find that they have no less right than you yourselves to those goods which are now in your possession. Nature, or to use more Christian phraseology, God, has from the beginning given an equal right to all over the things they need to maintain life. No one of us can boast of having more advantages than another by nature; but the insatiable desire for amassing and accumulating soon put an end to this beautiful fraternity. This led to division and to private property, the fruitful source of disputes and litigation: Hence the words *mine* and *thine* came into use, those "cold words," as St. John Chrysostom calls them.

Bossuet, 1627–1704

□

Mine, thine: "This dog is mine," said those poor children, "that is my place in the sun." Here is the beginning and the image of the usurpation of all the earth.

Pascal, 1623–1662

□

It is certain that the land among these people [the Indians of Hispaniola] is as common as the sun and water; that "mine" and "thine"—the seeds of all mischief—have no place with them. They are content with so little that, in so large a country, they have rather superfluity than scarceness; so that they seem to live in a golden world, without toil, in open gardens, neither intrenched, nor shut up by walls or hedges.

Peter Martyr, 1457–1526

□

Themistocles, when asked whether he would marry his daughter to a good poor man, or to a rich man of less respectable character, replied, "I, indeed, prefer the man who lacks money to the money that lacks a man."

Marcus Tullius Cicero, 106–43 B.C.

□

It is more endurable and easier not to acquire [money] than to lose it. Diogenes, that high-souled man, saw this, and made it impossible for anything to be snatched from him. Either I am deceived, or it is a regal thing to be the only one amid all the misers, the sharpers, the robbers, and plunderers who cannot be harmed. If anyone has any doubts about the happiness of Diogenes, he may likewise have doubts about the condition of the immortal gods as well.

Seneca, 4 B.C.?–A.D. 65

□

It is impossible to spend the smallest sum of money for any not absolutely necessary purpose, without a grave responsibility attaching to the manner of spending it. The object we ourselves covet may, indeed, be desirable and harmless, so far as we are concerned, but the providing us with it may, perhaps, be a very prejudicial occupation to someone else. And then it becomes instantly a moral question, whether we are to indulge ourselves or not. Whatever we wish to buy, we ought first to consider not only if the thing be fit for us, but if the manufacture of it be a wholesome and happy one; and if, on the whole, the sum we are going to spend will do as much good spent in this way as it would if spent in any other way. It may be said that we have not time to consider all this before we make a purchase. But no time could be spent in a more important duty; and God never imposes a duty without giving the time to do it. Let us, however, only acknowledge the principle; once make up your mind to allow the consideration of the *effect* of your purchases to regulate the *kind* of your purchase, and you will soon easily find grounds enough to decide upon.

Ruskin, 1819–1900

□

To forsake money with all one's heart should not be difficult for the heart; indeed there is no one who would willingly have money in his heart, for if the money were actually in it, the heart would assuredly die.

63

We observe, moreover, that a colored shield is not aware of its color, takes no pleasure in it and is devoid of all other color both as regards quantity and quality. The human senses, on the other hand, particularly the sense of sight, although it does not possess any color and indeed rejects it by its very nature, is aware of color, takes pleasure in color and is sensitive, both quantitatively and qualitatively, to all manner of colors. In the same way the just man, the more he forsakes and the less he possesses, the richer he is, the more he possesses, and the more pleasant is the possession.

Eckhart, 1260?–1327

☐

There are things that man can digest, and there are things that he cannot digest. It depends from what source they come. The Prophet calls wealth that can be digested *Halal,* and the wealth which can not be digested, he calls *Haram.* It makes a great difference whether one acquires it honestly or dishonestly, honorably or dishonorably: with force or with work. Money rightfully earned must certainly bring peace, but money earned by causing pain to another, by ruining the life of another, by dishonesty or by injustice, man cannot digest.

Hazrat Inayat Khan, 1882–1927

☐

The values of an acquisitive society have a metallic flavor.

Robert Heilbroner, 1956

☐

It is the higher accomplishment to use money well than to use arms, but not to need it is more noble than to use it.

Coriolanus, 5th cent. B.C.

THE RIGHT THING

☐

Of great riches there is no real use, except it be in the distribution; the rest is but conceit. Do you not see what feigned prices are set upon little stones and rarities? and what works of ostentation are undertaken, because there might seem to be some use of great riches? Seek not proud riches, but such as thou mayest get justly, use soberly, distribute cheerfully, and leave contentedly. Yet have no abstract or friarly contempt of them. The ways to enrich are many, and most of them are foul. Parsimony is one of the best, and yet is not innocent; for it witholdeth men from works of liberality and charity. Wealth is like muck. It is not good but if it be spread.*

Sir Francis Bacon, 1561–1626

☐

And yet if Riches be sanctified, they are great blessings, and singular advantages to honor God, and do good withall to others, if not, curses; being like poison, if corrected, physick, if not, death; and like dung, which while it lyeth upon a heap doth no good, but dispersed and cast abroad, maketh fields fruitful.

Thomas Goddard, 1661

☐

Wealth in the gross is death, but life diffus'd;
As Poison heals, in just proportion us'd:
In heaps, like Ambergrise, a stink it lies,
But well-dispers'd, is Incense to the Skies.

Alexander Pope, 1688–1744

☐

Affluence, being the manure and water for spiritual growth, is not to be avoided.

Gampopa, 1077–1152

65

□

It is written that it is very difficult for a rich man to enter the kingdom of Heaven. This does not refer to the possession of wealth, but to one's vain and avaricious life; for while man grows fat, God is forgotten. . . . The kingdom of God is in truth, justice, and love toward the needy. It condemns none who properly uses that which is his.*

Jakob Boehme, 1575–1624

□

I look upon this craze for wealth that possesses nearly all classes in our time as one of the most lamentable spectacles the world has ever seen.

Beyond the point of a moderate competency, wealth is a burden. A man may possess a competency; great wealth possesses him. He is the victim. It fills him with unrest; it destroys or perverts his natural relations to his fellows; it corrupts his simplicity.

For a rich man to lead the simple life is about as hard as for a camel to go through the needle's eye.*

John Burroughs, 1908

□

Our possessions are our limitations. He who is bent upon accumulating riches is unable, with his ego continually bulging, to pass through the gates of comprehension of the spiritual world. . . .

Tagore, 1861–1941

□

Accustom thyself to cut off all superfluities in the provision of thy life; for our desires will enlarge beyond the present possession so long as all the things of this world are unsatisfying; if, therefore, you suffer them to extend beyond the measures of necessity

66

or moderated conveniency, they will still swell; but you reduce them to a little compass, when you make nature to be your limit. We must more take care that our desires should cease, than that they should be satisfied, and therefore reducing them to narrow scantlings and small proportion is the best instrument to redeem their trouble. . . .

Jeremy Taylor, 1840

☐

Superfluous wealth can buy superfluities only. Money is not required to buy one necessary of the soul.

Thoreau, 1817–1862

☐

It is better to have fewer wants than to have larger resources.

St. Augustine, 354–430

☐

PLAYING POOR

Let us pass over the wealth that is almost poverty, let us come to the really rich. How many are the occasions on which they are just like the poor! And not only does the necessity of certain times and places put them on a level with the poor in actual want, but, when a weariness of riches happens to seize them, they even choose to dine on the ground, and use earthen vessels, refraining from gold and silver plate. Madmen!—this state which they always dread, they sometimes even covet. O what darkness of mind, what ignorance of truth blinds those who, harassed by the fear of poverty, for pleasure's sake simulate poverty!

Seneca, 4 B.C.?–A.D. 65

LESS IS MORE

□

Nineteenth-century America saw in the rags-to-riches motif not only the model for but *of* life. Indeed, to the quick, the able, and the bold wealth came liberally and fast. As might be expected, money earned with such abandon was spent with corresponding carelessness. As in every age, wealth suddenly acquired had to be advertised. Perhaps the nadir of taste was reached in the "poverty socials" which became the rage. The guests, attired in rags, ate scraps from wooden plates, used newspapers for napkins, and drank beer from old tin cans—all in the marble and glass settings of their hosts' resplendent homes.

Robert Heilbroner, 1956

□

Practicing Poverty

Practice poverty of spirit in the midst of riches, practice richness of spirit in real poverty.

St. François de Sales, 1567–1622

□

I know both how to be abased, and I know how to abound: Everywhere and in all things I am instructed both to be full and to be empty, both to abound and to suffer need.

Philippians 4:12

□

It is the mark of a noble spirit not to precipitate oneself into such things [the life of voluntary poverty] on the ground that they are better, but to practice for them on the ground that they are thus easy to endure; when, however, you come to them after

68

long rehearsal, they are even pleasant; for they contain a sense of freedom from care—and without this nothing is pleasant. I hold it essential, therefore, to do what great men have often done:

Set aside a certain number of days, during which you shall be content with the scantiest and cheapest fare, with coarse and rough dress, saying to yourself the while: "Is this the condition that I feared?" It is precisely in times of immunity from care that the soul should toughen itself beforehand for occasions of greater stress, and it is while Fortune is kind that it should fortify itself against her violence. . . .

You need not suppose that I mean meals like Timon's, or "pauper's huts," or any other device which luxurious million-aires use to beguile the tedium of their lives. Let the pallet be a real one, and the cloak coarse; let the bread be hard and grimy. Endure all this for three or four days at a time, sometimes for more, so that it may be a test of yourself instead of a mere hobby. . . .

There is no reason, however, why you should think that you are doing anything great; for you will merely be doing what many thousands of slaves and many thousands of poor men are doing every day. But you may credit yourself with this item— that you will not be doing it under compulsion, and that it will be as easy for you to endure it permanently as to make the experiment from time to time. Let us practice our strokes on the "dummy," let us become intimate with poverty, so that Fortune may not catch us off our guard. We shall be rich with all the more comfort, if we once learn how far poverty is from being a burden.*

Seneca, 4 B.C.?–A.D. 65

☐

In an orderly and peaceable democracy like the United States, where men cannot enrich themselves by war, by public office, or by political confiscation, the love of wealth mainly drives them into business and manufactures. Although these pursuits often bring about great commotions and disasters, they cannot prosper

without strictly regular habits and a long routine of petty uniform acts. The stronger the passion is, the more regular are these
habits, and the more uniform are these acts. It may be said that
it is the vehemence of their desires which makes the Americans
so methodical; it perturbs their minds, but it disciplines their
lives.

Alexis de Tocqueville, 1805–1859

□

A peaceful mind is your most precious capital.

Swami Sivananda, 1887–1963

□

Silence every motion proceeding from the love of money.

John Woolman, 1720–1772

□

We talk much about despising money, and we give advice on this
subject in the lengthiest of speeches, that mankind may believe
true riches to exist in the mind and not in one's bank account,
and that the man who adapts himself to his slender means and
makes himself wealthy on a little sum, is the truly rich man; but
our minds are struck more effectively when a verse like this is
repeated:

He needs but little who desires but little.

Even men in whose opinion nothing is enough, wonder and
applaud when they hear such words, and swear eternal hatred
against money. When you see them thus disposed, strike home,
keep at them, and charge them with this duty, dropping all
double meanings, syllogisms, hair-splitting, and the other side-
shows of ineffective smartness. Preach against greed, preach
against high living; and when you notice that you have made

70

progress and impressed the minds of your hearers, lay on still harder.*

Seneca 4? B.C.–A.D. 65
Ep. CVIII

□

THE POLITICAL COIL

When I found myself drawn into the political coil, I asked myself what was necessary for me in order to remain absolutely untouched by immorality, by untruth, by what is known as political gain. . . . It was a difficult struggle in the beginning and it was a wrestle with my wife and—as I can vividly recall—with my children also. Be that as it may, I came definitely to the conclusion that, if I had to serve the people in whose midst my life was cast and of whose difficulties I was witness from day to day, I must discard all wealth, all possession.

I cannot tell you with truth that, when this belief came to me, I discarded everything immediately. I must confess to you that progress at first was slow. And now, as I recall those days of struggle, I remember that it was also painful in the beginning. But, as days went by, I saw that I had to throw overboard many other things which I used to consider as mine, and a time came when it became a matter of positive joy to give up those things. And one after another then, by almost geometric progression, the things slipped away from me. And, as I am describing my experiences, I can say a great burden fell off my shoulders, and I felt that I could now walk with ease and do my work also in the service of my fellow-men with great comfort and still greater joy. The possession of anything then became a troublesome thing and a burden. . . .

And then I said to myself: Possession seems to me to be a crime; I can only possess certain things when I know that others, who also want to possess similar things, are able to do so. But we know—everyone of us can speak from experience—that such

71

a thing is an impossibility. Therefore, the only thing that can be possessed by all is non-possession.

You might then well say to me: But you are keeping many things on your body even as you are speaking about voluntary poverty and not possessing anything whatsoever! And your taunt would be right, if you only superficially understood the meaning of the thing that I am speaking about just now. It is really the spirit behind. Whilst you have the body, you will have to have something to clothe the body with also. But then you will take for the body not all that you can get, but the least possible, the least with which you can do. You will take for your house not many mansions, but the least cover that you can do with. And similarly with reference to your food and so on.

And those who have actually followed out this vow of voluntary poverty to the fullest extent possible (to reach absolute perfection is an impossibility, but the fullest possible extent for a human being), those who have reached the ideal of that state, they testify that when you dispossess yourself of everything you have, you really possess all the treasures of the world. . . .*

Gandhi, 1869–1948

□

VARIETIES OF ETHICAL POVERTY

The man that does good service to the state is not merely he who brings forward candidates and defends the accused and votes for peace and war, but he also who admonishes young men, who instills virtue into their minds, supplying the great lack of good teachers, who lays hold upon those that are rushing wildly in pursuit of money and of luxury, and draws them back, and, if he accomplishes nothing else, at least retards them—such a man performs a public service even in private life.

Seneca, 4 B.C.?–A.D. 65

□

SOCRATES: My occupation quite absorbs me, and I have no time to give either to any public matter of interest or to any concern of my own, but am in utter poverty by reason of my devotion to the god. . . . For I do nothing but go about persuading you all, old and young alike, not to take thought for your persons and your properties, but first and chiefly to care about the greatest improvement of the soul. I tell you that virtue is not given by money, but that from virtue comes money, and every other good of man, public as well as private. This is my teaching, and if this is the doctrine which corrupts the youth, I am a mischievous person. . . . And here is my witness: my poverty.*

Plato, 427?–347 B.C.

☐

Solon surely was a dreamer, and a man of simple mind;
When the gods would give him fortune,
He of his own will declined.

Solon, 638?–559? B.C.

☐

When Pythagoras entrusted his daughter Damo with the custody of his memoirs, he solemnly charged her never to give them to anyone outside his house. And, although she could have sold the writings for a large sum of money, she would not, but reckoned poverty and her father's solemn injunctions more precious than gold, for all that she was a woman.

Diogenes Laërtius, 3d cent.

☐

Letter to her master, or rather to her father; to her husband, or rather to her brother; his handmaid, or rather his daughter; his wife, or rather his sister: to Abélard:

You have condescended to recall some of the reasons why I sought to dissuade you from a fatal marriage, yet you say nothing of those which made me choose love rather than matrimony, freedom rather than a chain. As God is my witness, had Augustus, the master of the world, adjudged me worthy of marriage . . . being known as your courtesan would have seemed sweeter and nobler to me than being known as his empress. For it is not wealth or power that makes a man great. Wealth and power stem from luck. Greatness stems from merit. . . . To marry a rich man in preference to a poor man, and to value the advantages of a husband's rank more highly than his innate virtues, is tantamount to selling oneself. Certainly, a woman who is prompted to marry by any such covetousness deserves to be paid rather than loved, for it is obvious that her attachment is not to the man but to his riches and that, given the opportunity, she would gladly have prostituted herself to an even wealthier man. . . .*

Héloïse, 1101–1164

□

When the court is arrayed in splendor,
The fields are full of weeds,
and the granaries are bare.
Some wear gorgeous clothes,
Carry sharp swords,
and indulge themselves with food and drink:
They have more possessions than they can use.
They are robber barons.
This is certainly not the way of Tao.

Tao Te Ching

□

Non-possession is allied to non-stealing. A thing not originally stolen would have to be classified as stolen property if one continues to possess it without needing it. If somebody else possesses more than I do, let him. But so far as my own life has to be regu-

74

lated, I do say that I dare not possess anything which I do not need.

Gandhi, 1869–1948

□

Theft is punished by Thy Law, O Lord. . . . Yet I lusted to thieve, and did it, compelled by no hunger, nor poverty, but through *a cloyedness of well-doing, and a pamperedness of iniquity.* For I stole that of which I had enough, and much better.*

St. Augustine, 354–430

□

By the establishment of non-stealing,
All wealth comes to the yogi.

Patanjali, 2d cent. B.C.

□

I had no lock nor bolt but for the desk which held my papers, not even a nail to put over my latch or windows. I never fastened my door night or day, though I was to be absent several days. And yet my house was more respected than if it had been surrounded by a file of soldiers. I am convinced, that if all men were to live as simply as I then did, thieving and robbery would be unknown. These take place only in communities where some have got more than is sufficient while others have not enough.*

Thoreau, 1817–1862

□

With the abolition of want and the fear of want, the admiration of riches would decay, and men would seek the respect and ap-

75

probation of their fellows in other modes than by the acquisition and display of wealth.*

Henry George, 1839–1897

☐

They say that Solon, coming to Croesus who was decked with every possible rarity and curiosity, in ornaments of jewels, purple, and gold, that could make a grand and gorgeous spectacle of him, seemed not at all surprised, nor gave Croesus those compliments he expected, but showed himself to all discerning eyes to be a man that despised gaudiness and petty ostentation. Croesus commanded them to open all his treasure houses, and carry him to see his sumptuous furniture and luxuries, though he did not wish it; Solon could judge of him well enough by the first sight of him; and, when he returned from viewing all, Croesus asked him if ever he had known a happier man than he. And when Solon answered that he had known one Tellus, a fellow-citizen of his own, and told him that this Tellus had been an honest man, had had good children, a competent estate, and died bravely in battle for his country, Croesus took him for an ill-bred fellow and a fool, for not measuring happiness by the abundance of gold and silver, and preferring the life of a private and mean man before so much power and empire.

Plutarch, 46?–120?

☐

Property is now the most easily recognized evidence of a reputable degree of success as distinguished from heroic or signal achievement. It therefore becomes the conventional basis of esteem.

Thorstein Veblen, 1857–1929

☐

JUST DESSERTS

It is said that among the barbarians, where wealth is still measured by cattle, great chiefs are described as hundred-cow men. The manager of a great enterprise who is paid $400,000 a year, might similarly be described as a hundred-family man, since he receives the income of a hundred families. It is true that special talent is worth any price, and that a payment of $400,000 a year to the head of a business with a turnover of millions is economically a bagatelle. But economic considerations are not the only considerations. There is also "the point of honor." And the truth is that these hundred-family salaries are ungentlemanly.

No one has any business to expect to be paid "what he is worth," for what he is worth is a matter between his own soul and God. What he has a right to demand, and what concerns his fellow-men to see that he gets, is enough to enable him to perform his work. . . . If a man has important work, and enough leisure and income to enable him to do it properly, he is in possession of as much happiness as is good for any of the children of Adam.*

R. H. Tawney, 1880–1962

□

He thought that no poverty could befall him that enjoyed Paradise. For when all things are gone which man can give, a man is still as rich as Adam was in Eden, who was naked there. A naked man is the richest creature in all worlds, and can never be happy til he sees the riches of his very nakedness.

Thomas Traherne, 1637?–1674

□

What is a salary of ten thousand bushels to me, if I come by it against my principles? Shall I take this position because it offers me beautiful mansions and the service of a wife and concubines,

77

or because I shall be able to help my friends who knew me when I was poor? If formerly I refused to accept the post in the face of death (or starvation), and now I accept it in order to have a fine residence, if formerly I refused to accept this post in the face of death, and now I accept it in order to have the service of a wife and concubines, if formerly I refused this post in the face of death, and now I accept it in order to be able to help my friends who knew me when I was poor, would that not be something totally unnecessary? This is called "losing one's original heart."

Mencius, 372?–289 B.C.

□

So deeply rooted are past ideas that demanded a further increase in income that questioning this approach is still unfashionable except in certain very limited circles. It is difficult to accept that our income could be sufficient and that our feeling that we do not have enough comes from our failure to use the available resources well, rather than from our need for more.

Robert Theobald, 1961

□

The equalization of property is one of the things that tend to prevent the citizens from quarreling. Not that the gain in this direction is very great. For the nobles will be dissatisfied because they think themselves worthy of more than an equal share of honors. . . . And the avarice of mankind is insatiable: At one time two obols was pay enough; but now, when this sum has become customary, men always want more and more without end; for it is of the nature of desire not to be satisfied, and most men live only for the gratification of it. The beginning of reform is not so much to equalize property as to train the nobler sort of natures not to desire more. . . .*

Aristotle, 384–322 B.C.

BUSINESS MAN

My mind, through the power of truth, was in good degree weaned from the desire of outward greatness, and I was learning to be content with real conveniences that were not costly, so that a way of life free from much entanglement appeared best for me, though the income might be small. I had several offers of business that appeared profitable, but I did not see my way clear to accept them, believing they would be attended with more outward care and cumber than was required of me to engage in. I saw that an humble man, with the blessing of the Lord, might live on a little and that where the heart was set on greatness, success in business did not satisfy the craving; but that commonly with an increase of wealth the desire of wealth increased. There was a care on my mind so to pass my time that nothing might hinder me from the most steady attention to the voice of the true Shepherd.

Hath He who gave me a being attended with many wants unknown to brute creatures given me a capacity superior to theirs, and shown me that a moderate application to business is suitable to my present condition; and that this, attended with His blessing, may supply all my outward wants while they remain within the bounds He hath fixed, and while no imaginary wants proceeding from an evil spirit have any place in me? Attend then, O my soul! to this pure wisdom as thy sure conductor through the manifold dangers of this world.*

John Woolman, 1720–1772

☐

And it remains true, no matter whom the idea displeases, that no merchant lives at ease. He has put his heart into such a state of war that he burns alive to acquire more, nor will he ever have acquired enough. He has undertaken a wondrous task: He aspires to drink up the whole Seine, but he will never be able to drink so much that there will not remain more. This is the distress, the fire, the anguish which lasts forever; it is the pain, the battle which tears his guts and torments him in his lack: The more he acquires, the more he needs.

Lawyers and physicians are all shackled by this bond. They sell knowledge for pennies; they all hang themselves by this rope. They find gain so sweet and pleasant that the physician wishes he had sixty patients for the one he has, and the lawyer thirty cases for one, indeed two hundred or two thousand, so much covetousness and guile burn in their hearts.*

Roman de la Rose, 13th cent.

□

Ernest Bader started the enterprise of Scott Bader Co. Ltd. in 1920, at the age of thirty. Thirty-one years later, after many trials and tribulations during the war, he had a prosperous medium-scale business employing 161 people, with a turnover of about £625,000 a year and net profits exceeding £72,000. Having started with virtually nothing, he and his family had become prosperous. His firm had established itself as a leading producer of polyester resins and also manufactured other sophisticated products, such as alkyds, polymers, and plasticizers. As a young man he had been deeply dissatisfied with his prospects of life as an employee; he had resented the very ideas of a "labor market" and a "wages system," and particularly the thought that capital employed men, instead of men employing capital. Finding himself now in the position of employer, he never forgot that his success and prosperity were the achievements not of himself alone but of all his collaborators and decidedly also of the society within which he was privileged to operate. He decided to introduce "revolutionary changes" in his firm, "based on a philosophy which attempts to fit industry to human needs."

Mr. Bader realized at once that no *decisive* changes could be made without two things: first, a transformation of ownership—mere profit-sharing, which he had practiced from the very start, was not enough; and, second, the voluntary acceptance of certain self-denying ordinances. To achieve the first, he set up the Scott Bader Commonwealth in which he vested the ownership of his firm, Scott Bader Co. Ltd. To implement the second, he agreed with his new partners, that is to say, the members of the Commonwealth, his former employees, to establish a *constitution* not only to define the distribution of the "bundle of powers" which private ownership implies, but also to impose such restrictions on the firm's freedom of action as:

—the firm shall remain an undertaking of limited size, so that every person in it can embrace it in his mind and imagination. It shall not grow beyond 350 persons or thereabouts. If circumstances appear to demand growth beyond this limit, they shall be met by helping to set up new, fully independent units organized along the lines of the Scott Bader Commonwealth.

—the Commonwealth shall devote one-half of the appropriated profits to the payment of bonuses to those working within the operating company and the other half to charitable purposes outside the Scott Bader organization.

—none of the products of Scott Bader Co. Ltd. shall be sold to customers who are known to use them for war-related purposes.

When Mr. Ernest Bader and his colleagues introduced these revolutionary changes, it was freely predicted that a firm operating on this basis of collectivized ownership and self-imposed restrictions could not possibly survive. In fact, it went from strength to strength, although difficulties, even crises and setbacks, were by no means absent.

[While] no one has *acquired* any property, Mr. Bader and his family have nonetheless deprived themselves of their property. They have voluntarily abandoned the chance of becoming inordinately rich. Now, one does not have to be a believer in total equality, whatever that may mean, to be able to see that the existence of inordinately rich people in any society today is a very great evil. Some inequalities of wealth and income are no doubt "natural" and functionally justifiable, and there are few people who do not spontaneously recognize this. But here again, as in all human affairs, it is a matter of scale. Excessive wealth, like power, tends to corrupt. Even if the rich are not "idle rich," even when they work harder than anyone else, they work differently, apply

81

different standards, and are set apart from common humanity. They corrupt themselves by practicing greed, and they corrupt the rest of society by provoking envy. Mr. Bader drew the consequences of these insights and refused to become inordinately rich and thus made it possible to build a real *community*.*

E. F. Schumacher, 1973

□

The business of America is business.

Calvin Coolidge, 1872–1933

□

If all our inhabitants lived according to sound wisdom, laboring to promote universal love and righteousness, and ceased from every inordinate desire after wealth, and from all customs which are tinctured with luxury, the way would be easy for our inhabitants, though they might be much more numerous than at present, to live comfortably on honest employments, without the temptation they are so often under of being drawn into schemes to make settlements on lands which have not been purchased of the Indians, or of applying to that wicked practice of selling rum to them.

John Woolman, 1720–1772

□

I'm not in business for my health.

Anonymous

□

A man completely enslaved to wealth can never be honest.

Democritus, ca. 420 B.C.

THE RIGHT THING

□

Get not ill gains: Ill gains are even as disasters.

Hesiod, 8th cent. B.C.

□

In intercourse with others do not do all which you may lawfully do, but keep something within thy power; and because there is a latitude of gain in buying and selling, take not thou the utmost penny that is lawful, or which thou thinkest so; for although it be lawful, yet it is not safe; and he that gains all that he can gain lawfully this year, possibly next year will be tempted to gain something unlawfully.

Jeremy Taylor, 1840

□

An honest man has hardly need to count more than his ten fingers, or in extreme cases he may add his ten toes, and lump the rest. Simplicity, simplicity, simplicity! I say, let your affairs be as two or three, and not a hundred or a thousand; instead of a million count half a dozen, and keep your accounts on your thumb nail.

Thoreau, 1817–1862

□

As a peg is held fast in the joint between stones, so dishonesty squeezes in between selling and buying.

Ecclesiasticus 27:2

□

If there is neither excessive wealth nor immoderate poverty in a nation, then justice may be said to prevail.

Thales of Miletus, 640?–546 B.C.

LESS IS MORE

☐

When things are *even* there never can be war.

Solon, 638–559? B.C.

☐

One hears of the mechanical equivalent of heat. What we now need to discover in the social realm is the moral equivalent of war: something heroic that will speak to men as universally as war does, and yet will be as compatible with their spiritual selves as war has proved itself to be incompatible. I have often thought that in the old monkish poverty-worship, in spite of the pedantry which infested it, there might be something like that moral equivalent of war which we are seeking. May not voluntarily accepted poverty be "the strenuous life," without the need of crushing weaker peoples?

Poverty indeed *is* the strenuous life—without brass bands or uniforms or hysteric popular applause or lies or circumlocutions; and when one sees the way in which wealth-getting enters as an ideal into the very bone and marrow of our generation, one wonders whether a revival of the belief that poverty is a worthy religious vocation may not be "the transformation of military courage," and the spiritual reform which our time stands most in need of.

William James, 1842–1910

☐

Facts seem to me to point more strongly than ever to the importance of voluntary poverty today. At least we can avoid being comfortable through the exploitation of others. And at least we can avoid physical wealth as the result of a war economy. There may be ever-improving standards of living in the United States, with every worker eventually owning his own home and driving his own car; but our whole modern economy is based on preparation for war, and this surely is one of the great arguments for poverty in our time. If the comfort one achieves results in the death of millions in the future, then that comfort shall be duly paid for. Indeed, to be literal, contributing to the war (misnamed "defense") effort is very difficult to avoid. If you work in a textile mill making cloth, or in a factory making dungarees or blankets, your work is still tied up with war. If you raise food or irrigate the land to raise food, you may be feeding troops or liberating others to serve as troops. If you ride a bus you are paying taxes. Whatever you buy is taxed, so that you are, in effect, helping to support the state's preparations for war exactly to the extent of your attachment to worldly things of whatever kind.

Dorothy Day, 1963

□

Napier (1550–1617) acquired a great reputation as an inventor; for with his intellectual gifts he combined a fertile nimbleness in making machines. His constant efforts to fashion easier modes of arithmetical calculation led him to produce a variety of devices. But what impressed his friends was a piece of artillery of such appalling efficiency that it was able to kill all cattle within the radius of a mile. Napier, horrified, refused to develop this terrifying invention, and it was forgotten.

□

The current notion that it is possible to establish a collective peace and brotherhood among men who are individually filled with every manner of restlessness, would have seemed to [the Buddha] positively delirious. We are wont to deal with the question of war and peace at its extreme periphery; . . . the Buddhist would begin at the center . . . with the issue of war or peace in the heart of the individual. Any conquest that the individual may win over his inordinate desires will be reflected at once in his contact with other men.*

Irving Babbitt, 1865–1933

85

LESS IS MORE

□

"At first I thought the Cambodians were going to take us out and shoot us. But they were so nice, really kind. They fed us first and everything. . . ."

"I don't think anybody got sick on their food even though it wasn't what you would go into a restaurant and order. They served us first and ate the leftovers."

SS *Mayaguez* crewmen,
comments on their captors,
Time, May 26, 1975

□

Let me tell you one thing. When the white man prays, he prays for what *he* wants, for himself. When the Indian prays he prays for other people. The last words of the Indian prayer are these: *"If there is anything left, let it be for me."* You do not hear the Anglos pray that way. It is our way. We shall keep it our way.

Andy Abieta, Governor, Isleta Pueblo, New Mexico

□

"But increased production is important." Of course it is! That plenty is good and scarcity evil—it needs no ghost from the past to tell us that. But plenty consists upon cooperative efforts and cooperation upon moral principles. And moral principles are what the prophets of this dispensation despise. And so the world "continues in scarcity," because it is too grasping and too short-sighted to seek that "which maketh men to be of one mind in a house." The well-intentioned schemes for social reorganization put forward by its commercial teachers are abortive because they endeavor to combine incompatibles, and, if they disturb everything, settle nothing . . . and when their fit of feverish energy has spent itself, and there is nothing to show for it except disillusionment, they cry that reform is impracticable and blame human nature, when what they ought to blame is themselves.*

R. H. Tawney, 1880–1962

☐

Any discussion of world poverty that does not come round to demanding a radical change in our habits of consumption and waste, our tastes, our profligate standard of living, our values generally is a hypocrisy. There are no technical answers to ethical questions.

Theodore Roszak, 1972

☐

MAMMON AVENUE

As a society becomes increasingly affluent, wants are increasingly created by the process by which they are satisfied. . . . This higher level of production has, merely, a higher level of want creation necessitating a higher level of want satisfaction.

If the individual's wants are to be urgent they must be original with himself. They cannot be urgent if they must be contrived for him. And above all they must not be contrived by the process of production by which they are satisfied. For this means that the whole case for the urgency of production, based on the urgency of wants, falls to the ground. One cannot defend production as satisfying wants if that production creates the wants.

The fact that wants can be synthesized by advertising, catalyzed by salesmanship, and shaped by the discreet manipulations of the persuaders shows that they are not very urgent. The latter are effective only with those who are so far removed from physical want that they do not already know what they want. In this state alone men are open to persuasion.**

John Kenneth Galbraith, 1958

□

No one is content with that station in life from which he started. Simplicity, thrift, the art of making a little go a long way, the cultivation of the fireside have few votaries. The creation of new wants is one of the greatest of American industries, and is pursued with an energy, ingenuity, and prodigality which makes European performances in the same line look childish.

J. A. Spender, 1862–1942

□

Can the general level of taste and intelligence rise to permit society to see beyond the point of immediate cash value into some of those more aesthetic vistas proposed by the great teachers of humanity?

In the commercialism, the ugliness of taste, the mass mediocrity of so much contemporary society there is little to encourage a facile optimism.

Yet the matter is by no means certain, and there may well be forces in a Society of Wealth which would lead it to embrace a scale of values in which sheer profitability occupied a lower place.

In the centuries behind us the dark side of the quest for wealth could well be disregarded, for the acquisitive drive had an all-important task to perform—to propel society itself toward social abundance. But now and in the future, when that great purpose has neared its accomplishment, this urgency of need can no longer be used as the prime rationalization of the drive. As we march toward a Society of Wealth, the material justification of the acquisitive drive must diminish and its psychological and moral aspects must therefore rise higher in the balance.*

Robert Heilbroner, 1956

□

Spoken or printed, broadcast over the ether or on woodpulp, all advertising copy has but one purpose—to prevent the will from

88

ever achieving silence. Desirelessness is the condition of deliverance and illumination. The condition of an expanding and technologically progressive system of mass production is universal craving. Advertising is the organized effort to extend and intensify craving—to extend and intensify, that is to say, the workings of that force, which (as all the saints and teachers of all the higher religions have always taught) is the principal cause of suffering and wrong-doing and the greatest obstacle between the human soul and its divine Ground.

Aldous Huxley, 1894–1963

□

The heart of truth in our traditional philosophies was God or His equivalent. . . . The heart of truth in pecuniary philosophy is contained in the following three postulates:

Truth is what sells.
Truth is what you want people to believe.
Truth is that which is not legally false.*

Jules Henry, 1963

□

The superior man understands what is right,
The inferior man understands what will sell.
The superior man loves his soul,
The inferior man loves his property;
The superior man always remembers how he was punished for his
    mistakes,
The inferior man always remembers what presents he got.

Confucius, ca. 551–479 B.C.

□

It had been my general practice to buy and sell things really useful. Things that served chiefly to please the vain mind in

89

people, I was not easy to trade in; seldom did it; and whenever I did I found it weaken me as a Christian.

The increase of business became my burden; for though my natural inclination was toward merchandise, yet I believed truth required me to live more free from outward cumbers; and there was now a strife in my mind between the two. In this exercise my prayers were put up to the Lord, who graciously heard me, and gave me a heart resigned to his holy will. Then I lessened my outward business, and, as I had opportunity, told my customers of my intentions, that they might consider what shop to turn to; and in a while I wholly laid down merchandise, and followed my trade as a tailor by myself, having no apprentice. In merchandise it is the custom where I lived to sell chiefly on credit, and poor people often got in debt; when payment is expected, not having wherewith to pay, their creditors often sue for it at law. Having frequently observed occurrences of this kind, I found it good for me to advise poor people to take such goods as were most useful, and not costly.

John Woolman, 1720–1772

☐

TEACHING PEOPLE TO WANT THINGS

Salesmanship tries not only to make things attractive to you, but also it seeks to make buying easy for you. And in the last few years, in pursuit of the latter end, it has evolved the Installment System. This marks a new phase in distribution. Great multitudes of people are now in possession of goods that they partially own. They have paid an "advance"; they pay for two or three years to complete their purchase, and meanwhile, in case of default, the seller has the power of recovering the goods. They buy first instead of buying last or not at all.

The social consequences of this new method of distribution are still a matter for speculation.**

H. G. Wells, 1866–1946

THE RIGHT THING

□

WILLY LOMAN: They time those things. They time them so when you finally paid for them, they're used up.

Arthur Miller, *Death of a Salesman,* 1949

□

. . . From this process of accelerating obsolescence by technological progress flow the benefits we all share. . . .

Harlow Curtice, 1956
President, General Motors

□

It is true that the consumer is sometimes caught in a carefully engineered trap—an old product whose death has been deliberately hastened by its manufacturer, and the simultaneous appearance of a "new improved" model advertised as the latest heaven-sent triumph of advanced technology.*

Alvin Toffler, 1970

□

[We] appear to be in a trap in which we may become weary of the goods we have learned to miss not having, without having learned other than inchoately what we are missing when we do have them.

David Riesman, 1964

□

Aided and abetted by advertising and the installment plan, the two most fearsome social inventions of man since the discovery of gunpowder, selling has become the most striking activity of contemporary America. Against frugality, selling emphasizes prodigality; against asceticism, the lavishness of display.

Daniel Bell, 1956

☐

Every corner of the public psyche is canvassed by some of the nation's most talented citizens to see if the desire for some merchantable product can be cultivated. . . .*

John Kenneth Galbraith, 1958

☐

I think of a message displayed on TV and posters. It shows the face of an old Indian with a tear running down his cheek, and the caption: "Pollution: it's a crying shame." You see, it's not just that smog, like onions, brings tears to your eyes. It's that the lifestyle symbolized by the pollution we promote is so totally and viciously at variance with a life in harmony with the rhythm of the Earth.

And in the midst of an urgent need for radical alterations in our economy and lifestyle what do we do with television? We take the greatest communications system ever available to the human race, put a TV in nearly every home, and let it run six hours a day—to do what? To encourage increased consumption of sugar, meat, alcohol, coffee, and carcinogenic additives; the purchase of automobiles and other energy-guzzling appliances; and a lifestyle designed at every turn to encourage ill health, rapacious consumption of precious resources, a psychosis of materialism, creation of enormous quantities of pollution and trash, an inequitable distribution of wealth within the United States and an immoral distribution abroad—that's what we do with television.

Television: It's a crying shame.*

Nicholas Johnson, 1975

☐

92

THE RIGHT THING

Just as we are lowering our water table by ever-deeper artesian wells and in general digging ever deeper for other treasures of the earth, so we are sinking deeper and deeper wells into people in the hope of coming upon "motives" which can power the economy or some particular sector of it. I am suggesting that such digging, such forcing emotions to externalize themselves, cannot continue much longer without man running dry.

David Riesman, 1964

☐

As technological drivenness mines the earth of wealth, so it mines the desires of men: As the strip-shovel rips coal from the earth, as the pump sucks oil from the bed, so advertising dredges man's hidden needs and consumes them in the "hard sell."

Jules Henry, 1963

☐

It has occurred to me that I am employed in a dying industry. Advertising is not dying out for any of the usually advocated reasons—immoral or distasteful behavior in the marketplace. Perhaps it should be killed for those reasons but it will not be necessary. Advertising is a critical element encouraging an economic system committed to growth. However, there is only so much getting bigger possible.

I am prepared to bet that the ultimate answer to ecological problems is not cleverer technology. It will probably be less technology, at least of a certain sort, and I never would have thought five years ago that I'd be coming out on the side of the Luddites today.

Unlike them, however, I am not saying we should tear down factories, or that there should be no technology. Naturally. But I am saying there should probably be a lot less of it, and less people to be served by it, of course, but most important, *less emphasis on increase, starting now.* Less emphasis on acquisition and material wealth as any measure of anything good.

93

I hereby volunteer my own office to undertake the ad campaign for the government, free, whether it's contraceptives or reduced power, if the government would only be willing to recognize the importance of both.*

Jerry Mander, advertising executive, 1969

☐

Products created for short-term or one-time use are becoming more numerous and crucial to our way of life.

We develop a throw-away mentality to match our throw-away products. . . .

Alvin Toffler, 1970

☐

If we have only trash and trivialities to sell, we must produce trashy and trivial personalities to serve as consumers.

Lewis Mumford, 1944

☐

Clearly the attitudes and values which make production the central achievement of our society have some exceptionally twisted roots.

John Kenneth Galbraith, 1958

☐

The ethics of humanity's manhood will be neither "animal" ethics nor "*super*natural" ethics. It will not be a branch of zoology, the ethics of tooth and claw, the ethics of profiteering, the ethics of space-binding beasts fighting for "a place in the sun." It will be a branch of humanology, a branch of Human Engineering; it will be a time-binding ethics, the ethics of the entirely natural civilization-producing energies of humanity. "Survival of the fittest" in the sense of the *strongest* is a space-binding standard, the ethical standard of beasts; in the ethics of humanity's manhood survival of the fittest will mean survival of the *best* in competitions for excellence, and excellence will mean time-binding excellence—excellence in the production and right use of material and spiritual wealth. . . .*

Count Alfred Korzybski, 1879–1950

6

DESIRE/GREED, NECESSITY/NEED

THE TEN THOUSAND THINGS

The first developments of the heart were the effects of a new situation, which united husbands and wives, parents and children under one roof. The two sexes by living a little more at their ease began to lose somewhat of their usual ferocity and sturdiness; but if on the one hand individuals became less able to engage separately with wild beasts, they on the other were more easily got together to make a common resistance against them.

In this new state of things, the simplicity and solitariness of man's life, the limitedness of his wants, and the instruments which he had invented to satisfy them, leaving him a great deal of leisure, he employed it to supply himself with several conveniences unknown to his ancestors; and this was the first yoke he inadvertently imposed upon himself; for besides continuing in this manner to soften both body and mind, these conveniences having through use lost almost all their aptness to please, and even degenerated into real wants, the privation of them became far more intolerable than the possession of them had been agreeable; to lose them was a misfortune, to possess them no happiness.

As long as men remained satisfied with their rustic cabins; as long as they confined themselves to the use of clothes made of the skins of other animals, and the use of thorns and fish-bones, in putting these skins together; as long as they continued to consider feathers and shells as sufficient ornaments; in a word, as long as they undertook such works only as a single person could finish, and stuck to such arts as did not require the joint endeavors of several hands, they lived free, healthy, honest, and happy, as much as their nature would admit, and continued to enjoy with each other all the pleasures of an independent intercourse.

On the other hand, man, heretofore free and independent, was now in consequence of a multitude of new wants brought under subjection, as it were, to all nature. Mankind thus debased and harassed, and no longer able to retreat, or renounce the unhappy acquisitions it had made; laboring, in short, merely to its confusion by the abuse of those faculties, which in themselves do it so much honor, brought itself to the very brink of ruin and destruction.*

Jean Jacques Rousseau, 1712–1778

☐

If a man would guide his life by true philosophy, he will find ample riches in a modest livelihood enjoyed with a tranquil mind. Of that little he need never be beggared. Men craved for fame and power so that their fortune might rest on a firm foundation and they might live out a peaceful life in the enjoyment of plenty. An idle dream.

For what we have here and now, unless we have known something more pleasing in the past, gives the greatest satisfaction and is reckoned the best of its kind. Afterwards the discovery of something new and better blunts and vitiates our enjoyment of the old. So it is that we have lost our taste for acorns. So we have abandoned those couches littered with herbage and heaped with leaves. So the wearing of wild beasts' skins has gone out of fashion.

Skins yesterday, purple and gold today—such are the baubles that embitter human life with resentment and waste it with war. In this, I do not doubt, the greater blame rests with us. To the earth-born generation in their naked state the lack of skins meant real discomfort through cold; but we are in no way discommoded by going without robes of purple, brocaded with gold and generously emblazoned, so long as we have some plebeian wrap to throw around us. So mankind is perpetually the victim of a pointless and futile martyrdom, fretting life away in fruitless worries through failure to realize what limit is set to acquisition and to the growth of genuine pleasure. It is this discontent that has driven life steadily onward, out to the high seas, and has stirred up from the depths the surging tumultuous tides of war.*

Lucretius, 96?–55 B.C.

□

That which we miscall poverty is indeed nature; and its proportions are the just measures of a man, and the best instruments of content. But when we create needs that God or nature never made, we have erected to ourselves an infinite stock of trouble that can have no period. Sempronius complained of want of clothes, and was much troubled for a new suit, being ashamed to appear in the theatre with his gown a little threadbare: But when he got it, and gave his old clothes to Codrus, the poor man was ravished with joy, and went and gave God thanks for his new purchase; and Codrus was made richly fine and cheerfully warm by that which Sempronius was ashamed to wear; and yet their natural needs were both alike: The difference only was that Sempronius had some artificial and fantastical necessities superinduced, which Codrus had not.

God and nature made no more ends than they mean to satisfy, and he that will make more must look for satisfaction where he can.

Jeremy Taylor, 1840

□

There is not anything that is necessary to us, but we have it either cheap or gratis. . . . Providence has been kinder to us than to leave us to live by our wits, and to stand in need of invention and arts. So long as men contented themselves with their lot there was no violence, no engrossing or hiding of those benefits for particular advantages which were appointed for the community, but every man had as much care for his neighbor as for himself—no arms, or bloodshed; no war, but with wild beasts: But, under the protection of a wood or a cave, they spent their days without cares, and their nights without groans. Their innocence was their security and their protection. There were as yet no beds of state, no ornaments of pearl or embroidery, nor any of those remorses that attend them; but the heavens were their canopy, and the glories of them their spectacle. The motions of the orbs, the courses of the stars, and the wonderful order of Providence, was their contemplation. They had no palaces then like cities, but they had open air and breathing room—crystal fountains, refreshing shades, the meadows dressed up in their native beauty, and such houses as were afforded by nature, and wherein they lived contentedly, without fear either of loss or injury. These people lived without either solicitude or fraud. They had not as yet torn up the bowels of the earth for gold, silver, or precious stones; and, so far were they from killing any man, as we do, for a spectacle, that they were not as yet come to it, either in fear or anger. It is the wonderful benignity of nature that has laid open to us all things that may do us good, and only hid those things from us that may hurt us—as if she durst not trust us with gold and silver, or with iron, which is the instrument of war and contention for another's. It is we ourselves that have drawn out of the earth both the causes and the instruments of our dangers, and we are so vain as to set the highest esteem upon those things to which nature has assigned the lowest place. What can be more coarse and rude in the mine than these precious metals, or more slavish and dirty than the people that dig and work them? And yet they defile our minds more than our bodies, and make the possessor fouler than the artificer of them. Rich men, in fine, are only the greater slaves—both the one and the other wants a great deal.*

Seneca, 4? B.C.–A.D. 65

□

[If] in stable cultures all over the world almost every object, however bizarre it may seem to us, is found to have a complementary need, it is only common sense to suppose that human beings have the potential for developing an enormous variety of needs. If the Ashanti of West Africa, for example, need golden stools, the natives of the South American jungles need curare, intoxicating drugs, dyed parrots, feather cloaks, shrunken heads, and flutes several feet long and the Kwakiutl Indians needed totem poles, slat armor, engraved copper plates six feet square, and painted cedar boxes inlaid with mother of pearl, one can realize without even looking at Greece, Rome, Babylon, Egypt, and modern America that human beings have the capacity to learn to want almost any conceivable material object. Given, then, the emergence of a modern industrial culture capable of producing almost anything, the time is ripe for opening the storehouse of infinite need! But bear in mind that since our equation states that a necessary condition for cultural stability is perfect economic complementarity, it follows that lack of complementarity—a modern condition in which new objects are constantly seeking new needs, and new needs are constantly chasing after new objects—involves cultural *in*stability. Meanwhile, we know that the storehouse of infinite need is now being opened in America. It is the modern Pandora's box, and its plagues are loose upon the world.*

Jules Henry, 1963

☐

The senses are no longer satisfied; they are jaded. Instead of meeting with stimulating variations, we come face to face with bizarre and nauseating extravagance; this is why everything keeps changing continually and for no good reason: fashion, dress, customs, manners, and speech. The rich soon become insensible to new pleasures. The furnishings of their houses have the character of changeable stage settings; to dress up becomes a real task; their meals are pageants. In my opinion luxury is to them as much an affliction as poverty is to the poor.

Louis Mercier, 1740–1814

DESIRE/GREED, NECESSITY/NEED

☐

The wealth demanded by nature is both limited and easily procured; that demanded by idle imaginings stretches on to infinity.

Epicurus, 342?–270? B.C.

☐

Thirst for happiness being eternal,
Desires are without beginning.

Patanjali, 2d cent.? B.C.

☐

Everything is desire.

Sri Baba Hari Dass, 1965

☐

Desire is an acrid, astringent, attracting (contracting) quality. It is an active power, and without it, there would be nothing but tranquility. It contracts and fills itself with itself.

Jakob Boehme, 1575–1624

☐

By attributing worth to tangible objects, man becomes attracted to them; attraction to them brings desire for them; desire leads to competition and dispute amongst men. These rouse violent anger, and the result is delusion. Delusion completely overcomes man's sense of right and wrong.

Srimad Bhagavatam XI: xiv

☐

Thinking of sense-objects, man becomes attached thereto. From attachment arises longing and from longing anger is born. From anger arises delusion; from delusion, loss of memory is caused. From loss of memory, the discriminative faculty is ruined and from the ruin of discrimination, he perishes.

Bhagavad-Gita, II:60–63

☐

Riches destroy the foolish, if they look not for the other shore; by his thirst for riches the foolish man destroys himself as if he were his own enemy.

Dhammapada

☐

A Ch'i individual stole some money at a crowded bazaar. He was walking away with it when the police asked him why it was that he stole the money in the market. The thief replied that the sight of the money filled his mind to the exclusion of the policemen. So his desires made him forgetful of the nature of his act.

Huai-nan Tzû, d. 122 B.C.

☐

We are exposed to the corrupting power of *things,* the astonishing number and variety of things produced by the processes which we ourselves created: the supposedly neutral things which we *consume,* as the interesting word has it, and which enter into our substance and hold us in bondage. Technological dominion turns everything—the works of man and man himself—into things, into marketable commodities.

D. S. Carne-Ross, 1975

☐

DESIRE/GREED, NECESSITY/NEED

Things are in the saddle and ride mankind.

Emerson, 1803–1882

□

All things are full of weariness; man cannot utter it: the eye is not satisfied with seeing, nor the ear filled with hearing. That which hath been is that which shall be; and that which hath been done is that which shall be done: and there is no new thing under the sun.

Ecclesiastes 1:8–9

□

THINGS: THE THROW-AWAY SOCIETY

The ocean of man-made physical objects that surrounds us is set within a larger ocean of natural objects. . . . Their number is expanding with explosive force, both absolutely and relative to the natural environment. This will be even more true in super-industrial society than it is today.

The turnover of things in our lives thus grows even more frenetic. We face a rising flood of throwaway items, impermanent architecture, mobile and modular products, rental goods, and commodities designed for an almost instant death.**

Alvin Toffler, 1970

□

We forgot that the sensual objects were pleasant and cool only like the shade under the hissing hood of an angry serpent and we sought them as capable of giving us happiness.

Sri Chandrasekhara Bharati Swamigal, d. 1954

□

LESS IS MORE

Desire and satiety fill with distress
the regions above and below pleasure.

Michel de Montaigne, 1533–1592

□

As want is the constant scourge of the people, so ennui is that of
the fashionable world. In middle-class life ennui is represented
by the Sunday, and want by the six week days.

Thus between desiring and attaining all human life flows on
throughout. The wish is, in its nature, pain, the attainment soon
begets satiety: The end was only apparent; possession takes away
the charm; the wish, the need, presents itself under a new form;
when it does not, then follows desolateness, emptiness ennui,
against which the conflict is just as painful as against want.

Arthur Schopenhauer, 1788–1860

□

I put for a general inclination of all mankind a perpetual and
restless desire of power after power, that ceaseth only in death.
And the cause of this is not always that a man hopes for a more
intensive delight than he has already attained to, or that he cannot be content with a moderate power; but because he cannot
assure the power and means to live well which he hath present,
without the acquisition of more. And from hence it is that kings,
whose power is greatest, turn their endeavors to the assuring it
at home by laws, or abroad by wars; and, when that is done, there
succeedeth a new desire.

Thomas Hobbes, 1588–1679

□

Desire can't be satisfied by fulfilling. It grows more and more
and there is no end of desires. If a person becomes a king of a

104

country he desires other countries. But one who doesn't want to possess any thing possesses everything. The desires can be given up by understanding desires.

Sri Baba Hari Dass, 1973

□

To what end do men gather riches, but to multiply more? Do they not like Pyrrhus, the King of Epire, add house to house and lands to lands, that they may get it all? It is storied of that prince, that having conceived a purpose to invade Italy, he sent for Cineas, a philosopher and the King's friend: to whom he communicated his design, and desired his counsel. Cineas asked him to what purpose he invaded Italy? He said, to conquer it. And what will you do when you have conquered it? Go into France, said the King, and conquer that. And what will you do when you have conquered France? Conquer Germany. And what then? said the philosopher. Conquer Spain. I perceive, said Cineas, you mean to conquer all the World. What will you do when you have conquered all? Why then said the King we will return, and enjoy ourselves at quiet in our own land. So you may now, said the philosopher, without this ado. Yet could he not divert him till he was ruined by the Romans. Thus men get one hundred pound a year that they may get another; and having two covet eight, and there is no end of all their labor; because the desire of their Soul is insatiable. Like Alexander the Great they must have all: and when they have got it all, be quiet. And may they not do all this before they begin? Nay it would be well, if they could be quiet. But if after all, they shall be like the stars, that are seated on high, but have no rest, what gain they more, but labor for their trouble? It was wittily feigned that that young man sat down and cried for more worlds to conquer. So insatiable is man that millions will not please him. They are no more than so many tennis-balls, in comparison of the Greatness and Highness of his Soul.

Thomas Traherne, 1637?–1674

□

LESS IS MORE

The American chases after money with all his might, exactly as on the tennis court he tries to hit the ball.

Hugo Münsterberg, 1863–1916

☐

... Mad in pursuit, and in possession so;
    Had, having, and in quest to have, extreme. . . .

Shakespeare, 1564–1616

☐

For of a froward will, was a lust made; and a lust served, became custom; and custom not resisted, became necessity.

St. Augustine, 354–430

☐

Every moment Thou are delivering us, and again we are going to a snare, O Thou who art without want!

Rūmi, 1207–1273

☐

Seek among men, from beggar to millionaire, one who is contented with his lot, and you will not find one such in a thousand. Each one spends his strength in pursuit of what is exacted by the doctrine of the world, and of what he is unhappy not to possess, and scarcely has he obtained one object of his desires when he strives for another, and still another, in that infinite labor of Sisyphus which destroys the lives of men. Run over the scale of individual fortunes, ranging from a yearly income of three hundred rubles to fifty thousand rubles, and you will rarely find a person who is not striving to gain four hundred rubles if he have three hundred, five thousand if he have four hundred, and so on to the top of the ladder. Among them all you will scarcely find one who, with five hundred rubles, is willing to adopt the mode of life of him who has only four hundred. . . . Today we must buy an overcoat and galoshes, tomorrow, a watch and a chain; the next day we must install ourselves in an apartment with a sofa and a bronze lamp; then we must have carpets and velvet gowns; then a house, horses and carriages, paintings and decorations, and then—then we fall ill of overwork and die. Another continues the same task, sacrifices his life to this same Moloch, and then dies also, without realizing for what he has lived.*

Count Leo Tolstoy, 1828–1910

☐

What is the right way to live?

By lessening our demand.
Demand increases desires and desire makes demand which creates dissatisfaction. Dissatisfaction makes pain.

Sri Baba Hari Dass, 1973

☐

Hunger and impotence lead the poor to demand rapid industrialization and the defense of growing luxuries pushes the rich into more frantic production. Power is polarized, frustration is generalized, and the alternative of greater happiness at lower affluence is pushed into the blind spot of social vision.

Ivan Illich, 1973

☐

And now let us see whether riches really drive away need. Don't the wealthy become hungry and thirsty; don't they feel cold in the winter? You may argue that they have the means to satisfy their hunger and thirst, and to protect themselves against the

cold. Nevertheless, the needs remain, and riches can only minimize them. For if needs are always present and making demands
which must be met by spending money, clearly there will always
be some need which is unsatisfied. And here I do not press the
point that, although nature makes very modest demands, avarice
is never satisfied. . . . If riches cannot eliminate need, but on
the contrary create new demands, what makes you suppose that
they can provide satisfaction?*

Boethius, 480?–524?

□

Ballance: Men seek Wealth rather than Subsistence; and the
End of Cloaths is the least Reason of their Use. Nor is the satisfying of our Appetite our End in Eating, so much as the pleasing
of our Pallate. The like may also be said of Building, Furniture,
&c, where the Man rules not the Beast, and Appetite submits not
to Reason.

William Penn, 1644–1718

□

The rich man consumes no more food than his poor neighbor. In
quality it may be very different, and to select and prepare it may
require more labor and art; but in quantity it is very nearly the
same. But compare the spacious palace and the great wardrobe of
the one, with the hovel and the few rags of the other, and you
will be sensible that the difference between their cloathing, lodging, and household furniture, is almost as great in quantity as
it is in quality. The desire of food is limited in every man by
the narrow capacity of the human stomach; but the desire of the
conveniences and ornaments of building, dress, equipage, and
household furniture seems to have no limit or certain boundary.
What is over and above satisfying the limited desire, is given for
the amusement of those desires which cannot be satisfied, but
seem to be altogether endless. Hence arises a demand for every
sort of material which human invention can employ, either use-

fully or ornamentally; for the fossils and minerals contained in the bowels of the earth, the precious metals, and the precious stones. . . .

Adam Smith, 1723–1790

☐

Throw a crust of bread to a dog, he takes it open-mouthed, swallows it whole, and presently gapes for more. Just so do we with the gifts of fortune; down they go without chewing, and we are immediately ready for another chop. But what has avarice now to do with gold and silver, that is so much outdone by curiosities of a far greater value? Let us no longer complain that there was not a heavier load laid upon those precious metals, or that they were not buried deep enough, when we have found out ways by wax and parchments, and by bloody usurious contracts, to undo one another. It is remarkable that providence has given us all things for our advantage near at hand; but iron, gold, and silver (being both the instruments of blood and slaughter, and the price of it), nature has hidden in the bowels of the earth.

Seneca, 4? B.C.–A.D. 65

☐

The satisfaction of man's elemental material needs opens the way for new, more sophisticated gratifications. We are moving from a "gut" economy to a "psyche" economy because there is only so much gut to be satisfied.

Alvin Toffler, 1970

☐

I confess that I apprehend much less for democratic society from the boldness than from the mediocrity of desires. What appears to me most to be dreaded, is, that, in the midst of the small incessant occupations of private life, ambition should lose its vigor and its greatness; that the passions of man should abate, but at the same time be lowered; so that the march of society should every day become more tranquil and less aspiring.

Nothing conceivable is so petty, so insipid, so crowded with paltry interests, in one word, so anti-poetic, as the life of a man in the United States.

Alexis de Tocqueville, 1805–1859

☐

With the transformation of American culture into a consuming one, all inhibitory emotions, all feelings that contribute in any way to an austere view of life and to the constriction of impulse, had to go.

Jules Henry, 1963

☐

The cloyed will,—
That satiate yet unsatisfied desire, that tub
Both fill'd and running,—ravening first the lamb,
Longs after the garbage.

Shakespeare, 1564–1616

☐

I can remember when the bison were so many that they could not be counted, but more and more Wasichus [white men] came to kill them until there were only heaps of bones scattered where they used to be. The Wasichus did not kill them to eat; they killed them for the metal that makes them crazy, and they took only the hides to sell. Sometimes they did not even take the hides, only the tongues; and I have heard that fireboats came down the Missouri River loaded with dried bison tongues. You can see that the men who did this were crazy. Sometimes they did not even take the tongues; they just killed and killed because they liked to do that. When we hunted bison, we killed only what we needed. And when there was nothing left but heaps of bones, the Wasichus came and gathered up even the bones and sold them.

Black Elk, 1931

□

The profit-making incentive still endures as a magnet for the greedy.

Jack Newfield, 1975

□

... Stung to the quick with gain's elusive itch
And pining with the thirst of getting rich ....

Horace, 65–8 B.C.

□

How could we even begin to disarm greed and envy? Perhaps by being much less greedy and envious ourselves; perhaps by resisting the temptation of letting our luxuries become needs; and perhaps by even scrutinizing our needs to see if they cannot be simplified and reduced.

E. F. Schumacher, 1973

□

Wherefore do ye spend money for that which is not bread?

Isaiah 55:2

□

Industrious habits in each bosom reign,
And industry begets a love of gain.
Hence all the goods from opulence that springs,
With all those ills superfluous treasure brings,

111

Are here displayed. Their much lov'd wealth imparts
Convenience, plenty, elegance, and arts;
But view them closer, craft and fraud appear,
Ev'n liberty itself is bartered here.
At gold's superior charms all freedom flies,
The needy sell it, and the rich man buys. . . .

Oliver Goldsmith, 1728–1774

□

[Our artificers were never so excellent in their trades as at this present. As their workmanship was never more fine and curious to the eye, so was it never less strong and substantial for the continuance and benefit of the buyers.] Neither is there anything that hurteth the common sort of our artificers more than haste, and a barbarous or slavish desire to turn the penny, and, by ridding their work, to make speedy utterance of their wares: which enforceth them to bungle up and despatch many things they care not how so they be out of their hands, whereby the buyer is often sore defrauded, and findeth to his cost that haste maketh waste, according to the proverb. Oh, how many trades and handicrafts are now in England whereof the commonwealth hath no need!

Holinshed's *Chronicles*, 1577

□

He that maketh haste to be rich shall not be innocent.

Proverbs 28:20

□

The handicraftsmen of democratic ages endeavor not only to bring their useful production within the reach of the whole community, but they strive to give to all their commodities attractive qualities which they do not in reality possess. In the confusion of all ranks, every one hopes to appear what he is not, and makes great exertions to succeed in this object. The hypocrisy of virtue is of every age, but the hypocrisy of luxury belongs more particularly to the ages of democracy. To satisfy these new cravings of human vanity, the arts have recourse to every species of imposture; and these devices sometimes go so far as to defeat their own purpose. Imitation diamonds are now made which may be easily mistaken for real ones; as soon as the art of fabricating false diamonds shall become so perfect that they cannot be distinguished from real ones, it is probable that both will be abandoned, and become mere pebbles again.*

Alexis de Tocqueville, 1805–1859

□

If consumers can no longer distinguish clearly between the real and the simulated, if whole stretches of one's life may be commercially programmed, we enter into a set of psycho-economic problems of breathtaking complexity. These problems challenge our most fundamental beliefs, not merely about democracy, but about the very nature of rationality and sanity.

Alvin Toffler, 1970

□

The strenuous and foolish things that people in our time seek to do with history—to multiply thermonuclear overkill endlessly, to raise up economics of limitless growth, to build conglomerate empires that straddle the globe, to turn the planet into one vast industrial artifact, to produce without limit, to consume beyond all sane need . . . all this is what people use to fill the emptiness inside them.*

Theodore Roszak, 1975

□

Will any man hesitate to endure poverty in order to free his mind from madness?

Seneca, 4? B.C.–A.D. 65

☐

If you must be mad, why should you be mad for the things of the world? If you must be mad, be mad for God alone.

Sri Ramakrishna, 1834–1886

☐

Since desire is more compelling than reason, it is important and necessary for man to know and manage his desire. To what extent, then, can he through reason satisfy his desire, or divert, thwart, or postpone its fulfillment—if that is his wish?

Dr. Jonas Salk, 1972

7

CONTROLLED FOLLY

ENOUGH IS ENOUGH

The "logic of production" is neither the logic of life nor that of
society. It is a small and subservient part of both. The destructive
forces unleashed by it cannot be brought under control, unless
the "logic of production" itself is brought under control—so that
destructive forces cease to be unleashed. It is of little use trying
to suppress terrorism if the production of deadly devices continues to be deemed a legitimate employment of man's creative
powers. Nor can the fight against pollution be successful if the
patterns of production and consumption continue to be of a
scale, a complexity, and a degree of violence which, as is becoming more and more apparent, do not fit into the laws of the universe, to which man is just as much subject as the rest of creation.
Equally, the chance of mitigating the rate of resource depletion
or of bringing harmony into the relationships between those in
possession of wealth and power and those without is nonexistent
as long as there is no idea anywhere of enough being good and
more-than-enough being evil.

E. F. Schumacher, 1973

☐

My last year's poverty was not poverty enough;
My poverty this year is poverty indeed.
In my poverty last year there was room for a gimlet's point;
But this year even the gimlet has gone.

Kyōgen Shikan, 9th cent.

LESS IS MORE

☐

He who but asks "Enough" defies
Wild waves to rob him of his ease;
He fears no rude shocks when he sees
Arcturus set or Haedus rise.

Horace, 65–8 B.C.

☐

He who knows he has enough is rich.

Tao Te Ching

☐

Enough! or Too Much.

William Blake, 1757–1827

☐

Too few know when they have enough; and fewer know how to employ it.

William Penn, 1644–1718

☐

Here is the test with every man, of whether money is the principal object with him, or not. If in midlife he could pause and say, "Now I have enough to live upon, I'll live upon it; and having well-earned it, I will also well spend it, and go out of the world poor, as I came in to it," then money is not principal with him; but if, having enough to live upon in the manner benefiting his character and rank, he still wants to make more, and to *die* rich, then money is the principal object with him, and it becomes a curse to himself, and generally to those who spend it after him.

Ruskin, 1819–1900

CONTROLLED FOLLY

□

Lord! who would live turmoiled in the court
And may enjoy such quiet walks as these?
This small inheritance my father left me,
Contenteth me, and worth a monarchy.
I seek not to wax great by others waning,
Or gather wealth I care not with what envy:
Sufficeth that I have maintains my state,
And sends the poor well pleased from my gate.

Shakespeare, 1564–1616

□

Whatever is enough is abundant in the eyes of Nature.

Seneca 4? B.C.–A.D. 65
Ep. LXXXIV

□

At a certain season of our life we are accustomed to consider
every spot as the possible site of a house. I have thus surveyed
the country on every side within a dozen miles of where I live.
In imagination I have bought all the farms in succession, for all
were to be bought, and I knew their price. An afternoon sufficed
to lay out the land into orchard, woodlot, and pasture, and to
decide whence each blasted tree could be seen to the best advantage, and then I let it lie, fallow perchance, for a man is rich
in proportion to the number of things which he can afford to
let alone. I found thus that I had been a rich man without any
danger to my poverty.*

Thoreau, 1817–1862

□

When some desire comes, consider it. Then, suddenly, *quit it.*

Shiva

☐

We live happily indeed, free from greed among the greedy!
Among men who are greedy, let us dwell free from greed!
We live happily indeed, though we call nothing our own!
We shall be like the bright gods, feeding on happiness!

Dhammapada

☐

[I resolved] always to attempt the mastery over myself rather
than over fortune, to try to alter my desires rather than the
course of the world. For, as our will naturally only tends to desire
those things which the understanding represents as possible to it,
it is certain that, if we look upon all external goods as equally
outside our power, we should no more regret the loss of what
seems due to our birth, if we have been deprived of it through
no fault of our own, than we regret not being in possession of
the realms of China and Mexico.*

René Descartes, 1596–1650

☐

I have not Peru in my desires.

Sir Thomas Browne, 1605–1682

☐

Ask of Me everything, for I possess everything; do not ask of Me
a single thing, for I do not approve of thy having a single thing.

Niffari, d. ca. 965

☐

It is due to the greed of the soul that it wants to grasp and possess many things, and thus it lays hold of time and corporeality

and multiplicity and loses precisely what it possesses. For as long as more and more is in you, God can never dwell and act in you. These things must always come out if God is to enter, unless you possess them in a higher and better way, namely, if multiplicity has become one in you. Then, the more multiplicity is in you, the more unity there will be, for the one has been changed into the other.

St. Augustine, 354–430

☐

How happy is the man who abides steadfast against multiplicity.

Blessed Henry Suso, 1295–1365

☐

Those who are steadfast in the face of multiplicity, behold what light and grace are revealed to them!

Eckhart, 1260?–1327?

☐

As it is written, he that had gathered much had nothing over, and he that had gathered little had no lack.

II Corinthians 8:15

☐

He who has little will receive.
He who has much will be embarrassed.

Tao Te Ching

☐

Those who have little, if they are good at managing, must be counted among the rich.

Socrates, 470?–399 B.C.

☐

To have what we want is riches, but to be able to do without is power.

George Macdonald, 1824–1905

☐

Each individual who resists the drive for financial success means less pressure for growth in our berserk economic system.

Paul and Anne Ehrlich, 1974

☐

Of all manifestations of power, restraint impresses men most.

Thucydides, 471?–400? B.C.

☐

The True Sublime: It must be understood, my dear friend, that, as in everyday life nothing is great which it is considered great to despise, so is it with the sublime. Thus riches, honors, reputation, sovereignty, and all the other things which possess in marked degree the external trappings of a showy splendor, would not seem to a sensible man to be great blessings, since contempt for them is itself regarded as a considerable virtue; and indeed people admire those who possess them less than those who could have them but are high-minded enough to despise them.

Longinus, 213?–273

☐

To wiser desires it is satisfaction enough to deserve, though not to enjoy, the favors of Fortune.

Sir Thomas Browne, 1605–1682

☐

FORTUNA: *STOPPING THE WHEEL*

I am an exile declared an outlaw, surrendered to poverty. . . . Though it is already the fourth year of my exile, and the third that I am an outlaw, every day I am less shocked by the whirlwind of fortune and less moved by disasters. . . . Much freer than when I was oppressed by the burden of earthly possessions, in a happy condition, if not to say happy poverty, I experience the teaching of philosophy that every soil is a fatherland for the strong. My condition is not only tolerable for me, but even pleasant.*

John of Salisbury, d. 1180

☐

When Zeno heard that the only ship he had left had been lost at sea with all its freight, he said, "Fortune, you are doing me a kindness, limiting me to a threadbare cloak and the life of a philosopher." He has leisure, can take walks, read, sleep undisturbed, and say like Diogenes, "Aristotle dines when Philip chooses, Diogenes when Diogenes chooses."

Plutarch, 46?–120?

☐

You have placed yourself in Fortune's power; now you must be content with the ways of your mistress. . . . Would you indeed attempt to stay the force of Fortune's turning wheel? O you most dull-witted of mortals, if Fortune begins to stand still, she is no longer Fortune!

When Fortune turns her wheel with her proud right hand, she is as unpredictable as the flooding Euripus. She heeds no tears, but wantonly mocks the sorrow her cruelty causes. This is her sport, thus she proves her power. She shows her servants the marvel of a man despairing and happy within a single hour.*

Boethius, 480?–524?

☐

Your Magnificence shall know that the motive of my coming into this realm of Spain was to traffic in merchandise: and that I pursued this intent about four years: during which I saw and knew the inconstant shiftings of Fortune: and how she kept changing those frail and transitory benefits: and how at one time she holds man on the summit of the wheel, and at another time drives him back from her, and dispoils him of what may be called his borrowed riches: so that, knowing the continuous toil which man undergoes to win them, submitting himself to so many anxieties and risks, I resolved to abandon trade, and to fix my aim upon something more praiseworthy and stable: whence it was that I made preparation for going to see part of the world and its wonders. . . .

Amerigo Vespucci, 1454–1512

☐

Fortune is a woman who to be kept under must be beaten and roughly handled; and we see that she suffers herself to be more readily mastered by those who so treat her than by those who are more timid in their approaches.

Niccolò Machiavelli, 1469–1527

☐

Fortune, who loves her cruel game,
   Still bent upon some heartless whim,
Shifts her caresses, fickle dame,
   Now kind to me, and now to him:

CONTROLLED FOLLY

She stays; 't is well: but let her shake
　　Those wings, her presents I resign,
Cloak me in native worth, and take
　　Chaste Poverty undower'd for mine.

Horace, 65–8 B.C.

□

Contentment with poverty is Fortune's best gift.

Fu Hsüan, 3d. cent.

□

Seek not to be Rich, but Happy. The one lies in Bags, the other in Content: which Wealth can never give.

William Penn, 1644–1718

□

SWEET CONTENT

Art thou poor, yet hast thou golden slumbers?
　　O sweet content!
Art thou rich, yet is thy mind perplex'd?
　　O punishment!
Dost thou laugh to see how fools are vex'd
To add to golden numbers golden numbers?
　　O sweet content! O sweet content!

Work, apace, apace, apace, apace;
Honest labour bears a lovely face;
Then hey nonny nonny—hey nonny nonny!

Canst drink the waters of the crisped spring?
　　O sweet content!
Swim'st thou in wealth, yet sink'st in thine own tears?

123

LESS IS MORE

O punishment!
Then he that patiently want's burden bears,
No burden bears, but is a king, a king!
O sweet content!, O sweet, O sweet content!

Thomas Dekker, 1572?–1632?

□

In India there is a particular type of man who delights in having
as few needs as possible. He carries with him only a little flour
and a pinch of salt and chillies tied in his napkin. He has a *lota*
and a string to draw water from the well. He needs nothing else.
He walks on foot covering ten-twelve miles a day. He makes the
dough in his napkin on the embers. It is called *bati*. I have tasted
it and found it most delicious. . . . Such a man has God as his
companion and friend and feels richer than any king or emperor.
Contentment is his treasure.*

Gandhi, 1869–1948

□

Can anything be so elegant as to have few wants and to serve
them one's self?

Emerson, 1803–1882

□

To be content with what one has is to be rich.

Tao Te Ching

□

If thou wilt tear out this vice of avarice by the very roots, then
having victual, clothing and a roof to cover thee, therewith be
content.

Gerald Zerbolt of Zutphen, d. 1398

124

☐

From contentment comes supreme happiness.

Patanjali, 2d cent. B.C.

☐

TEMPERANTIA: *THE HAPPY MEDIUM*

To be temperate is the great virtue.

Heraclitus, d. 484 B.C.

☐

Temperantia means knowing when enough is enough.

E. F. Schumacher, 1973

☐

The temperance of the hero proceeds from the wish to do no dishonor to the worthiness he has. But he loves it for its elegancy, not for its austerity. It seems not worth his while to be solemn and denounce with bitterness flesh-eating or wine-drinking, the use of tobacco, or opium, or tea, or silk, or gold. A great man scarcely knows how he dines, how he dresses, but without railing or precision his living is natural and poetic. The essence of greatness is the perception that virtue is enough. Poverty is its ornament.

Emerson, 1803–1882

☐

Be both poor and rich appropriately; if a lord squanders, that is not lord-like; if he hoards treasure too much, that is dishonor also. Make your rule the true mean.

Wolfram von Eschenbach's *Parzival*, 12th cent.

□

THE GOLDEN MEAN: *THE MIDDLE WAY*

Nothing in excess.

*The Golden Mean
Inscribed at Delphi*

□

Philosophy consists in avoiding excess in everything.

Pythagoras, 6th cent. B.C.

□

Give me neither poverty nor riches. . . .

Proverbs 30:8

□

There is a *mean* in things, fixed limits on either side of which right living cannot get a foothold.

Horace, 65–8 B.C.

□

The name of the mean is sufficiency.

Roman de la Rose, 13th cent.

□

The Perfect Way is only difficult for those who pick and choose;
Do not like, do not dislike; all will then be clear.
Make a hairsbreadth difference,
and Heaven and Earth are set apart.

Seng-ts'an, ca. A.D. 600

□

Frugality is good if Liberality be join'd with it. The first is leaving off superfluous Expences; the last bestowing them to the Benefit of others that need. The first without the last begins Covetousness; the last without the first begins Prodigality: Both together make an excellent Temper. Happy the Place where ever that is found.

Were it universal, we should be Cur'd of two Extreams, Want and Excess: and the one would supply the other, and so bring both nearer to a Mean; the just Degree of earthly Happiness.

William Penn, 1644–1718

□

Frugality too has a limit, and the man who disregards it is in like case with him who errs through excess.

Epicurus, 342?–270 B.C.

□

Within the earth, a mountain:
The image of *Modesty*.
Thus the Superior Man reduces that which is too much,
And augments that which is too little.
He weighs things and makes them equal.

I Ching

□

A man had need, if he be plentiful in some kind of expense, to be saving again in some other. As if he be plentiful in diet, to be saving in apparel; if he be plentiful in the hall, to be saving in the stable; and the like.

Sir Francis Bacon, 1561–1626

□

LESS IS MORE

Your folly should be moderate,
Proportioned to a small estate.

Horace, 65–8 B.C.

□

The Master said: "The highest good is to hold fast the *Golden Mean*. Amongst the people it has long been rare."

Confucius, ca. 551–479 B.C.

□

I look upon Avarice and Prodigality in the Society as I do upon two contrary Poisons in Physick, of which it is certain that the noxious Qualities being by mutual Mischief corrected in both, they may assist each other, and often make a good Medicine between them.

Bernard Mandeville, 1670?–1733

□

Somewhere between a pinching thrift and a heedless luxury lies the humanistic goal of wealth as a means to be apportioned between progress and pleasure. It is a philosopher's quest, perhaps, but one with which no healthy society can afford to dispense.**

Robert Heilbroner, 1956

□

The rule of Poverty must be applied to the temper of normal consciousness as well as to the tastes and possessions of the self. Under this tonic influence, real life will thrive; unreal life will wither and die.

Evelyn Underhill, 1875–1941

CONTROLLED FOLLY

☐

The opposition between the men who *have* and the men who *are* is immemorial. Though the gentleman, in the old-fashioned sense of the man who is well-born, has usually in point of fact been predaceous and reveled in lands and goods, yet he has never identified his essence with these possessions, but rather with the personal superiorities, the courage, generosity, and pride supposed to be his birthright.

This ideal of the well-born man without possessions was embodied in knight-errantry and templardom; and, hideously corrupted as it has always been, it still dominates sentimentally, if not practically, the military and aristocratic view of life. We glorify the soldier as the man absolutely unincumbered. Owning nothing but his bare life, and willing to toss that up at any moment when the cause commands him, he is the representative of unhampered freedom in ideal directions.

In short, lives based on having are less free than lives based either on doing or on being, and in the interest of action people subject to spiritual excitement throw away possessions as so many clogs. Only those who have no private interests can follow an ideal straight away. Sloth and cowardice creep in with every dollar or guinea we have to guard.

But beyond this more worthily athletic attitude involved in doing and being, there is, in the desire of not having, something profounder still, something related to that fundamental mystery of religious experience.*

William James, 1842–1910

☐

The more we spend being on having the less we *are*.

☐

All that is contrary to essential being must be relinquished.

Karlfried, Graf von Dürckheim, 1971

129

LESS IS MORE

□

He must increase, but I must decrease.

John 3:30

□

VIA NEGATIVA: THE ART OF REFUSING

Human moods and reactions to the encounter with Nothingness
vary considerably from person to person, and from culture to
culture. The Chinese Taoists found the Great Void tranquiliz-
ing, peaceful, even joyful. For the Buddhists in India, the idea
of Nothing evoked a mood of universal compassion for all creatures caught in the toils of an existence that is ultimately ground-
less. In the traditional culture of Japan the idea of Nothingness
pervades the exquisite modes of aesthetic feeling displayed in
painting, architecture, and even the ceremonial rituals of daily
life. But Western man, up to his neck in *things,* objects, and the
business of mastering them, recoils with anxiety from any possible encounter with Nothingness. . . .

William Barrett, 1962

□

That thou mayest possess all things, seek to possess nothing. In
detachment the spirit finds quiet and repose, for coveting nothing, nothing wearies it by elation, and nothing oppresses it by
dejection, because it stands in the center of its own humility. For
as soon as it covets anything, it is immediately fatigued thereby.

St. John of the Cross, 1542–1591

□

No soul is rested till it is made naught as to all things that are made.

Julian of Norwich, 1343–1413?

☐

Thou shalt love the naughting and flee the self.

Mechthild of Magdeburg, 1210–1297

☐

Nothing is left to Saichi.
Except a joyful heart nothing is left to him.
Neither good nor bad has he,
All is taken away from him:
Nothing is left to him!
To have nothing—how completely satisfying!

Saichi, fl. 1800

☐

As for me, I shall despise riches alike when I have them and when I have them not, being neither cast down if they shall lie elsewhere, nor puffed up if they shall glitter around me. For indeed the wise man does not deem himself undeserving of any of the gifts of Fortune. He does not love riches, but he would rather have them; he does not admit them to his heart, but to his house, and he does not reject the riches he has, but he keeps them and wishes them to supply ampler material for exercising his virtue.*

Seneca, 4? B.C.–A.D. 65

☐

The individual avoids mistakes because he possesses as if he possessed nothing.

I Ching

131

□

DETACHMENT: *BREAKTHROUGH*

Righteousness is not all in fasting, nor in eating, but you are righteous if everything is alike to you, contempt or praising, poverty or riches, hunger and need, or delight and dainties.

Richard Rolle, ca. 1300

□

I have learned in whatsoever state I am, therewith to be content. I know how both to be abased, and I know how to abound: every where and in all things I am instructed, both how to be full and to be hungry, both to abound and to suffer need.

Philippians 4:11–12

□

For him who is freed from attachment to worldly luxuries, it is the same whether he practice asceticism or not.

Gampopa, d. 1151

□

It is self-evident that no terrestrial possessions of any kind will benefit the spirit, but the acquisition of such possessions will not be an obstacle for us, provided that we possess them and do not permit ourselves to be possessed by them.

Jakob Boehme, 1575–1624

□

CONTROLLED FOLLY

A Sufi was asked: "Who is a Sufi?"
He replied: "He who neither possesses nor is possessed."

Al-Kalâbâdhi, ca. 1000

□

What is detachment? That which clings to nothing. Spiritual poverty clings to nothing, and nothing clings to it.

Johannes Tauler, 1300?–1361

□

I am alone and nothing is mine,
nor do I pertain to anything else;
I can find none whose I am or who is mine.

Sri Devikalottara, 6th cent.

□

When our Lord wanted to speak of the beatitudes, He placed poverty of spirit at the head of them all, and it was the first as a sign that all beatitude and perfection have their origin in poverty of spirit. For the more detached we are, the more we possess, as St. Paul has it: We shall possess as if we possessed not and yet possess all things.

Eckhart, 1260?–1327?

□

I saw Indian Brahmans living upon the earth and yet not on it, and fortified without fortifications, and possessing nothing, yet having the riches of all men.

Apollonius of Tyana, 1st cent.

□

The Fenni are squalidly poor. The men and women alike are supplied by the chase . . . neither arms nor homes have they; the little children have no shelter from wild beasts and storms but a covering of interlaced boughs. Their food is herbs, their clothing skins, their bed the earth. Yet they count this greater happiness than groaning over field labor, toiling at building and poising the fortunes of themselves and others between hope and fear. Heedless of men, heedless of gods, *they have attained that hardest of results, the not needing so much as a wish. . . .**

Tacitus, 55?–120?

☐

Socrates was wont to say, *They are most happy and nearest the gods that need nothing,* and coming once up into the Exchange at Athens, they that traded asked him, *What will you buy; what do you lack?* After he had gravely walked up into the middle, spreading forth his hands and turning about, *Good Gods,* saith he, *who would have thought there were so many things in the world which I do not want!*

☐

For a man's life consisteth not in the abundance of things he possesseth.

Luke 12:15

☐

BEING VS. HAVING

Man is not complete; he is yet to be. In his *to be* he is infinite, there is his heaven, his deliverance. His *is* is occupied every moment with what it can get and have done with; his *to be* is

134

hungering for something which is more than can be got, which he never can lose because he never has possessed.

Thus to get is always to get partially, and it can never be otherwise. So this craving for acquisition belongs to our finite self.

But that side of our existence whose direction is toward the infinite seeks not wealth, but freedom and joy. There the reign of necessity ceases, and there our function is not to get but to be.*

Tagore, 1861–1941

□

Lives based on having are less free than lives based either on doing or being.

William James, 1842–1910

□

The more we have the less we own.

Eckhart, 1260?–1327?

□

Possessions give me no more than I have already.

Pascal, 1623–1662

□

Meditation is the chief possession of the gnostic.

Al-Muhâsibi, d. 857

□

The mere capacity to project and thus to "possess" does not bring with it a necessity to acquire. One need only think of St.

135

Francis or Thoreau or Cezanne, each of whom identified with the physical world to an extraordinary degree, but no one of whom felt motivated to use that quality of possessiveness in an acquisitive fashion.

Robert Heilbroner, 1956

☐

I'd like to become less acquisitive altogether, to be able to see some exquisite piece of porcelain in some other man's house and be wholly glad that it was there and not mine.

Gabriel Fielding, 1965

☐

Where is freedom? In always doing more and more or in doing fewer things to do them better? That, of course, amounts to asking if the very abundance of material goods may not result in a loss of freedom.

Robert Redfield, b. 1897

☐

True freedom is to be found in the absence of all material goods.

Johannes Tauler, 1300?–1361

☐

Poverty is naught to have, and nothing to desire: but all things to possess in the spirit of liberty.

Jacopone da Todi, 1230?–1306

☐

CONTROLLED FOLLY

Desirelessness is liberation.

Sri Baba Hari Dass, 1973

☐

Desire is slavery; renunciation is freedom.

Hermes Trismegistus

☐

The root of evil is attachment which has sprung from the seed
called desire—the prime cause of ignorance. The eradication of
desire and attachment is called liberation.

Swami Ramdas, 1886–1963

☐

GIVING IT UP: *THE GREAT RENUNCIATION*

Whatever you do, do in moderation.
Be easily pleased and easily sustained.
Run like a wild animal from whatever would entrap you.

Atisa, 10th cent.

☐

Money and dainties are the devil's envoys.
Association with them is pernicious.
Renounce them and all other things that bind you.

Milarepa, 1052–1135

☐

LESS IS MORE

The Power of Renunciation

If enough Americans refused to buy a new car for one given year it would permanently alter the American economy. . . . Learn to break the habit of unnecessary possessions—but avoid a self-abnegating anti-joyous self-righteousness. Simplicity is light, carefree, neat, and loving—not a self-punishing ascetic trip.*

Keith Murray, 1970

□

To every man comes, sooner or later, the great renunciation.

Bertrand Russell, 1872–1970

□

Renunciation! —Learn, man, to forego!
This is the lasting theme of themes,
That soon or late will show its power. . . .

Goethe's *Faust*, ca. 1774

□

Evangelical poverty in its final profundity is a *radical* renunciation.

Pie-Raymond Régamey, 1954

□

The knowledge which results in renunciation *(zuhd)* consists of the realization that what is renounced is of little value in comparison with what is received.

Al-Ghazali, d. 1111

□

One day two dervishes were arguing.

Ibrahim ben Adam said to one of them: "The life of renunciation has been wasted upon you. You got it cheaply, and so you do not value it."

The dervish sneered and said: "And what price, pray, did you pay for being a dervish?"

Ibrahim said: "I exchanged it for the kingdom of Balkh, and even then I regard that as a cheap price, brother."

Group Recitals

□

To abound in wealth, to have fine houses and rich clothes, to be beautiful in our persons, to have titles of dignity, to be above our fellow-creatures, to overcome our enemies with power, to subdue all that oppose us, to set out ourselves in as much splendor as we can, to live highly and magnificently, to eat, and drink, and delight ourselves in the most costly manner, these are the great, the honorable, the desirable things, to which the spirit of the world turns the eyes of all people. And many a man is afraid of standing still, and not engaging in the pursuit of these things, lest the same world should take him for a fool.

William Law, 1686–1761

□

In the eyes of the world the people who renounce their pleasures, comforts, and happiness, seem to be foolish; but there is nothing that man has renounced and not received a greater gain. And yet renunciation for gain can be called nothing but greed. Renunciation for the pleasure of renunciation is the only renunciation that is worthwhile.

Hazrat Inayat Khan, 1882–1927

□

Really to give up anything on which we have relied, to give it up definitely, "for good and all" and forever, signifies a radical alteration of character. . . . In it the inner man rolls over into an entirely different position of equilibrium, lives in a new center of energy from this time on.

William James, 1842–1910

☐

All our belongings assume a weight by the ceaseless gravitation of our selfish desires; we cannot easily cast them away from us. They seem to belong to our very nature, to stick to us as a second skin, and we bleed as we detach them.

Tagore, 1861–1941

☐

Desires and attachments affect the soul as the remora is said to affect a ship; that is but a little fish, yet when it clings to the vessel it effectively hinders its progress.

St. John of the Cross, 1542–1591

☐

LETTING GO: *GIVING IT AWAY*

To you, all you have seems small: To me, all I have seems great. Your desire is insatiable, mine is satisfied. See children thrusting their hands into a narrow-necked jar, and striving to pull out the nuts and figs it contains: If they fill the hand, they cannot pull it out again, and then they fall to tears. —"Let go a few of them, and then you can draw out the rest!" —You, too, let your desire go! Covet not many things, and you will obtain.

Epictetus, 60?–100?

☐

CONTROLLED FOLLY

Receive wealth and prosperity without arrogance, and be ready to let it go.

Marcus Aurelius, 121–180

☐

No man is free until he is free at the center. When he lets go there he is free indeed. It is life's supreme strategic retreat. Asking for nothing, if anything comes to him, it is all sheer gain. Then life becomes one constant surprise.

Eli Stanley Jones, 1884–1973

☐

Know that no man in this life ever gave up so much that he could not find something else to let go.

Eckhart, 1260?–1327?

☐

Gandhiji's advocacy of *aparigraha* or non-possession was based not merely on ethical grounds, but also on humanitarian grounds. Quite early in his own life, in South Africa, he had set a striking example of non-possession. In his eyes, possession of hoards of jewelry was the sign of inordinate attachment to material wealth; bedecking oneself with ornaments and flaunting them constituted an ugly manifestation of social inequality. This was the significance of his appeal to the conscience of the "caste" Hindus to divest themselves of gold for the Harijan cause. The response to his call was spectacular; it had a spiritual and uplifting character.

The enthusiasm of the people everywhere has far exceeded expectations. At all places visited up till now, the meetings have been the largest ever held in them. Thousands of peasants swarm from villages to the nearest place which Gandhiji visits. Women attend in hundreds. Many part with some of their ornaments.*

Harijan, 1933

LESS IS MORE

☐

I would like to thank the thousands of sisters who attend my meetings to give me most, if not all, of the jewelry they wear. In this country of semistarvation of millions, the wearing of jewelry is an offense to the eye. A woman in India has rarely any cash which she can call her own. But the jewelry she wears does belong to her, though even that she will not, dare not, give away, without the consent of her lord and master. It ennobles her to part with, for a good cause, something she calls her own. Moreover, most of this jewelry has no pretension to art, some of it is positively ugly. In my opinion, the wearing of expensive jewelry is a distinct loss to the country. It is so much capital locked up or, worse still, allowed to wear away. And in this movement of self-purification, the surrender of jewelry by women or men I hold to be a distinct benefit to society. Those who give do so gladly. My invariable condition is that on no account should the jewelry donated be replaced. Indeed, women have blessed me for inducing them to part with things which had enslaved them. And in not a few cases men have thanked me for being an instrument for bringing simplicity into their homes. I admit I have been instrumental in making paupers of doctors, lawyers, and merchants. I do not repent. On the contrary, I rejoice that many have embraced poverty voluntarily. In a poor country like India, where people walk for miles to get a dole of one pice per day, as they are doing in Orissa today, it does not behove anybody who cares for the poor to wear costly ornaments. In no other way can we identify ourselves with the Harijans.*

Gandhi, 1869–1948

☐

The property of riches is to be given liberally.

Pascal, 1623–1662

☐

CONTROLLED FOLLY

As with anything else in this kind of work, such as the practice of meditation, you have to be fully involved, you have to become one with what you are doing. So it is with giving things away; no matter how small the thing is in terms of value, one must be fully involved in the giving so that a part of one's Ego is also given away.

Chogyam Trungpa, 1969

☐

Wealth is the abundance of worldly goods and poverty is lack of them: all goods belong to God: when the seeker bids farewell to property, the antithesis disappears and both terms are transcended.

Hujwiri, d. 1063

☐

Accept Poverty, demolish ownership, the very "to have" in every mood and tense, and this downward drag is at an end. At once the Cosmos belongs to you, and you to it. You escape the heresy of separateness, are "made one." Then, a free spirit in a free world, the self moves upon its true orbit; undistracted by the largely self-imposed needs and demands of ordinary earthly existence.*

Evelyn Underhill, 1875–1941

☐

Turn yourself into gold and then live wherever you please.

Sri Ramakrishna, 1834–1886

☐

LESS IS MORE

Anyone whose aim, in conquering the earth, has really been to subject a little more matter to spirit has, surely, begun to take leave of himself at the same time as taking possession of himself. This is also true of the man who rejects mere enjoyment, the line of least resistance, the easy possession of things and ideas, and sets out courageously on the path of work, inward renewal and the ceaseless broadening and purification of his ideal.

Pierre Teilhard de Chardin, 1881–1955

8

ECO-LOGIC

HOLDING BACK: *THE LIMITS OF GROWTH*

The West seems to take a pride in thinking that it is subduing nature; as if we are living in a hostile world where we have to wrest everything we want from an unwilling and alien arrangement of things. This sentiment is the product of the city-wall habit and training of mind. For in the city-life man naturally directs the concentrated light of his mental vision upon his own life and works, and this creates an artificial dissociation between himself and the Universal Nature within whose bosom he lies. Deprived of the background of the whole, his poverty loses its one great quality, which is simplicity, and becomes squalid and shamefaced. His wealth is no longer magnanimous; it grows merely extravagant. His appetites do not minister to his life, keeping to the limits of their purpose; they become an end in themselves.*

Tagore, 1861–1941

□

Wealth is what Nature gives us and what a reasonable man can make out of the gifts of Nature for his reasonable use. The sunlight, the fresh air, the unspoiled face of the earth, food, raiment and housing necessary and decent; the storing up of knowledge of all kinds, and the power of disseminating it; means of free communication between man and man; works of art, the beauty which man creates when he is most a man, most aspiring and

thoughtful—all things which serve the pleasure of people. . . .
This is wealth. Nor can I think of anything worth having which
does not come under one or other of these heads.

William Morris, 1834–1896

☐

How long shall we covet and oppress, enlarge our possessions,
and account that too little for one man which was formerly
enough for a nation? And our luxury is as insatiable as our
avarice. Where's that lake, that sea, that forest, that spot of land
that is not ransacked to gratify our palate? The very earth is
burthened with our buildings; not a river nor a mountain escapes
us. Oh that there should be such boundless desires in our little
bodies! Would not fewer lodgings serve us? We lie but in one,
and where we are not, that is not properly ours. What with our
hooks, snares, nets, and dogs, we are at war with all living creatures, and nothing comes amiss but that which is either too
cheap or too common; and all this is to gratify a fantastical
palate. Our avarice, our ambition, our lusts, are insatiable; we
enlarge our possessions, swell our families; we rifle sea and land
for matter of ornament and luxury. A bull contents himself with
one meadow, and one forest is enough for a thousand elephants;
but the little body of a man devours more than all other living
creatures. We do not eat to satisfy hunger, but ambition; we are
dead while we are alive, and our houses are so much our tombs,
that a man might write our epitaphs upon our very doors.

Seneca, 4? B.C.–A.D. 65

☐

Simplicity and nonviolence are obviously closely related. As
physical resources are everywhere limited, people satisfying their
needs by means of a modest use of resources are obviously less
likely to be at each other's throats than people depending upon a
high rate of use. Nonrenewable goods must be used only if they
are indispensable, and then only with the greatest care and the

most meticulous concern for conservation. To use them heedlessly or extravagantly is an act of violence, and while complete non-violence may not be attainable on this earth, there is nonetheless an ineluctable duty on man to aim at the ideal of nonviolence in all he does.*

E. F. Schumacher, 1973

☐

The surface of the earth can be profoundly altered without desecrating it or decreasing its fitness for life; man also can be changed in ways that would enrich his humanness.

René Dubos, 1972

☐

Can we do no more than cut and trim the forest? Can we not assist in its interior economy, in the circulation of the sap?

Thoreau, 1817–1862

☐

Earth provides enough to satisfy every man's need, but not enough for every man's greed.

Gandhi, 1869–1948

☐

Poverty, brought into conformity with the law of Nature, is great wealth.

Epicurus, 342?–270 B.C.

☐

Unfortunately all our drive and optimism are bound up with continuous growth; "growth addiction" is the unwritten and unconfessed religions of our times. . . . The insane quantitative growth must stop. Innovation must not stop—it must take an entirely new direction. Instead of working blindly toward things bigger and better, it must work toward improving the quality of life . . . toward a new harmony, a new equilibrium.*

Dennis Gabor, 1963

□

Withdrawal from growth mania will be painful, but mostly for members of the generation which has to experience the transition and above all for those most disabled by consumption. If their plight could be vividly remembered, it might help the next generation avoid what they know would enslave them.

Ivan Illich, 1973

□

Mankind has become a locust-like blight on the planet that will leave a bare cupboard for its own children—all the while in a kind of addict's dream of affluence, comfort, eternal progress—using the great achievements of science to produce software and swill.*

Keith Murray, 1970

□

Overcoming the addiction to quantitative growth, fortunately, is compatible with great qualitative changes.

René Dubos, 1972

□

To those who clamor, as many now do, "Produce! Produce!" one simple question may be addressed—"Produce what?" Food, clothing, house-room, art, knowledge? By all means! But if the nation is scantily furnished with these things had it not better stop producing a good many others which fill shop windows? . . . What can be more childish than to urge the necessity that productive power should be increased, if part of that productive power which exists already is misapplied? Is not *less* production of futilities as important as, indeed a condition of, more production of things of moment? Would not "Spend less on private luxuries" be as wise a cry as "produce more"?*

R. H. Tawney, 1880–1962

□

It is possible that progress might be nothing more than the development of an error.

Jean Cocteau, 1889–1963

□

We are in for completely automated success once we get over the idea that survival and enjoyment solutions must come through politics and recognize that they can come only through unbiased, intelligently organized competence and physical redesigning of the use of the world's resources to do so much more with so much less as to be able to supply everybody with all that they need. Quite clearly it is only going to come through the development of a world consciousness of what constitutes the true problem.

R. Buckminster Fuller, 1969

□

Beyond the need for limiting growth lies a need for a conceptual change in the way we use the resources of the planet. Present-day economics including their power requirements, food-production, shelter, heating and/or cooling, transport, and manufacture are predicated on finite substances including fossil fuels and potentially dangerous nuclear materials. There is no precedent in human history for whole civilizations based on nonrenewable fuels. . . .

In part this realization is arising out of a waning confidence in the ability of science and technology to salvage an industrialized growth-oriented society in an ultimately finite world. It is becoming apparent that a science of steady states is needed to prepare us for the future. It will be different from the one we now know, having been created within a framework of ethical and moral considerations.*

John Todd, 1975

☐

With increasing necessity and demand for efficiency, integration, and minimizing of waste in the economic world, there will be increasing demand for efficiency, integration, and minimizing of waste in the social world. These changes will have marked effects upon the ways in which men live. It seems clear that the first major penalty man will have to pay for his rapid consumption of the earth's nonrenewable resources will be that of having to live in a world where his thoughts and actions are ever more strongly limited, where social organization has become all-pervasive, complex, and inflexible, and where the state completely dominates the actions of the individual.

Harrison Brown, 1954

☐

The lure of quantity is the most dangerous of all. When once the individual loses control of method, it is taken over by society.

Simone Weil, 1909–1943

☐

The alternative to managerial fascism is a political process by which people decide how much of any scarce resource is the most any member of society can claim; a process in which they agree to keep limits relatively stationary over a long time, and by which they set a premium on the constant search for new ways to have an ever larger percentage of the population join in doing ever more with ever less. Such a political choice of a frugal society remains a pious dream unless it can be shown that it is not only necessary but also possible.

Ivan Illich, 1973

☐

With world population doubling time a little more than 30 years, and decreasing, society will be hard put to meet the needs and expectations of so many more people in so short a period. We are likely to try to satisfy these demands by overexploiting our natural environment and further impairing the life-supporting capacity of the earth. Hence, on both sides of the man-environment equation, the situation will tend to worsen dangerously. We cannot expect technological solutions alone to get us out of this vicious circle. . . .

Club of Rome Report, 1972
The Limits of Growth

☐

What we do about ecology depends on our ideas of the man-nature relationship. More science and more technology are not going to get us out of the present ecologic crisis until we find a new religion, or rethink our old one. The beatniks, who are the basic revolutionaries of our time, show a sound instinct in their affinity for Zen Buddhism, which conceives the man-nature relationship as very nearly the mirror-image of the Christian view.

The greatest spiritual revolutionary in Western history, Saint Francis, proposed what he thought was an alternative Christian view of nature and man's relation to it: He tried to substitute the idea of equality of all creatures, including man, for the idea of man's limitless rule of creation. He failed. Both our present

science and our present technology are so tinctured with ortho-
dox Christian arrogance toward nature that no solution for our
ecologic crisis can be expected from them alone. Since the roots
of our trouble are so largely religious, the remedy must also be
essentially religious, whether we call it that or not. We must
rethink and refeel our nature and our destiny. The profoundly
religious, but heretical, sense of the primitive Franciscans for
the spiritual autonomy of nature may point a direction. I propose
Francis as a patron saint for ecologists.*

Lynn White, Jr., 1967

□

Economic thought is the language of the time. It is our meta-
phor; it is the logical calculus upon which the metaphysics of
industrial society must rest. We are in love with the law of supply
and demand, the idea of economies of scale, and the rule of
diminishing returns. We are fascinated with the power implied
in the process of compounding. We look forward to ever
more. . . .

The market economy is not a creature suited to an environment where materials and energy are increasingly scarce. The
market is geared to "more and more," not to more from less. Yet
the reality of our limited natural resources requires precisely
that: more from less. The household, not the market, is the institution for such a condition.*

Scott Burns, 1975

□

For the prosperity of fools shall destroy them.

Proverbs 1:32

□

Few men have been permitted to lay aside prosperity gently. The
rest all fall, together with the things amid which they have come

into eminence, and they are weighted down by the very things which had before exalted them. For this reason foresight must be brought into play, to insist upon a limit or upon frugality in the use of these things, since licence overthrows and destroys its own abundance. That which has no limit has never endured, unless reason, which sets limits, has held it in check.

Seneca, 4? B.C.–A.D. 65
Ep. LXXII

□

There is a limit to all things—which may be trite but is nevertheless true. There is a limit to bigness, a limit to speed, a limit to numbers and a limit to complexity—not theoretically, which is in the realm of imagination, but practically in the sense that beyond a certain limit the penalty for further advance is greater than the advantage. And it is this general condition we are rapidly approaching.

N. J. Berrill, 1961

□

If anyone gives too great power to anything, too large a sail to a vessel, too much food to the body, too much authority to the mind, and does not observe the mean, everything is overthrown, and in the wantonness of excess runs in the one case to disorders, and in the other to injustice, which is the child of excess.

Plato, 427?–347 B.C.

□

People at present think that five sons are not too many and each son has five sons also, and before the death of the grandfather there are already twenty-five descendants. Therefore people are more and wealth is less.

Han Fei-Tzu, ca. 500 B.C.

☐

LOVE VS. PEOPLE: *POPULATION CHECK*

It seems to me that we can picture our past up to the beginning of neolithic times as a small group of climbers laboriously climbing the precipitous slopes of a high mountain, with one after another falling to death as the hazards increased. Then far from the top, on a wide mountain meadow in the lush warmth of unexpected sunshine, the survivors relax, forget about the climb and settle down for good, or they so think, in a garden of Eden in which they busily propagate their kind. It has been a nice interlude, but the garden is getting full and we have spread out horizontally almost to the limit. We look down over the heights our somewhat remote ancestors have climbed and begin to realize there are also heights above us which can give us a far wider and deeper view of the universe than that we can see from here. The analogy is not too far-fetched. The essence of man is his quality, not his quantity, and this is no place to stop, half-way between ape and angel.

N. J. Berrill, 1961

☐

"You seem to have solved your economic problems pretty successfully."

"Solving them wasn't difficult. To begin with, we never allowed ourselves to produce more children than we could feed, clothe, house, and educate into something like full humanity. Not being overpopulated, we have plenty. But, although we have plenty, we've managed to resist the temptation that the West has now succumbed to—the temptation to overconsume. And while you people are overconsuming the rest of the world sinks more and more deeply into chronic disaster. Ignorance, militarism and breeding, these three—and the greatest of these is breeding. No

154

hope, not the slightest possibility, of solving the economic problem until *that's* under control."*

Aldous Huxley, 1894–1963

☐

We *can* control our population and thus decrease our per capita use of power. Population may be stabilized, and use of power reduced to what is necessary for a high quality of life. But population control will take time. We can begin now by ceasing to use power for trivial purposes.

Garrett De Bell, 1970

☐

The concept of zero growth, first for population, later for resource use and now for energy in particular, has caught the attention of many citizens. This stems in part from a growing concern that we are rapidly approaching the limits to growth on our planet. Besides the concern over physical limits, there is growing dissatisfaction with the automatic acceptance of "progress" as well as a feeling of "dehumanization" that stems from disillusionment with ever-growing consumption of material goods, and with the huge bureaucracies which produce, dispense, regulate, and otherwise service those goods. . . .

One reason for zero energy growth in the United States is simply that the rich nations of the world may limit their energy consumption either by choice or necessity so that the poor nations have a better opportunity, especially when it comes to using nonrenewable resources, of achieving a decent standard of living. Because of its influence in world affairs, America could take the lead in restraining its consumption of resources.

The idea of *zero energy growth* sometimes evokes the image of Spartan austerity. The ZEG future we envision does not match this image. An energy consumption level of 100 quadrillion Btu's per year in 2000 would provide 10 percent more energy per person than the United States uses today. And the energy would be used more efficiently, thus providing more benefits to society. There is nothing inherent in the ZEG scenario which would preclude national redistribution of the "energy income." Those who do not have an adequate standard of living need not be stopped from achieving one because of lack of energy. Nor is there any inherent reason why those in the middle to high energy brackets would have to give up any of the things they enjoy today. It would, however, mean an end to the "more is better" philosophy, replacing it with one saying "enough is best."*

Exploring Energy Choices, 1974
[Report from Ford Foundation
Energy Policy Project]

☐

ALTERNATIVE ENERGIES

Our descendants might well blame us for our wasteful extravagances in the use of these most important natural resources. They might say, "You consumed gasoline in 200-hp engines simply to carry one person to his office and back. You talked about the folly of burning for fuel cow dung which should be used for fertilizer, yet you burned the limited supply of organic fossil fuel that should have been used as raw material for making petrochemicals. You used it not only for concentrated energy in engines at high temperatures but even for low-temperature operations such as cooking, heating and cooling of houses, and distillation of water that could often be as well done by the sun, thereby saving more of the coal, oil, and gas for us."

Farrington Daniels, 1964

☐

Direct Use of the Sun: I had now come into the first stretches of the desert, about two miles from the Nile. As a guide, I had one of the brothers who had a good knowledge of the region. We arrived at the dwelling of an old man who lived at the foot of a mountain. Here we found something that is very rare in those parts, a well. The old man owned an ox, whose work consisted entirely in turning a wheel for drawing water. The garden there was full of vegetables. These were what the ox, along with his master lived on, and from this same abundant supply, the holy man gave us dinner. I tell there something you Gauls will perhaps not believe: The pot filled with the vegetables that were being prepared for dinner was boiling without any fire. The sun's heat is so great that there is no cook who would not find it sufficient even for preparing God's specialties.

Sulpicius Severus, 360?–410?

□

Like the wasps, before I finally went into winter quarters in November, I used to resort to the northeast side of Walden, which the sun, reflected from the pitch-pine woods and the stony shore, made the fireside of the pond; it is so much pleasanter and wholesomer to be warmed by the sun while you can be, than by an artificial fire. I thus warmed myself by the still glowing embers which the summer, like a departed hunter, had left.

Thoreau, 1817–1862

□

The term "standard of living" as used by utility spokesmen in the United States today generally means abundant luxuries, such as the following, for the affluent: electric blenders, toothbrushes and can openers, power saws, toys and mowers, dune buggies, luxury cars and golf carts, electric clothes dryers and garbage grinders. . . .

Are these necessary for a high quality of life? We must realize that a decision made to purchase one of these "conveniences" is also a decision to accept the environmental deterioration that results from the production, use, and disposal of the "convenience."

We can make the ecologically sensible decision to reject the concept of increasing perpetually the "standard of living" regardless of the human or ecological consequences. We can replace the outmoded industrial imperative—the "standard of living" concept—by the more human "quality of life" concept.*

Garrett De Bell, 1970

□

Thou shalt judge value by the energies spent, the energies stored, and the energy flow which is possible, turning not to the incomplete measure of money.

Howard T. Odum

□

The prize of the Olympian games, that called forth the most strenuous exertions of all Greece, was but a wreath of wild olive; for a bit of ribbon men have over and over again performed services no money could have bought.

Shortsighted is the philosophy which counts on selfishness as the master motive of human action. Self-interest is, as it were, a mechanical force—potent, it is true; capable of large and wide results. But there is in human nature what may be likened to a chemical force; which melts and fuses and overwhelms; to which nothing seems impossible. "All that a man hath will he give for his life"—that is self-interest. But in loyalty to higher impulses men will give even life.

And this force of forces—that now goes to waste or assumes perverted form—we may use for the strengthening, and building up, and ennobling of society, if we but will, just as we now use physical forces that once seemed but powers of destruction.*

Henry George, 1839–1897

ECO-LOGIC

☐

The more the energy is released from the driving necessity of getting more and more and yet more things that are half-used, and is turned to making a good life out of what one has, the less there is that psychic dependence on the means of livelihood which makes the typical "worry" of the businessman. . . .

Marjorie B. Greenbie, 1935

☐

The economics of humanity's manhood will know and will teach that the characteristic energies of man as man are by *nature* civilizing energies, wealth-producing energies, time-binding energies, the peaceful energies of inventive mind, of growing knowledge and understanding and skill and light; it will know and will teach that these energies of existing men united with one billion six hundred million available "sun-man" powers united with the ten billion living "man-powers of the dead," if they be not wasted by ignorance and selfishness, by conflict and competition characteristic of beasts, are more than sufficient to produce a high order of increasing prosperity everywhere throughout the world. . . .*

Count Alfred Korzybski, 1879–1950

☐

What is the nature of the luxury which enervates and destroys nations? Are we sure that there is none of it in our own lives? The philosopher is in advance of his age even in the outward form of his life. He is not fed, sheltered, clothed, warmed, like his contemporaries. How can a man be a philosopher and not maintain his vital heat by better methods than other men?

Thoreau, 1817–1862

☐

LESS IS MORE

THE ART OF WARMING ONESELF WITHOUT FIRE UP IN THE SNOWS

To spend the winter in a cave amidst the snows at altitudes between 11,000 and 18,000 feet, clad in a thin cotton garment or even naked, and escape freezing, is a somewhat difficult achievement. Yet many Tibetan and Hindu monks and hermits do so, ascribing their endurance to the power they have acquired to generate *tumo,* the inner heat. This art is a method of extracting *prana* (life-breath) from the inexhaustible *pranic* reservoir in Nature, and storing it up in the human-body battery, and then employing it to produce a psychophysical heat which permeates the entire body. Everyman is a portable generator of this kind, and the instructions for use are to be found in the traditional *Knowledge of the Path.*

After a prescribed series of very elaborate meditations, postures, breathings, thought-directing and physical exercises, there follow visualizations whereby, for example, a sun is imagined in the palm of each hand, on the sole of each foot, and below the navel.

"By rubbing together of the suns of the hands and feet, fire flareth up."

This strikes the sun below the navel which in turn fills the whole body with warmth.

A kind of examination concludes the training whereby, on a frosty, windy, moonlit night, neophytes are taken to a lakeshore. If the water is frozen, a hole is made in the ice. The naked neophytes sit cross-legged on the ground. Sheets are dipped in the icy water and each man wraps himself in one and must dry it on his body. As soon as the sheet becomes dry, the exercise is repeated. Witnesses have reported as many as forty sheets a night to have been dried by a practitioner.

Another test to determine the degree of warmth a yogin can generate consists of sitting in the snow, the quantity of snow melted in his radius indicating his proficiency.

Once the art is mastered, the production of heat becomes a natural function of the organism which works all by itself as soon as the weather grows cold and may be practiced anywhere at any time.

Yogic immunity to extreme heat is obtained through "Fire-Cooling" mantras and time-tested yogic techniques for inner and outer illumination ("every Buddha can light up the whole universe with the tuft of hair which grows between his eyebrows") further demonstrate man's built-in, costless, and omnipresent abilities which, when correctly practiced, leave him well beyond the mercy of any worldly energy crises.

Disgusted with the worldly life,
I sought solitude on the slopes of Lachi Kang. . . .
Then, it snowed continually for nine days and nights,
The biggest flakes were as big as the fleece of wool,
They came down flying like birds. . . .
The greatness of the snowfall was beyond all expression. . . .
The snow, the wintry blast and my thin cotton garment fought against
    each other on the white mountain.
The snow as it fell on me, melted into a stream,
The roaring blast was broken against the thin cotton robe which
    enclosed fiery warmth. . . .
And I, having won the victory, left a landmark for the hermits
Demonstrating the great virtue of *tumo.* *

Milarepa, 1052–1135

One meditates at midnight "on the idea of the sun's entering the heart by way of the mouth, and lighting the whole interior of the heart, so that the heart is as bright as the sun; one leaves heart and sun together for a certain time, and one feels the heart growing warm.

Nourishing the Vital Principle
[Taoist text]

LESS IS MORE

□

THE FLAMING MONKS

Once Abba Joseph stretched his hands toward Heaven and his fingers became like two flames of fire. Then, turning to one of the monks, he said: "If you wish, you may become entirely like fire!"

The Baptism of Fire

□

If thou wouldst complete the diamond body with no outflowing,
Diligently heat the roots of consciousness and life.
Kindle light in the blessed country ever close at hand,
And there hidden, let thy true self always dwell.

Liu Hua-yang, 1794

□

The direct kindling of creative energy from soul to soul. . . . is no doubt the ideal way.*

Arnold Toynbee, 1889–1975

□

When a man is warmed by the several modes which I have described, what does he want next? Surely not more warmth of the same kind, as more and richer food, larger and more splendid houses, finer and more abundant clothing, more numerous incessant and hotter fires, and the like. When he has obtained those things which are necessary to life, there is another alternative than to obtain the superfluities; and that is, to adventure on life now.

Thoreau, 1817–1862

□

CONSERVATION: *WANT NOT, WASTE NOT*

The fact is that America wastes nearly half the energy it produces. It would certainly be cheaper, safer and more sensible to try to save that wasted power than to build more and more nuclear plants.

John M. Blatt, 1976

□

An economy of abundance is under present rules also an economy of waste and repetition—indeed without this waste the economy would slump. Nobody, however, can be optimistic about the survival of a society with such values.

Robert Theobald, 1961

□

The world is too much with us; late and soon,
Getting and spending, we lay waste our powers. . . .

William Wordsworth, 1770–1850

□

Part of the goods which are annually produced, and which are called wealth is, strictly speaking, waste, because it consists of articles which, though reckoned as part of the income of the nation, either should not have been produced until other articles had already been produced in sufficient abundance, or should not have been produced at all. And some part of the population is employed in making goods which no man can make with happiness, or indeed without loss of self-respect, because he knows that they had much better not be made, and that his life is wasted in making them.

R. H. Tawney, 1880–1962

☐

Wise work is *useful*. No man minds, or ought to mind, its being hard, if only it comes to something. . . . Yet do we ever ask ourselves, personally, or even nationally, whether our work is coming to anything or not? . . . Of all wastes, the greatest waste you can commit is the waste of labor.

Ruskin, 1819–1900

☐

The prosperity of this country has produced a wastefulness that has extended to the laboring multitude. . . . It is, indeed, important that the standard of living in all classes should be high; that is, it should include the comforts of life, the means of neatness and order in our dwellings, and such supplies of our wants as are fitted to secure vigorous health. But how many waste their earnings on indulgences which may be spared. How many among them sacrifice improvement to appetite! How many sacrifice it to the love of show, to the desire of outstripping others, and to habits of expense which grow out of this insatiable passion! In a country so thriving and luxurious as ours, the laborer is in danger of contracting artificial wants and diseased tastes; and to gratify these he gives himself wholly to accumulation, and sells his mind for gain. Our unparalleled prosperity has not been an unmixed good. It has inflamed cupidity, has diseased the imagination with dreams of boundless success and plunged a vast multitude into excessive toils, feverish competitions and exhausting cares.*

William Ellery Channing, 1780–1842

☐

The more goods people procure, the more packages they discard and the more trash that must be carried away. If the appropriate sanitation services are not provided, the counterpart of increasing opulence will be deepening filth. The greater the wealth the thicker will be the dirt.

John Kenneth Galbraith, 1958

☐

The environment can absorb a man's organic wastes, and even turn them to good use; and as to his psychic pollution, what difference do fantasies make? Let him project his evil-heartedness wherever he likes—what does it matter?

The danger arises when a man's psychic excretions are given material form—when his projections appear as physical objects. We cannot ignore his fantasies of super-potency when they are represented by overpowered automobiles that claim a thousand lives a week; his paranoid fears when they are expressed in bugging devices and security data banks; his hatreds when they appear in the form of a nuclear arsenal capable of eliminating vertebrate life on our planet.

Our psychic excretions, in other words, show an annoying tendency to become part of our real environment, so that we are forced to consume our own psychic wastes in physical form.

Philip Slater, 1974

☐

Under the selective surveillance of the law of conspicuous waste there grows up a code of accredited canons of consumption, the effect of which is to hold the consumer up to a standard of expensiveness and wastefulness in his consumption of goods and in his employment of time and effort.

Thorstein Veblen, 1857–1929

☐

LESS IS MORE

When I came to build my chimney I studied masonry. My bricks
being second-hand ones required to be cleaned with a trowel,
so that I learned more than usual of the qualities of bricks and
trowels. Many of the villages of Mesopotamia are built of second-
hand bricks of a very good quality, obtained from the ruins of
Babylon, and the cement on them is older and probably harder
still. As my bricks had been in a chimney before, though I did
not read the name of Nebuchadnezzar on them, I picked out as
many fireplace bricks as I could find, to save work and waste, and
I filled the spaces between the bricks about the fireplace with
stones from the pond shore, and also made my mortar with the
white sand from the same place. I lingered most about the fireplace, as the most vital part of the house. Indeed, I worked so
deliberately, that though I commenced at the ground in the
morning, a course of bricks raised a few inches above the floor
served for my pillow at night.*

Thoreau, 1817–1862

□

It must be demonstrated ceaselessly that a continually "growing
economy" is no longer healthy, but a cancer. And that the criminal waste which is allowed in the name of competition—especially that ultimate in wasteful needless competition, hot wars
and cold wars with "communism" (or "capitalism")—must be
halted totally with ferocious energy and decision. Economics
must be seen as a small sub-branch of ecology, and production/
distribution/consumption handled by companies or unions with
the same elegance and spareness one sees in nature.

Keith Murray, 1970

□

Use it up, wear it out, Make it do or do without.

New England Proverb

□

166

ECO-LOGIC

Make do with what you have.

Dr. John Moore, 1976

□

They who are possessed by desire suffer much and enjoy little, as the ox that drags a cart gets but a morsel of grass. For the sake of this morsel of enjoyment, which falls easily to the beast's lot, man, blinded by his destiny, wastes this brief fortune, that is so hard to win.

Santi-deva, 7th cent.

□

Having obtained the difficult-to-obtain, free and endowed human body, it would be a cause of regret to fritter life away.

from *The Ten Causes of Regret,*
Precepts of the Gurus, 12th cent.

□

It is a pity when man is not aware of this privilege of being human; and every moment in life that he passes in this error of unawareness is a waste, and is to his greatest loss.

Hazrat Inayat Khan, 1882–1927

□

Moral precepts, which to a superficial view appear arbitrary, and seem to spoil our zest for life, have really but one object—to preserve us from the evil of having lived in vain. That is why they are constantly leading us back into the same paths; that is why they all have the same meaning: *Do not waste your life.*

Charles Wagner, 1895

□

167

A monk and an old master were once walking in the mountains. They noticed a little hut upstream. The monk said, "A wise hermit must live there" and the master said, "That's no wise hermit, you see that lettuce leaf floating down the stream, he's a waster." Just then an old man came running down the hill with his beard flying and caught the floating lettuce leaf.

Keith Murray, 1970

☐

Gather up the fragments that remain, that nothing be lost.

John 6:12

9

VOLUNTARY POVERTY
AND SPACE

THE ART OF TRAVELING LIGHTLY

> Take nothing for your journey,
> neither staves, nor scrip,
> neither bread, neither money;
> neither have two coats apiece.

Luke 9:3

□

The Brotherhood of the Road

Ordo Vagorum, Gyrovagus: world-walkers, the most ancient of elites. Wandering fools and scholars, peripatetic saints, preaching minstrels, itinerant thinkers, rainmakers, back-packing dreamers, tinkers, errant monk-knights, mendicant artists, peregrinating dancers, easy riders, minnesingers and noble hobos, goliards, bhikkus, troubadours, Wandervogel, gypsy hippies, sannyasins, journeymen and women, dharma bums of the legendary trip trap, roving poets, God-mad nomads, Eastern Wayfarers, staff-bearing sadhus, footloose renouncers, Never-Returners, supertramps, pilgrims of the guru-circuit, holy hikers: thousand-faced heroes rambling empty-handed, the easier to scale celestial walls.

169

Garbed in ochre robes or folded togas, kimonos, astral-blue jeans, Sufi-patched, cloaked and sporting a Christic cockle-shell or "clothed in space," naked as the way is long: the Bodhisattva remains at large, wholly engaged in questing the warm-blooded grail of the sacred self.

For love of Lady Poverty or of the irresistible open road, the prince leaves his palace forever in the dead of night, the commoner his solidstate hearth, saying *no* to owning, yes to *being*, in total response to the call to mystic adventure. Birds of passage, these visionary vagabonds have always mapped the spiritual routes, migrating from Bamboo Grove to Celtic caves, across the vast American flats, ever in search of the miraculous, traveling as lightly as possible, the better to be everywhere and no where at home.

☐

Provide neither gold, nor silver, nor brass in your purses, nor scrip for your journey, neither two coats, nor yet staves. . . .

Matthew 10:9–10

☐

As the wayfarer's step is the jauntier the lighter he travels, so in this journey of life that man is happier who lightens his needs by poverty and does not groan under the burden of riches.

Minucius Felix, 3d cent.

☐

I cannot call riches better than the baggage of virtue. The Roman word is better, *impedimenta*. For as the baggage is to an army, so is riches to virtue. It cannot be spared nor left behind, but it hindereth the march; yea, and the care of it sometimes loseth or disturbeth the victory.

Sir Francis Bacon, 1561–1626

VOLUNTARY POVERTY AND SPACE

☐

For my part, as I grow older I am more and more inclined to reduce my baggage, to lop off superfluities. I become more and more in love with simple things and simple folk—a small house, a hut in the woods, a tent on the shore. The show and splendor of great houses, elaborate furnishings, stately halls, oppress me, impose upon me. . . .

John Burroughs, 1837–1921

☐

You possess only whatever will not be lost in a shipwreck.

Al-Ghazali, 12th cent.

☐

I was shipwrecked before I got aboard. [The] journey showed me this: how much we possess that is superfluous; and how easily we can make up our minds to do away with things whose loss, whenever it is necessary to part with them, we do not feel.

So I shall now become silent, at least with reference to superfluous things like these; doubtless the man who first called them "hindrances" *(impedimenta)* had a prophetic inkling that they would be the very sort of thing they now are.*

Seneca, 4? B.C.–A.D. 65

☐

The bundle I carried on my thin, bony shoulders was the cause of my first discomfort on this journey. I had intended to set off just as I was; however, a kimono to protect me from the cold at night, a waterproof, writing materials and so on—all these things I received from my friends as parting gifts, and I could hardly leave them behind, but they were necessarily a cause of discomfort and vexation all the way.

Bashō, 1644–1694

171

LESS IS MORE

☐

As life carries its own bundle in the form of the body . . .
So does the monk carry a travelling bundle over his shoulder.

Shunryu Suzuki, 1970

☐

Walk simply, do not desire repose of the spirit too earnestly and
you will have the more of it. I recommend to you holy simplicity:
look before you and regard not those dangers which you see afar
off.

St. François de Sales, 1567–1622

☐

Every step towards progress and rise, is a step of renunciation.
The poverty of the one who has renounced, is real riches compared with the riches of the one who holds them fast. One could
be rich in wealth and poverty-stricken in reality, and one can
be penniless and yet richer than the rich of the world. . . .

This philosophy was lived in life by the ascetics who traveled
from place to place. All happiness, comforts, and good friends
they made in one place, they enjoyed all that for the moment,
and left it, lest it might bind them for ever.*

Hazrat Inayat Khan, 1882–1927

☐

Faithful to our instructions, we lived like pilgrims [with only
the usual linen haversack on our backs] and made no use of
those contrivances which spring into existence in a world deluded
by money, number and time, and which drain life of its content.

Hermann Hesse, 1877–1962

☐

VOLUNTARY POVERTY AND SPACE

By riding the horse of the magic *prana*-mind,
Thus, my son, you should travel in India.

Milarepa, 1052–1135

☐

Several years ago, a close friend and associate belonging to a rich, prosperous family, who had received a high degree of education and had travelled and seen much in different parts of the world, solemnly abjured the use of all vehicular and other means of transport and has ever since stuck to his resolve through all vicissitudes of weather and health. His testimony should, therefore, command our respect. Kindred spirits in all climes and ages have borne similar testimony to the joy and beauty of travelling on foot and renouncing all worldly possessions.

"Of the many vows that I took, I have found the one about travelling on foot to be the most beneficial. It has afforded me the richest experience. As a result of it, my faith in God today is much stronger than it was when I set out from Ahmedabad about a couple of years ago.

"Having had experience of both riches and poverty, I am in a position to testify today that, whilst I have almost always found pride and licence threatening the life of the rich and whilst those who wielded authority could not without difficulty escape the intoxication of power, poverty alone left enough scope for a spontaneous and natural devotion to God, a spirit of service and the capacity to suffer and to endure. I have now clearly realized that the state of voluntary poverty is really a blessed state and that riches, in the worldly sense, are nothing in comparison. May God always keep me in poverty and keep me free from the slightest desire for possession, or from the care for the morrow."

Gandhi, 1869–1948

☐

How the Brothers Are to Travel in this World

. . . with neither purse, nor sack, nor bread, nor money, nor staff.
When they stop let them eat and drink what their hosts offer.
Do not put up resistance to offenses.
If one strikes on the right cheek, offer the other.
If one takes away your cloak, offer your mantle.
Give what is asked of you, and if someone takes from you, do not ask for it back.
No brother who is traveling (and this goes for clerics as well as lay brothers) is to have a horse or accept a ride on one. The only exception to this rule is in case of great urgency or illness.

The Rule, Order of the Friars Minor, ca. 1210

☐

Saint Bernard was reproached by his enemies with the inconsistency of preaching evangelical poverty while making his journeys from place to place on a magnificently caparisoned mule, which had been lent to him by the Cluniac monks. He expressed great contrition: but said that he had never noticed what it was that he rode upon.

☐

Release from the world; solitude for the following of the ways of prayer; a lively seeking after knowledge; a passion for sacrifice and self-denial; a driving concern for the souls of their fellowmen—these were the marks of early medieval saints. For these ends they wandered wherever their time called them.

They might be seen, sometimes in small companies of two or three, often alone, tramping along the lanes and trails, struggling through the forest, plunging through the stretches of bog and marsh, climbing the mountains. On their feet they wore sandals of hide; their monkish habit was of skins roughly sewn together, with a hood to protect them from cold and rain; in their hands they carried a staff, and from their shoulders hung the pack which held the small store of food, the cup, the books of prayer for Mass and Office. Their food they begged from the peasants of the cottages they passed, who often willingly gave a meal to a holy man in return for his blessing upon them and their home. In lonely and inhospitable places they sat in the evening to eat what they had gathered as they walked from fruit trees growing wild, from bark, from the leaves of some wholesome plant. At night they made a bed of boughs under the open sky; sometimes a cottager gave them a lodging upon the hay of his barn and a drink of milk from his cow before they left at dawn.

Eleanor Duckett, 1959

□

And what rule do you think I walked by? Truly a strange one, but the best in the whole world. I was guided by an implicit faith in God's goodness: and therefore led to the study of the most obvious and common things. Then I began to enquire what things were most common: Air, Light, Heaven and Earth, Water, the Sun, Trees, Men and Women, Cities, Temples, &c. These I found common and obvious to all: Rubies, Pearls, Diamonds, Gold and Silver; these I found scarce, and to the most denied. Then began I to consider and compare the value of them which I measured by their serviceableness, and by the excellencies which would be found in them, should they be taken away. And in conclusion, I saw clearly, that there was a real valuableness in all the common things; in the scarce, a feigned.

Thomas Traherne, 1637?–1674

□

In short, all good things are wild and free.

Thoreau, 1817–1862

□

LESS IS MORE

Attar was in his shop one day, among his numerous and varied merchandise, when a wandering Sufi appeared at the door, gazing in with his eyes filled with tears. The chemist at once told the man to be gone. "It is not difficult for me," replied the traveler. "I have nothing to carry; nothing but this cloak. But you, you with your costly drugs? You would do well to consider your own arrangements for going your way."

Attar was so profoundly impressed that he renounced his shop and his work, and withdrew into a Sufi settlement for retreat.

Daulet-Shah

☐

It seems sad that at times the obsession with owning something blinds a person to the object's true worth. When the obsession is absent, however, more time and energy can be directed toward discovering and appreciating the real meaning of the thing. I, for one, do not want a whole attic full of possessions attaching themselves to me. Rather, I want the mobility to be able to explore all things, the mobility that a closet full of shoes and the complete leatherbound works of Shakespeare cannot give.

Linda Konner, 1975

☐

And whatever be his road, to make toward his goal, the traveler must not lose himself in crossways, nor hamper his movements with useless burdens. Let him heed well his direction and forces, and keep good faith; and that he may the better devote himself to the essential—which is to progress—at whatever sacrifice, let him simplify his baggage.

Charles Wagner, 1895

☐

When I have met an immigrant tottering under a bundle which contained his all—looking like an enormous wen which had grown out of the nape of his neck—I have pitied him, not because that was his all, but because he had all *that* to carry. If I have got to drag my trap, I will take care that it be a light one and do not nip me in a vital part. But perchance it would be wisest never to put one's paw into it.

Thoreau, 1817–1862

□

If you are wise, you will dread a prosperity which only loads you with more.

Emerson, 1803–1882

□

[When I travel] I carry
Only my Guru's instructions—lighter
Than feathers, I shoulder them with ease;
More handy than gold, I conceal them
Where I please.

Milarepa, 1052–1135

□

By concentrating on the relation of the body to the all-pervading ether, and, thinking of small and light objects such as the fibres of cotton-wool, the yogi is able to travel through space.

Patanjali, 2d cent. B.C.

□

I met my first *lung-gom-pa* runner in Northern Tibet. [We] were riding leisurely across a wide tableland, when I noticed a moving speck which my field-glasses showed to be a man. I felt astonished. For the last ten days we had not seen a human being. Moreover, men on foot and alone do not, as a rule, wander these

immense solitudes. But as I continued to observe him, I noticed
that the man proceeded at an unusual gait and especially, with
extraordinary swiftness. What was to be done if he really was a
lung-gom-pa? I wanted to talk with him, question him, photo-
graph him, [but I was told] "Your Reverence will not stop the
lama, nor speak to him. This would certainly kill him. These
lamas when travelling must not break their meditation." I had
to remain satisfied with the sight of the uncommon traveller. By
that time he had nearly reached us; I could clearly see his perfectly calm face and wide-open eyes with their gaze fixed on some
invisible far-distant object. The man did not run. He seemed
to lift himself from the ground, proceeding by leaps. He wore
the usual monastic robe and toga, both rather ragged. My servants dismounted and bowed their heads to the ground as the
lama passed before us, but he went his way apparently unaware
of our presence.*

Alexandra David-Neel, 1929

☐

Jesus said: Become passers-by.

The Gospel According to Thomas

☐

It is a great joy to realize that the Path to Freedom which all
the Buddhas have trodden is ever-existent, ever unchanged, and
ever open to those who are ready to enter upon it.

Gampopa, d. 1152 A.D.

☐

If we practice a "Toward the One," whatever be the goal or purpose, walking becomes much easier.

Sufi Ahmed Murad, 1970

☐

Where the way is hardest, there go thou: and what the world casteth away, that take thou up. What the world doth, that do thou not; but in all things walk thou contrary to the world. So thou comest the nearest way to that which thou art seeking.

Jakob Boehme, 1575–1624

□

Travel light!

Robert Louis Stevenson, 1850–1894

□

Let thy walk be an interior one.

Blessed Henry Suso, ca. 1295–1365

□

On this path, it is only the first step that counts.

M. Vianney, 1864

10

VOLUNTARY POVERTY
AND TIME

INSTANT NOW: *LIVING THE MOMENT*

Possession implies provision for the future. A seeker after Truth,
a follower of the Law of Love cannot hold anything against
tomorrow. God never stores for the morrow; He never creates
more than what is strictly needed for the moment. . . . Our
ignorance or negligence of the Divine Law, which gives to man
from day to day his daily bread and no more, has given rise to
inequalities with all the miseries attendant upon them.*

Gandhi, 1869–1948

☐

Is it really wise to be always guarding against future misfortune?
Is it prudent to lose all enjoyment of the present through thinking of the disasters that may come at some future date?

Bertrand Russell, 1872–1970

☐

It is better for you to be free of fear lying upon a pallet, than to
have a golden couch and a rich table and be full of trouble.

Epicurus, 342?–270 B.C.

☐

VOLUNTARY POVERTY AND TIME

There is no avarice without some punishment, over and above that which it is to itself. How miserable is it in the desire! How miserable even in the attaining of our ends! For money is a greater torment in the possession than it is in the pursuit. The fear of losing it is a great trouble, the loss of it a greater, and it is made a greater yet by opinion. Nay, even in the case of no direct loss at all, the covetous man loses what he does not get. It is true, the people call the rich man a happy man, and wish themselves in his condition; but can any condition be worse than that which carries vexation and envy along with it?

Seneca, 4? B.C.–A.D. 65

□

Whether it be a question of food, dress, or dwelling, simplicity of taste is also a source of independence and safety. The more simply you live, the more secure is your future; you are less at the mercy of surprises and reverses. An illness or a period of idleness does not suffice to dispossess you: a change of position, even considerable, does not put you to confusion. Having simple needs, you find it less painful to accustom yourself to the hazards of fortune. You remain a man, though you lose your office or your income, because the foundation on which your life rests is not your table, your cellar, your horses, your goods and chattels, or your money.

Charles Wagner, 1895

□

Lay up for yourself treasures in heaven, where neither moth nor rust doth corrupt, and where thieves do not break through nor steal.

Matthew, 6:20

□

LESS IS MORE

The less money, the less trouble.

Seneca, 4? B.C.–A.D. 65

☐

He who has few things to desire cannot have many to fear.

William Blake, 1757–1827

☐

It is when I possess least that I have the fewest worries and the Lord knows that, as far as I can tell, I am more afflicted when there is an excess of anything than when there is lack of it.

St. Teresa of Avila, 1515–1582

☐

So, if in dread
Of want, one has one's freedom forfeited—
Freedom more precious than a mine outspread—
A master he will carry for his greed,
And always be a slave because indeed
He knows not how to make a little do.
. . . His master or his slave is each man's hoard,
And ought to follow, not to pull, the cord.*

Horace, 65–8 B.C.

☐

For myself, let the "sweet muses" lead me to their sacred retreats . . . far away from anxieties and cares and the necessity of doing every day something repugnant to my heart. Let me no longer tremblingly experience the madness and perils of the forum and the pallors of fame. Let me not be anxious about the future, have to make a will to secure my wealth. Let me not possess more than what I can leave to whom I please.*

Tacitus, 55–120?

VOLUNTARY POVERTY AND TIME

☐

Wealth heaped on wealth,
  Nor truth nor safety buys,
The dangers gather as the treasures rise.

Samuel Johnson, 1709–1784

☐

[In] a world of enslavement through installment buying and mortgages, the only way to live in any true security is to live so close to the bottom that when you fall you do not have far to drop, you do not have much to lose.

Dorothy Day, 1963

☐

Deep in the sea are riches beyond compare,
But if you seek safety, it is on the shore.

Saadi of Shiraz, 1184–1291

☐

A serious hindrance to our peace of mind is failure to proportion our desires to our means, and spread of too much sail, as it were, in hopes of great things. People want not only to be rich and learned and strong and convivial and attractive, and friends of kings and governors of cities, but they are dissatisfied if their dogs and horses and quails and cocks are not the finest and the best.

Plutarch, 46?–120?

☐

Peace is only possible in poverty.

D. T. Suzuki, 1949

LESS IS MORE

□

Fearful of poverty,
I sought for riches;
The inexhaustible Seven Glorious
and Holy Jewels are the riches I found
and now of poverty I have no fear.

Milarepa, 1052–1135

□

Be interested in the universe. Do not cling to this world. Do not want to possess anything. Never think of your 'pension'.

Okada Torajiro, 1915

□

The goal of tranquillisation is to be reached not by suppressing all mind activity but by getting rid of discriminations and attachments.

Lankavatara Sutra, VIII

□

Riches prick us with a thousand troubles in getting them, as many cares in preserving them, and yet with more anxiety in spending them, and with grief in losing them.

St. François de Sales, 1567–1622

□

There is no gain without pain.

Poor Richard, 18th cent.

□

184

VOLUNTARY POVERTY AND TIME

Where there is no property, there can be no injury.

John Locke, 1632–1704

□

We should not go about acquiring things we regard as valuable, and always be trembling for fear of losing them because they are valuable, and yet, while we have them, neglect and think little of them. We should use them constantly for our pleasure and enjoy them, so that we may bear their loss, if that happens, with more equanimity.

Plutarch, 46?–120?

□

Why should you trouble yourself about the future? You do not even properly know about the present. Take care of the present, the future will take care of itself.

Sri Ramana Maharshi, 1879–1950

□

Therefore I say unto you, Take no thought for your life, what ye shall eat, or what ye shall drink; nor yet for your body, what ye shall put on. Is not the life more than meat, the body more than raiment?

Matthew 6:25

□

Life-maintaining food and raiment in some manner will be found, so devote yourselves, most earnestly, to the *Dharma*.

Guru Phadampa Sangay, fl. 11th cent.

□

185

The Sufi is the son of the moment, O comrade: it is not the rule of the Way to say "tomorrow."

Rūmi, 1207–1273

□

Be here now.

Mikaël, Bhagavan Das, 1965

□

HOMO LUDENS: *LEISURE VS. IDLENESS*

As soon as want and suffering permit rest to a man, ennui is at once so near that he necessarily requires diversion. The striving after existence is what occupies all living things and maintains them in motion. But when existence is assured, then they know not what to do with it; thus the second thing that sets them in motion is the effort to get free from the burden of existence, to make it cease to be felt, "to kill time," *i.e.,* to escape from ennui. Accordingly we see that almost all men who are secure from want and care, now that at last they have thrown off all other burdens, become a burden to themselves, and regard as a gain every hour they succeed in getting through, and thus every diminution of the very life which, till then, they have employed all their powers to maintain as long as possible.

Arthur Schopenhauer, 1788–1860

□

As if you could kill time without injuring eternity.

Thoreau, 1817–1862

□

VOLUNTARY POVERTY AND TIME

Only those who take leisurely what the people of the world are busy about can be busy about what the people of the world take leisurely.

Chang Ch'ao, ca. 1676

☐

Ease, rest, owes its deliciousness to toil; and no toil is so burdensome as the rest of him who has nothing to task and quicken his powers.

Channing, 1780–1842

☐

Neither in thy actions be sluggish, nor in thy conversation without method, nor wandering in thy thoughts, nor let there be in thy soul inward contention nor external effusion, nor in life be so busy as to have no leisure.

Marcus Aurelius, 121–180

☐

Come then, my friend, an hour to pleasure spare
And quit awhile your business and your care.
The day is all our own; come and forget
Bonds, interest, all; the credit and the debt . . . .

Juvenal, 60?–140?

☐

If possible, withdraw yourself from all the business of which you speak; and if you cannot do this, tear yourself away. We have dissipated enough of our time already. . . . Why wait until there is nothing left for you to crave? That time will never come. We hold that there is succession of causes, from which fate is woven; similarly, you may be sure, there is a succession in our desires; for one begins where its predecessor ends. You have been thrust into an existence which will never of itself put an end to your wretchedness and your slavery. Withdraw your chafed neck from the yoke. . . . If you retreat to privacy, everything will be on a smaller scale, but you will be satisfied abundantly. "But," you say, "how can I take my leave?" Any way you please. Reflect how many hazards you have ventured for the sake of money. . . . You must dare something to gain leisure, also.*

Seneca, 4? B.C.–A.D. 65
Ep. XIX

□

In some societies, work is viewed as an interruption of free time in order to make the pleasure of leisure possible. In America, work was the continuum interrupted by leisure. Thus, the consecration of work exalted success, success intensified the importance of work, and in varying degrees, depending on the individual, leisure became a slave of status rather than a liberator for self-fulfillment.

Richard M. Huber, 1971

□

Work is the antonym of free time. But not of leisure. Leisure and free time live in two different worlds. We have got into the habit of thinking them the same. Anybody can have free time. Not everybody can have leisure. Free time refers to a special way of calculating a special kind of time. Leisure refers to a state of being.*

Sebastian De Grazia, 1962

□

Contemplation, like leisure, or being itself leisure, brings felicity. The man in contemplation is a free man. He needs nothing.

Therefore nothing determines or distorts his thought. He does whatever he loves to do, and what he does is done for its own sake.*

Aristotle, 384–322 B.C.

□

Can one compare any joy to that of taking things quietly, patiently and easily? All other joys come from outward sources, but this happiness is one's own property.

Hazrat Inayat Khan, 1882–1927

□

I joyed in lowly leisure.

Vergil, 70–19 B.C.

□

Even the leisure of some men is engrossed; in their villa or on their couch, in the midst of solitude, although they have withdrawn from all others, they are themselves the source of their own worry; we should say that these are living, not in leisure, but in busy idleness.

Seneca, 4? B.C.–A.D. 65

□

Idleness, in the old sense of the word, so far from being synonymous with leisure, is more nearly the inner prerequisite which renders leisure impossible: it might be described as the utter absence of leisure, or the very opposite of leisure. Leisure is only possible when a man is at one with himself.

Leisure, it must be clearly understood, is a mental and spiritual attitude—it is not simply the result of external factors, it is not the inevitable result of spare time, a holiday, a week-end or a vacation. It is, in the first place, an attitude of mind, a condition of the soul. . . .

Compared with the exclusive ideal of work as activity, leisure implies an attitude of non-activity, of inward calm, of silence; it means not being 'busy', but letting things happen.

Leisure is a form of silence, of that silence which is the pre-requisite of the apprehension of reality. . . . For leisure is a receptive attitude of mind, a contemplative attitude, and it is not only the occasion but also the capacity for steeping oneself in the whole of creation.

Leisure, like contemplation, is of a higher order than the *vita activa*. [It] is the power of stepping beyond the workaday world, and in doing so touching upon the superhuman life-giving powers which, incidentally almost, renew and quicken us for our everyday tasks. It is only in and through leisure that the 'gate to freedom' is opened and man can escape from the closed circle of that 'latent dread and anxiety' . . . the mark of the world of work.*

Joseph Pieper, 1952

☐

Owing to our belief that *work* is what matters, we have become unable to make our amusements anything but trivial. . . . If excellence is to survive, we must become more leisurely, more just, less utilitarian, and less "progressive." And the first step toward this end is the general diffusion of a less energetic conception of the good life.**

Dora and Bertrand Russell, 1923

☐

Abundance could be the prelude to bread and circuses. A degrading leisure would be society's substitute for a degrading work. . . . On the other hand, there could be a new kind of leisure and a new kind of work, or more precisely, a range of activities that would partake of the nature of both leisure and work.

This latter development will not simply happen. A society with a cybernated revolution and a conservative mentality is not going to make new definitions of leisure and work. It is much simpler, and in keeping with the current wisdom, to vulgarize the neo-Keynesian ethic and to provide a market for the products of machines by simply injecting quantities of money into the economy, without any planning for the use of this productivity. Such a course would be defended in the name of allowing the individual freedom of choice. In reality, it would tend to constrict that freedom to its basest and most commercial options.

But on the other side there are enormous possibilities. Activities which are now regarded as hobbies, like photography, gardening, and fishing, could be seen as important human occupations in a society where machines did all the drudgery. So could the practice of the arts, of scientific research, of politics and education. To the Athenians, these latter employments were indeed the truly human work of man. But the Greek ideal rested, as Aristotle made so clear in the *Politics,* upon the degradation of the slaves. That fatal immorality of the Aristotelian scheme is no longer necessary—as Aristotle himself realized when he said that the appearance of the Statues of Daedalus would obviate the need for slaves. The machine slaves, the modern statues of Daedalus, are now coming into existence.*

Michael Harrington, 1965

☐

It is quite possible to arrange things so as to produce a good deal fewer gadgets and instead to enjoy more leisure. And, although blasphemous to utter, it is also possible to train fewer scientists and engineers without our perishing from the face of the earth. Nor do we *need* to capture world markets in the hope of being able to lower costs; or to lower costs in the hope of capturing world markets. We can, while acting as rational beings, deliberately choose to reduce our foreign trade and in some lines, therefore, to produce smaller quantities at a somewhat higher cost. . . .

We can decide even to reduce the strains of competition and opt for an easier and more leisurely life. Such choices as these, and many others also, can be translated into perfectly practical alternatives whenever public opinion is ready to consider them.*

E. J. Mishan, 1967

☐

There is an art of life which, in many times and lands, has guided or builded this essential activity into beauty, into power—into habitual experience and collective achievements which appear superhuman and miraculous.

Leisure should be uncompelled, voluntary, uncalculating, free. Yet leisure is fatally emasculated if it be divorced from work. From world's work, I mean, as distinct from the restricted labor called wage work.

Nothing short of world's work can make the searching, irresistible appeal to our voluntary nature, on which a great leisure must depend.

John Collier, 1931

☐

Appreciation of life is not easy. One says he must earn a living—but why? It seems as though a great many who do earn the living or have it given them do not get much out of it. A sort of aimless racing up and down in automobiles, and aimless satisfaction in amassing money, an aimless pursuit of "pleasure," nothing personal, all external. . . . It takes wit, and interest and energy to be happy. A man must become interesting to himself and must become actually expressive before he can be happy.*

Robert Henri, 1923

☐

I had this advantage, at least, in my mode of life, over those who were obliged to look abroad for amusement, to society and the theatre, that my life itself was become my amusement and never ceased to be novel. It was a drama of many scenes and without an end. If we were always indeed getting our living, and regulating our lives according to the last and best mode we had learned, we should never be troubled with ennui. Follow your genius closely enough, and it will not fail to show you a fresh prospect every hour.

Thoreau, 1817–1862

□

Pleasure and simplicity are two old acquaintances.

Charles Wagner, 1895

□

The truly wise man must be as intelligent and expert in the use of natural pleasures as in all the other functions of life. So the sages live, gently yielding to the laws of our human lot, to Venus and to Bacchus. Relaxation and versatility, it seems to me, go best with a strong and noble mind, and do it singular honor. There is nothing more notable in Socrates than that he found time, when he was an old man, to learn music and dancing, and thought it time well spent.

Montaigne, 1533–1592

□

SIMPLE PLEASURES

Joy is not in things, it is in us, and I hold to the belief that the causes of our present unrest, of this contagious discontent spreading everywhere, are in us at least as much as in exterior conditions.

To give one's self up heartily to diversion one must feel himself on a solid basis, must believe in life and find it within him. And here lies our weakness. How do you think a man can be amused while he has his doubts whether after all life is worth living? Besides this, one observes a disquieting depression of vital force, which must be attributed to the abuse man makes of his sensations. Excess of all kinds has blurred our senses and poisoned our faculty for happiness. Most ingenious means have been invented; it can never be said that expense has been spared. Everything has been tried, the possible and the impossible. But in all these complicated alembics no one has ever arrived at distilling a drop of veritable joy. We must not confound pleasure with the instruments of pleasure. To be a painter, does it suffice to arm one's self with a brush, or does the purchase at great cost of a Stradivarius make one a musician? No more, if you had the whole paraphernalia of amusement in the perfection of its ingenuity, would it advance you upon your road. But with a bit of crayon a great artist makes an immortal sketch. It needs talent or genius to paint; and to amuse one's self, the faculty of being happy: whoever possesses it is amused at slight cost. This faculty is destroyed by scepticism, artificial living, over-abuse; it is fostered by confidence, moderation and normal habits of thought and action.*

Charles Wagner, 1895

☐

For every Pleasure Money is useless.

William Blake, 1757–1827

☐

This life which has leisure
Is more precious than the Wishing-Jewel;
So difficult to find, it is as quickly gone
    as lightning in the sky.
Thus realize that all worldly activities

194

VOLUNTARY POVERTY AND TIME

Are like chaff in the wind,
And seize the essence of leisure and opportunity
    day and night.
Listen with clear mind, you fortunate ones,
Who direct your minds to the path pleasing to Buddha,
Who strive to make good use of leisure and opportunity
And are not attached to the joys of samsara.
Thus from the outset seek Renunciation.
Leisure and opportunity are difficult to find.
There is no time to waste: reverse attraction to this life.

The Three Principles of the Path

COMMENTARY

To have leisure is to have the time to practice the Holy Dharma.
Therefore this life of leisure and opportunity is very important.
Therefore, having obtained this life of leisure and opportunity,
which is so important and difficult to find, I will utilize its
essence without wasting it senselessly. . . . "For lower beings—
four-legged animals and such—even to obtain rebirth in the
happy states of men or gods seems almost impossible. Even among
beings who have been born in those happy states, to have obtained
leisure and opportunity is as rare as a star in the daytime. Therefore, as I have obtained such a life, which is so difficult to come
by, I will make good use of it without wasting it senselessly."*

Geshé Wangyal, 1973

□

Obviously time on one's hands is not enough to make leisure.

Sebastian De Grazia, 1962

□

Seeing that when we die we must depart empty-handed . . . it is
useless to labor and to suffer privation in order to make for oneself a home in this world.*

Precepts of the Gurus

195

LESS IS MORE

☐

Naked I reached the world at birth;
Naked I pass beneath the earth:
Why toil I, then, in vain distress,
seeing the end is nakedness?

Palladas, ca. 360–430

☐

Work is the opiate of the masses. If you must work for something,
it is not worth having. I don't believe in things—possessions.
There are only two kinds of people who are happy—those who
have so much that no matter how much is taken from them, they
still have plenty, and those who don't have anything. Those in
the middle are the unhappy ones. That's why I say, don't work:
enjoy life.

Mark Landsberg, 1974

☐

HOMO LABORANS: *RIGHT LIVELIHOOD*

Sweat is the ornament of virtue's face.

Hesiod, 8th cent. B.C.

☐

In the sweat of thy face shalt thou eat bread. . . .

Genesis 3.19

☐

Do without attachment the work you have to do.

Bhagavad-Gita

VOLUNTARY POVERTY AND TIME

☐

Let not to get a living be thy trade, but thy sport.

Thoreau, 1817–1862

☐

Our traditions are always alive among us, even when we are not dancing; but we only work in order to be able to dance.

The Uitoto Cannibals

☐

Life without work is robbery; work without art is brutality.

Ruskin, 1819–1900

☐

Work without hope draws nectar in a sieve.

Coleridge, 1772–1834

☐

Work without devotion is sand.

Sri Baba Hari Dass, 1972

☐

Let us consider the way in which we spend our lives. This world is a place of business. What an infinite bustle! It would be glorious to see mankind at leisure for once. It is nothing but work, work, work. I cannot easily buy a blank-book to write thoughts in; they are commonly ruled for dollars and cents.

The ways by which you may get money almost without exception lead downward. To have done anything by which you earned money *merely* is to have been truly idle or worse. If the laborer gets no more than the wages which his employer pays him, he is cheated, he cheats himself.

The aim of the laborer should be, not to get his living, to get "a good job," but to perform well a certain work.

Perhaps I am more than unusually jealous with respect to my freedom. I feel that my connection with and obligation to society are still very slight and transient. Those slight labors which afford me a livelihood, and by which it is allowed that I am to some extent serviceable to my contemporaries, are as yet commonly a pleasure to me, and I am not often reminded that they are a necessity. So far I am successful. But I foresee that if my wants should be much increased, the labor required to supply them would become a drudgery. If I should sell both my fore-noons and afternoons to society, as most appear to do, I am sure that for me there would be nothing left worth living for. I trust that I shall never thus sell my birthright for a mess of pottage. I wish to suggest that a man may be very industrious, and yet not spend his time well. There is no more fatal blunderer than he who consumes the greater part of his life getting a living.*

Thoreau, 1817–1862

☐

Some men throughout their lives gather together the means of life, for they do not see that the draught swallowed by all of us at birth is a draught of death.

Epicurus, 342?–270 B.C.

☐

We do not content ourselves with the life we have in ourselves and in our own being; we desire to live an imaginary life in the mind of others, and for this purpose we endeavor to shine. We labour unceasingly to adorn and preserve this imaginary existence, and neglect the real.

Pascal, 1623–1662

VOLUNTARY POVERTY AND TIME

☐

The typical American has not been taught that life is a legitimate progress toward spiritual or intellectual ends. . . . He has had it embedded in his mind that the getting of a living is not a necessity incidental to some higher and more disinterested end, but that it is the prime and central end.*

Van Wyck Brooks, 1886–1963

☐

By means of occupation worthy of a beast abundance of riches is heaped up, but a miserable life results.

Epicurus, 342?–270 B.C.

☐

Drive thy business! Let not that drive thee!

Benjamin Franklin, 1706–1790

☐

PERNICIOUSNESS OF OVER-WORKING

Let us suppose, then, that the man's way of life and manner of work have been discreetly chosen: then the next thing to be required is, that he do not over-work himself therein. I am not going to say anything here about the various errors in our systems of society and commerce, which appear (I am not sure if they ever do more than appear) to force us to over-work ourselves merely that we may live; nor about the still more fruitful cause of unhealthy toil—the incapability, in many men, of being content with the little that is indeed necessary to their happiness.

Ruskin, 1819–1900

199

LESS IS MORE

☐

He who has enough to satisfy his wants and nevertheless ceaselessly labors to acquire riches, either in order to obtain a higher
social position, or that subsequently he may have enough to live
without labor, or that his sons may become men of wealth and
importance—all such are incited by a damnable avarice, sensual-
ity, and pride.

Henry of Langenstein, 14th cent.

☐

For seeing they bestow but six hours in work, perchance you may
think that the lack of some necessary things hereof may ensue.
But this is nothing so. For that small time is not only enough
but also too much for the store and abundance of all things that
be requisite, either for the necessity, or commodity of life.

Sir Thomas More, 1478–1535

☐

In every man's life we may read some lesson. What may be read
in mine? If I myself see correctly, it is this: that one may have a
happy and not altogether useless life on cheap and easy terms;
that the essential things are always near at hand; that one's own
door opens upon the wealth of heaven and earth; and that all
things are ready to serve and cheer one. Life is a struggle, but not
a warfare, it is a day's labor, but labor on God's earth, under the
sun and stars with other laborers, where we may think and sing
and rejoice as we work.

John Burroughs, 1837–1921

☐

Believe it if you can, we were fostered among a gay people. In
those days a workyard was a spot on earth where men were happy.

VOLUNTARY POVERTY AND TIME

Today a workyard is a spot on earth where men find fault, wish each other ill, fight; kill each other. In most of the corporations, one sang. Today, one balks. In those days, one earned scarcely anything, so to speak. No one has any idea how low salaries were. And yet everyone had enough grub. In the humblest cottages reigned a sort of ease, the memory of which is lost. At bottom, no one reckoned. And there was nothing to reckon about. One earned nothing. One spent nothing. And everybody lived.

We have known an honor of work exactly similar to that which in the Middle Ages ruled hand and heart. The same honor had been preserved, intact underneath. We have known this care carried to perfection, a perfect whole, perfect to the last infinitesimal detail. We have known this devotion to *l'ouvrage bien fait,* to the good job, carried and maintained to its most exacting claims. During all my childhood I saw chairs being caned exactly in the same spirit, with the same hand and heart as those with which this same people fashioned its cathedrals.

Everything was the long event of a beautiful rite. These workmen would have been much surprised and what would have been —not even their disgust, their incredulity—if they had been told that a few years later in the workyards, the workmen, the journeymen, would officially propose to do as little as possible. And that they would consider this a great victory. Such an idea, supposing that they could conceive of such a thing, would have struck directly at them, at their being. It would have been a doubt cast upon their capacity, for it would have inferred that they did not do as much as they could. It is like supposing of a soldier that he will not be victorious. *

Charles Péguy, 1873–1914

□

I look on that man as happy, who, when there is question of success, looks into his work for a reply, not into the market, not into opinion, not into patronage. In every variety of human employment, in the mechanical and in the fine arts, in navigation, in farming, in legislating, there are among the numbers who do their task perfunctorily, as we say, or just to pass, and as badly as they dare,—there are the working-men on whom the burden of the business falls,—those who love work, and love to see it rightly done, who finish their task for its own sake. Men talk as if victory were something fortunate. Work is victory. Wherever work is done, victory is obtained.

Emerson, 1803–1882

□

What shows that *work*—if it is not of an inhuman kind—is meant for us is its joy, a joy which even our exhaustion does not lessen. The workers are reluctant to confess to this joy—because they have the impression that it might lead to a reduction of wages!

Simone Weil, 1909–1943

□

Work apace, apace, apace;
Honest labor bears a lovely face;
Then hey nonny nonny—hey nonny nonny!

Thomas Dekker, 1572?–1632?

□

A man must work from *love* of the work. If a person takes life as usual, in the ordinary way—that is, always receives impressions in the same mechanical way and speaks from them in the same mechanical way—then nothing can change in the person. Such people cannot evolve. They do not see where the point of working on themselves lies. They think work is something outside them.

Maurice Nicoll, 1884–1953

□

VOLUNTARY POVERTY AND TIME

Work is not what people think it is. It is not just something which, when it is operating, you can see from outside.

Rūmī, 1207–1273

□

I'm quite willing to work here as a flunky, and pull weeds, or do anything of the kind. But when it comes to the dancing class, then I'm the Master, not in anything else.

Sufi Ahmed Murad, 1970

□

Do not resent manual labour or farmwork, for it was ordained by the Most High.

Ecclesiasticus 7:15

□

And the Lord God took the man, and put him into the garden of Eden to dress it and to keep it.

Genesis 2:15

□

We may talk what we please of lillies, and lions rampant, and spread-eagles, in fields d'or or d'argent; but, if heraldry were guided by reason, a plough in a field arable would be the most noble and antient arms.

Abraham Cowley, 1618–1667

□

How can a man, who does not do body labour, have the right to eat?

LESS IS MORE

A millionaire cannot carry on for long, and will soon get tired of his life, if he rolls in his bed all day long, and is even helped to his food. He, therefore, induces hunger by exercise. If everyone, whether rich or poor, has thus to take exercise in some shape or form, why should it not assume the form of productive, i.e. bread labour?

This labour can truly be related to agriculture alone. But at present at any rate, everybody is not in a position to take to it. A person can therefore spin or weave, or take up carpentry or smithery, instead of tilling the soil, always regarding agriculture, however, to be the ideal.*

Gandhi, 1869–1948

□

The great men among the ancients understood very well how to reconcile manual labour with affairs of state, and thought it no lessening to their dignity to make the one the recreation to the other. That indeed which seems most generally to have employed and diverted their spare hours, was agriculture. *Gideon* among the *Jews* was taken from threshing, as well as *Cincinnatus* amongst the *Romans* from the plough, to command the armies of their countries . . . and, as I remember, *Cyrus* thought *gardening* so little beneath the dignity and grandeur of a throne, that he shew'd *Xenophon* a large field of fruit-trees all of his own planting. . . . *Delving, planting, inoculating,* or any the like profitable employments, would be no less a *diversion* than any of the idle sports in fashion, if men could but be brought to delight in them.*

John Locke, 1632–1704

□

A person who undertakes to grow a garden at home, by practices that will preserve rather than exploit the economy of the soil, has his mind precisely against what is wrong with us. . . .

What I am saying is that if we apply our minds directly and

competently to the needs of the earth, then we will have begun to make fundamental and necessary changes in our minds. We will begin to understand and to mistrust *and to change* our wasteful economy, which markets not just the produce of the earth, but also the earth's ability to produce.*

Wendell Berry, 1970

□

KARMA-YOGA: *WORK AS MEDITATION*

Dig and sow, that you may have the wherewithal to eat and drink and be clothed; for where sufficiency is, there is stability, and where stability is, there is religion.

Abbot Luan, 6th cent.

□

Idleness is the enemy of the soul. And therefore, at fixed times, the brothers ought to be occupied in manual labor, and, again at fixed times, in sacred reading.

St. Benedict of Nursia, 480?–543?
Rule XLVIII, Benedictine Order

□

There is no law of place; wherever the mind is concentrated, there worship should be performed.

Vyāsa-*Sutras*

□

Work for work's sake. There are some who are really the salt of the earth in every country and who work for work's sake, who do not care for name, or fame, or even to go to heaven. . . . He

205

works best who works without any motive, neither for money, nor for fame, nor for anything else; and when a man can do that, he will be a Buddha, and out of him will come the power to work in such a manner as will transform the world. This man represents the very highest ideal of *Karma-Yoga.* *

Swami Vivekananda, 1862–1903

☐

The true husbandman will cease from anxiety, as the squirrels manifest no concern whether the woods will bear chestnuts this year or not, and finish his labor with every day, relinquishing all claim to the produce of his fields, and sacrificing in his mind not only his first but his last fruits also.

Thoreau, 1817–1862

☐

To work alone thou hast the right, but never the fruits
thereof. Let your reward be in the actions themselves.
Abiding under the Rule of Yoga and casting off attachment,
O Wealth-Winner,
Perform your actions, indifferent alike to gain or loss.

Bhagavad-Gita

☐

Man ought not to work for any why, not for God nor for his glory nor for anything at all that is outside him, but only for that which is his being, his very life within him.

Brhadaranyaka Upanishad

☐

Have no ulterior purpose in thy work.

Eckhart, 1260?–1327?

VOLUNTARY POVERTY AND TIME

☐

Work is the worship of the Lord. Do not make any distinction between menial and respectable work.

Swami Sivananda, 1887–1963

☐

Of all the precious things in my possession, I reckon this the choicest, that were I robbed of my whole present stock, there is no work so mean, but it would amply serve to furnish me with sustenance.

Antisthenes, 441?–371 B.C.

☐

We must have an antagonism in the tough world for all the variety of our spiritual faculties or they will not be born. Manual labor is the study of the external world.

Emerson, 1803–1882

☐

Free from attachment to the fruit of actions, everlastingly content, unconfined, even though he be engaged in work he does no work at all. Having no desires, his mind under control, his possessions forsworn, performing works through the body's action only, such a one incurs no defilement. Content with what chance brings him, passed beyond the dualities of pleasure and pain, of hot and cold; void of envy, indifferent alike to gain or loss, even in action he remains unfettered. In such a one who, being without attachments, liberated, and possessing a mind established in wisdom, does work as a sacrifice, all work is dissolved.

Bhagavad-Gita

☐

The pyramid, the obelisk, the tower, the arch, the dome, the steeple, the groined vault, the flying buttress, the stained-glass window—all these are examples of untrammeled technical audacity, brought into play, not by the satisfaction of physical needs or the desire for material wealth, but by the more fundamental pursuit of significance.

Lewis Mumford, 1966

□

In the cathedrals, where all medieval thought took visible shape, knowledge and manual labor are given a place of equal honour.

The cathedral teaches that work of any kind demands respect. Another lesson it would teach men is to expect neither riches from manual labour nor fame from learning. Work and knowledge are the instruments of man's inner perfection, and the things which his activities gain for him are of a material and fleeting nature.

Emile Mâle, 1913

□

IN PRAISE OF MANUAL LABOR

I laboured with my hands and I wish so to labour; and I most sincerely hope that all the other brothers will work at any task that is honest.

St. Francis of Assisi, 1182–1226
Testament

□

And those brothers who know how to work shall work. . . . For their labour they may accept what is necessary, but not money.*

The Rule, Order of the Friars Minor, ca. 1210

VOLUNTARY POVERTY AND TIME

☐

For the man whose delight is in the immortal Self, who is contented with Self, and is glad of the Self, there is nothing for him to work for. He has indeed nothing to gain or lose either in action or inaction, nor do his purposes depend on people of this earth. Therefore without attachment do the work you have to do, for the man who does his work without attachment wins to the Supreme.

Bhagavad-Gita

☐

The fact is that the work which improves the condition of mankind, the work which extends knowledge and increases power, and enriches literature, and elevates thought, is not done to secure a living. It is not the work of slaves, driven to their task either by the lash of a master or by animal necessities. It is the work of men who perform it for its own sake, and not that they may get more to eat or drink, or wear, or display.

Henry George, 1839–1897

☐

I do not believe that any greater good could be achieved for the country, than the change in public feeling on this head, which might be brought about by a few benevolent men, undeniably in the class of "gentlemen," who would, on principle, enter into some of our commonest trades, and make them honorable; showing in the best sense, a gentleman, though part of his time was every day occupied in manual labor.

Ruskin, 1819–1900

☐

A man must needs exercise himself in the labour of his hands, seeing that for his frailty he cannot always nor long continue in spiritual exercises.

Thou must often choose, as thou makest thine ascent, some bodily or manual labour, nay, verily, thou must so order thine exercises that thou train thyself every day and at set times in manual toil, and also at their own set times make progress in the upgoings of thine heart, although perhaps thou shalt not be hindered from making this progress even whilst thou dost labour with thine hands.

For thou canst pray, meditate and exercise thyself in fear and desires whiles thou art at labour.

Although to some small degree such toil may withdraw thee from leisure and contemplation, yet will it make thee more able for it afterwards.

Manual labour doth subserve the spiritual ascent in proportion as it doth remove the obstacles thereto. Also, thine heart is very unstable, and as a little boat is tossed hither and thither in the waves of the sea, so is the heart shaken by divers affections and thoughts. Therefore, as saith Cassianus, "It doth beseem thee to make fast thine heart, as with an anchor, that is, with the weight or occupation of manual toil."

Furthermore, as saith Bernard, this same labour doth often as it were press down the body by its weight and mass, and so sometimes expresseth a sweeter essence of compunction and maketh it purer. For these and many other reasons it is that our Holy Fathers, especially those in Egypt, did labour so faithfully, and for this are they so highly extolled by the saints.

Gerard Zerbolt of Zutphen, 1367–1398

☐

So when the abbot Paul, revered among the Fathers, was living in that vast desert of Porphyrio secure of his daily bread from the date palms and his small garden, and could have found no other way of keeping himself (for his dwelling in the desert was seven days' journey and more from any town or human habitation, so that more would be spent in conveying the merchandise than the work he had sweated on would fetch), nevertheless did he gather palm leaves, and every day exacted from himself just such a measure of work as though he lived by it. And when his cave would be filled with the work of a whole year, he would set fire to it and burn each year the work so carefully wrought: and thereby he proved that without working with his hands a monk cannot endure to abide in his place, nor can he climb any nearer the summit of holiness: and though necessity of making a livelihood in no way demands it, let it be done for the sole purging of the heart, the steadying of thought, perseverance in the cell, and the conquest and final overthrow of *accidie* itself.

Cassian of Marseilles, 4th cent.

☐

It becomes a question of life and death for society to replace the detail worker of today, crippled by life-long repetition of one and the same trivial operation, and thus reduced to the mere fragment of a man, by the fully developed individual, fit for a variety of labours, ready to face any change of production, and to whom the different social functions he performs are but so many modes of giving free scope to his own natural and acquired powers.

Karl Marx, 1818–1883

☐

Bodily labor . . . has everywhere been changed into an instrument of strange perversion; for dead matter leaves the factory ennobled and transformed where men are corrupted and degraded.*

Pope Pius XI, reign 1922–1939

☐

211

ELEVATION OF THE WORKING CLASS

The crisis can be solved only if we learn to invert the present
deep structure of tools; if we give people tools that guarantee
their right to work with high, independent efficiency, thus simultaneously eliminating the need for either slaves or masters and
enhancing each person's range of freedom. People need new
tools to work with rather than tools that "work" for them. They
need technology to make the most of the energy and imagination
each has, rather than more well-programmed energy slaves.

Ivan Illich, 1973

☐

Instead of developing techniques for maximum profit, try to
develop those that will give the maximum of freedom: an *entirely*
new approach.

Simone Weil, 1909–1943

☐

. . . Where money beareth all the swing, there are many vain and
superfluous occupations must needs be used, to serve only for
riotous superfluity and unhonest pleasure. For the same multitude that is now occupied in work, if they were divided into so
few occupations as the necessary use of nature requireth; in so
great plenty of things as then of necessity would ensue, doubtless
the prices would be too little for the artificers to maintain their
livings. But if all these, that be now busied about unprofitable
occupations, with all the whole flock of them that live idly and
slothfully, which consume and waste every one of them more of
these things that come by other men's labour, then two of the
workmen themselves do: if all these (I say) were set to profitable
occupations, you easily perceive how little time would be enough,

yea and too much to store us with all things that may be requisite
either for necessity, or for commodity, yea or for pleasure, so
that the same pleasure be true and natural. And this in Utopia
the thing itself maketh manifest and plain. . . .*

Sir Thomas More, 1478–1535

□

Have the factory and the workshop at the gates of your fields and
gardens, and work in them. Not those large establishments, of
course, in which huge masses of metals have to be dealt with and
which are better placed at certain spots indicated by Nature,
but the countless variety of workshops and factories which are
required to satisfy the infinite diversity of tastes among civilised
men . . . factories and workshops into which men, women and
children will not be driven by hunger, but will be attracted by
the desire of finding an activity suited to their tastes, and where,
aided by the motor and the machine, they will choose the branch
of activity which best suits their inclinations. . . . Very soon
you will yourselves feel interested in that work, and you will
have occasion to admire in your children their eager desire to
become acquainted with Nature and its forces, their inquisitive
inquiries as to the powers of machinery, and their rapidly developing inventive genius.*

Prince Peter Kropotkin, 1842–1921

□

The great question is: how much work does industrialism save
that we really need to have done at all; and how much more does
it do that we would rather have done on a handicraft or inter-
mediate technologies basis—for the sake of conserving other
values? For most people, work is a bore and a burden; it is done
for other people's profit and to other people's specifications. It
is done for money, rarely for love. So of course everyone rushes

to unload their labor on to the machines and the big systems. These in turn justify their existence by grinding out the swanky garbage which the official economics tallies up into a statistical mystery called "the standard of living." And the void that is left behind when the machines have taken over the drudgery that no one ever wanted to do in the first place is called "leisure"—a vacuum rapidly filled with cheerless, obsessive getting and spending.

But where work becomes a personal project and is done in community, its character is wholly transformed. It can even become, as it was for the Christian monks and has been for most primitive peoples, a form of prayer. Work can be the chance to innovate, fraternize, and serve. Its tools and patterns can be filled with transcendent symbolism. It can be a fulfilling expression of the personality. But we are a long, long way from that.*

Theodore Roszak, 1972

☐

By the elevation of the laborer, I do not understand that he is to be raised above the need of labor. Manual labor is a school in which men are placed to get energy of purpose and character. Even if we do not work with the hands, we must undergo equivalent toil in some other direction. The capacity of steady, earnest labor is, I apprehend, one of our great preparations for another state of being.

Manual labor is a great good; let us not fight against it. We need this admonition, because at the present moment there is a general disposition to shun labor; and this ought to be regarded as a bad sign of our times. The city is thronged with adventurers from the country, and the liberal professions are overstocked, in the hope of escaping the primeval sentence of living by the sweat of the brow; and to this crowding of men into trade we owe not only the neglect of agriculture, but, what is far worse, the demoralization of the community. It generates excessive competition, which of necessity generates fraud. Trade is turned to gambling; and a spirit of mad speculation exposes public and private interests to a disastrous instability. It is, then, no part of the philanthropy which would elevate the laboring body, to exempt them from manual toil. In truth, a wise philanthropy would, if possible, persuade all men of all conditions to mix up a measure of this toil with their other pursuits. The body as well as the mind needs vigorous exertion, and even the studious would be happier were they trained to labor as well as thought. Let us learn to regard manual toil as the true discipline of a man. Not a few of the wisest, grandest spirits have toiled at the workbench and the plough.*

Channing, 1780–1842

□

The Buddhist point of view takes the function of work to be at least threefold: to give a man a chance to utilise and develop his faculties; to enable him to overcome his ego-centredness by joining with other people in a common task; and to bring forth the goods and services needed for a becoming existence. To organise work in such a manner that it becomes meaningless, boring, stultifying, or nerve-racking for the worker would be little short of criminal; it would indicate a greater concern with goods than with people, an evil lack of compassion and a soul-destroying degree of attachment to the most primitive side of this worldly existence. Equally, to strive for leisure as an alternative to work would be considered a complete misunderstanding of one of the basic truths of human existence, namely that work and leisure are complementary parts of the same living process and cannot be separated without destroying the joy of work and the bliss of leisure.

It is clear, therefore, that Buddhist economics must be very different from the economics of modern materialism, since the Buddhist sees the essence of civilisation not in a multiplication of wants but in the purification of human character. Character, at the same time, is formed primarily by a man's work. And work, properly conducted in conditions of human dignity and freedom, blesses those who do it and equally their products.*

E. F. Schumacher, 1973

LESS IS MORE

☐

Two men I honour and no third. First, the toil-worn Craftsman
that with earth-made Implement laboriously conquers the Earth,
and makes her man's. Venerable to me is the hard Hand; crooked,
coarse; wherein notwithstanding lies a cunning virtue, indefeasi-
bly royal, as of the Scepter of this Planet.

A second man I honor, and still more highly Him who is
seen toiling for the spiritually indispensable; not daily bread,
but the bread of Life. Is not he too in his duty; endeavoring
towards inward Harmony; revealing this, by act or by word,
through all his outward endeavors, be they high or low? Highest
of all, when his outward and his inward endeavor are one: when
we can name him Artist; not earthly Craftsman only, but inspired Thinker, who with heaven-made Implement conquers
Heaven for us! These two, in all their degrees, I honor: all else
is chaff and dust, which let the wind blow wither it listeth.

Unspeakably touching is it, however, when I find both dig-
nities united; and he that must toil outwardly for the lowest of
man's wants, is also toiling inwardly for the highest.*

Thomas Carlyle, 1795–1881

☐

I have now said what I do not mean by the elevation of the
laboring classes. It is not an outward change of condition. It is
not release from labor. It is not struggling for another rank. It is
not political power. I understand something deeper. The only
elevation of a human being consists in the exercise, growth,
energy of the higher principles and powers of his soul. Such is the
elevation I desire for the laborer, and I desire no other. This
elevation is indeed to be aided by an improvement of his outward condition, and in turn it greatly improves his outward lot;
and thus connected, outward good is real and great; but supposing it to exist in separation from inward growth and life, it would
be nothing worth, nor would I raise a finger to promote it.

I know it will be said, that such elevation as I have spoken of

216

is not and cannot be within the reach of the laboring multitude, and of consequence they ought not to be tantalized with dreams of its attainment. It will be said that the principal part of men are plainly designed to work on matter for the acquisition of material and corporeal good, and that, in such, the spirit is of necessity too wedded to matter to rise above it.*

Channing, 1780–1842

☐

To supply the necessary energy to the dreams and ambitions of the nineteenth century, work had to be secularized. For the first time in his history, man assumed this very harsh task of "doing better and quicker than Nature," without having at his disposal the liturgical dimension which in other societies made work bearable. And it is in work finally secularized, in work in its pure state, numbered in hours and units of energy consumed, that man feels the implacable nature of temporal duration, its full weight and slowness. . . . The secularization of work is like an open wound in the body of modern society. There is, however, nothing to indicate that a resanctification may not take place in the future.*

Mircea Eliade, 1956

☐

Observe the phases of history: the most fruitful epochs, those most clearly filled with life and genius, have always seen a flourishing artisan class. A renewal of consciousness will only be achieved through craftsmanship, not by doctrines. Mechanized civilization is the agony of the world.

R. A. Schwaller de Lubicz, 1963

☐

Man gains, through work, the insight into nature he needs to transmute work into artifacts and symbols that have a use beyond

ensuring his immediate animal survival. The ultimate justification of work lies not alone in the performance of the product
but in the realm of the arts and sciences. . . .

Ritual, art, poetry, drama, music, dance, philosophy, science,
myth, religion, are accordingly all as essential to man as his daily
bread: man's true life consists not alone in the work activities
that directly sustain him, but in the symbolic activities which
give significance both to the processes of work and their ultimate
products and consummations. There is no poverty worse than
that of being excluded, by ignorance, by insensibility, or by a failure to master the language, from the meaningful symbols of one's
culture. For it is through the effort to achieve meaning, form,
and value that the potentialities of man are realized, and his
actual life in turn is raised to a higher potential.*

Lewis Mumford, 1944

□

There must become a haven where men need no longer degrade
their art, their science and their technique for the sake of livelihood or of governmental power-plays. They shall be given the
opportunity of working for the sake of perfection in work, without attachment to results.

Then, dedicated people will apply their talents and skills, their
knowledge and craft, to prove within their specialties the many
ways which will exalt the quality of matter.

André VandenBroeck, 1965

□

Thus the Great Work will be perfected.

Hermes Trismegistus

11

CHOOSING THE IMAGE: LIFE/STYLE

SIMPLICITY: *THE POWER OF THE MINIMAL*

There is nothing the busy man is less busied with than living;
there is nothing that is harder to learn. . . . It takes the whole
of life to learn how to live, and—what will perhaps make you
wonder more—it takes the whole of life to learn how to die.
Many very great men, having laid aside all their encumbrances,
having renounced riches, business, and pleasures, have made it
their own aim up to the very end of life to know how to live. . . .*

Seneca, 4? B.C.–A.D. 65

☐

We are living in a strange civilization. Our minds and souls are
so overlaid with fear, with artificiality, that often we do not even
recognize beauty. It is this fear, this lack of direct vision of truth
that brings about all the disaster the world holds, and how little
opportunity we give any people for casting off fear, for living
simply and naturally. When they do, first of all we fear them,
then we condemn them. It is only if they are great enough to
outlive our condemnation that we accept them.

Robert Henri, 1923

☐

LESS IS MORE

When Socrates heard one of his friends saying how expensive Athens was, how "Chian wine costs a mina, a purple robe three minas, a half pint of honey five drachmas," he took him to the bread shops. "Half a peck of barley meal for an obol? Athens is cheap!" Then to the vest maker. "A sleeveless vest for only ten drachmas? Athens is cheap!" So when we hear anyone saying of us that we live in a small way and are terribly unfortunate because we are not consuls or governors, we may answer, "We live in a grand way and our lot is enviable. We do not beg, we bear no heavy burdens, we toady to no one."

Plutarch, 46?–120

☐

To have a life that is in any way detached from the megatechnic complex, to say nothing of being cockily independent of it, or recalcitrant to its demands, is regarded as nothing less than a form of sabotage. Hence the fury evoked by the Hippies—quite apart from any objectionable behavior. On megatechnic terms complete withdrawal is heresy and treason, if not evidence of unsound mind. The arch-enemy of the Affluent Economy would not be Karl Marx but Henry Thoreau.

Lewis Mumford, 1964

☐

The most difficult aspect of coming to an ecological understanding of the world is in changing one's own life style to conform to the new comprehension. The kinds of change necessary to make American society ecologically and humanly sane are truly gargantuan. But they begin in one place and in one form—in our own heads and in our own day to day actions.*

Kenneth P. Cantor, 1970

☐

CHOOSING THE IMAGE: LIFE/STYLE

The most beautiful life possible, wherein there is no sordidness, is only attainable by effort. To be free, to be happy and fruitful, can only be attained through sacrifice of many common but over-estimated things.

Robert Henri, 1923

☐

A certain hermit named Kyo-yu owned nothing whatever: even water he drank out of his hand. Seeing this, someone gave him a bowl made of a gourd. One day, he hung it on the branch of a tree but the wind made it bang about and rattle noisily, so he took it and threw it away and drank water out of his hand as before.

Yoshida Kenkō, 1283–1350

☐

One day, observing a child drinking out of his hands, Diogenes cast away the cup from his wallet with the words, "A child has beaten me in plainness of living." He also threw away his bowl when in like manner he saw a child who had broken his plate taking up his lentils with the hollow part of a morsel of bread.

Diogenes Laërtius, 3d cent.

☐

The wallet and cloak and the barley-dough thickened with water, the staff planted before his feet, and the earthenware cup, are estimated by the wise Dog as sufficient for the needs of life, and even in these there was something superfluous; for, seeing the countryman drinking from the hollow of his hand, he said, "Why, thou earthen cup, did I burden myself with thee to no purpose?" . . . Even brass is aged by time, but not all the ages, Diogenes, shall destroy thy fame, since thou alone didst show to mortals the rule of self-sufficiency and the easiest path of life.*

Antiphilus of Byzantium, 1st cent. A.D.

221

LESS IS MORE

□

Remember that I teach you the principle of poverty with my life.

Diogenes, 412?–323 B.C.

□

We can only imagine Plato and Aristotle in grand academic robes. They were honest fellows, like others, laughing with their friends; and, when they amused themselves with writing their *Laws* and their *Politics,* they did so as a game. That was the least serious part of their lives. The most philosophic was living simply and tranquilly. If they wrote on politics, it was like making rules for a lunatic asylum.

Pascal, 1623–1662

□

To be a philosopher is not merely to have subtle thoughts, nor even to found a school, but so to love wisdom, as to live according to its dictates, a life of simplicity.

Thoreau, 1817–1862

□

As for myself, whenever I look back upon the great examples of antiquity, I am ashamed to seek any consolations for poverty, since in these times luxury has reached such a pitch that the allowance of exiles is larger than the inheritance of the chief men of old.

Will any one say, therefore, that these men lived poorly without seeming from his very words to be the poorest wretch alive?

With such defenders, therefore, as these the cause of poverty becomes not only safe, but greatly favoured.

Seneca, 4? B.C.–A.D. 65

CHOOSING THE IMAGE: LIFE/STYLE

☐

In the world when people call any one simple they generally mean a foolish, ignorant, credulous person. But real simplicity, so far from being foolish, is almost sublime. All good men like and admire it, are conscious of sinning against it, observe it in others, and know what it involves, and yet they could not precisely define it. I should say that simplicity is an uprightness of soul which prevents self-consciousness.

Verily such simplicity is a great treasure! How shall we attain to it?

François Fénelon, 1651–1715

☐

In everything, love simplicity.

St. François de Sales, 1567–1622

☐

To have but few desires and to be satisfied with simple things is the sign of a superior man.

Gampopa, d. 1152

☐

Unless a man is simple, he cannot recognize God, the Simple One.

Bengali song

☐

It would be an error to suppose that the simplicity we seek has anything in common with that which misers impose upon themselves through cupidity, or narrow-minded people through false

223

austerity. To the former the simple life is the one that costs least;
to the latter it is a flat and colorless existence, whose merit lies
in depriving one's self of everything bright, smiling, seductive.

Charles Wagner, 1895

☐

We are lovers of the beautiful, yet simple in our tastes. . . .
Wealth we employ, not for talk and ostentation, but when there
is a real use for it.

Thucydides, 471?–400? B.C.

☐

I am bound to praise the simple life, because I have lived it and
found it good. When I depart from it, evil results follow. I love
a small house, plain clothes, simple living. Many persons know
the luxury of a skin bath—a plunge in the pool or the wave
unhampered by clothing. That is the simple life—direct and
immediate contact with things, life with the false wrappings torn
away—the fine house, the fine equipage, the expensive habits, all
cut off. How free one feels, how good the elements taste, how
close one gets to them, how they fit one's body and one's soul!
To see the fire that warms you, or better yet, to cut the wood that
feeds the fire that warms you; to see the spring where the water
bubbles up that slakes your thirst, and to dip your pail into it;
to see the beams that are the stay of your four walls, and the tim-
bers that uphold the roof that shelters you; to be in direct and
personal contact with the sources of your material life; to want
no extras, no shields; to find the universal elements enough; to
find the air and the water exhilarating; to be refreshed by a morning walk or an evening saunter; to find a quest of wild berries
more satisfying than a gift of tropic fruit; to be thrilled by the
stars at night; to be elated over a bird's nest, or over a wild flower
in spring—these are some of the rewards of the simple life.

John Burroughs, 1837–1921

CHOOSING THE IMAGE: LIFE/STYLE

☐

How happy in his low degree,
How rich in humble Poverty is he
Who leads a quiet Country life,
Discharged of business, void of strife,
And from the griping Scrivener free!
Thus, ere the seeds of vice were sown,
Lived men in better ages born,
Who plowed with oxen of their own
Their small paternal field of corn . . .
The clamors of contentious Law,
And Court and State he wisely shuns;
Nor bribed with hopes, nor dared with awe,
To servile salutations runs . . . .*

Horace, 65–8 B.C.

☐

I saw an ancient Corycian who owned
a few acres, which were not fertile
for plowing, opportune for flocks or Bacchus.
As he placed herbs about the bushes
with white lilies, vervain and thin poppy,
he equalled the mind of kings and coming home
late at night would pile up free delicacies.
He was first to pick spring roses and fall apples,
and when morose winter was yet breaking
rocks and closing waters with ice,
he was soon selecting gentle hyacinth,
scolding lingering summer and dawdling Zephyr.
Thus he was also first with mother bees
and an abundant swarm, to press honey
foaming from the comb; lush were his limes,
and of all the fruits his fertile tree had on
early, as many were held in mature autumn.
He laid out the grown elms,
hard pear trees, spines with plums
and the plane transplanted for drinkers.

225

LESS IS MORE

I, excluded by these narrow limits,
relinquish this theme for others after me.

Vergil, 70–19 B.C.

☐

I think I could turn and live with animals, they are so placid and
self contained. . . .
Not one is dissatisfied, not one is demented with the mania of owning
things. . . .

Walt Whitman, 1819–1892

☐

From the summit of the years I look back over my life, and see
what I have escaped and what I have missed, as a traveler might
look back over his course from a mountaintop. . . . I have escaped
the soul-killing and body-wrecking occupations that are the fate
of so many men in my time. I have escaped the greed of wealth,
the "mania of owning things," as Whitman called it. . . .*

John Burroughs, 1837–1921

☐

Simplicity of life, even the barest, is not misery but the very foundation of refinement.

William Morris, 1834–1896

☐

I do not think that any civilization can be called complete until
it has progressed from sophistication to unsophistication, and
made a conscious return to simplicity of thinking and living.

Lin Yutang, 1938

☐

CHOOSING THE IMAGE: LIFE/STYLE

Needless to say, wealth, education, research, and many other things are needed for any civilization, but what is most needed today is a revision of the ends which these means are meant to serve. And this implies, above all else, the development of a life-style which accords to material things their proper, legitimate place, which is secondary and not primary.

E. F. Schumacher, 1973

☐

I went to the woods because I wished to live deliberately, to front only the essential facts of life, and see if I could not learn what it had to teach, and not, when I came to die, discover that I had not lived. I did not wish to live what was not life, living is so dear, nor did I wish to practise resignation, unless it was quite necessary. I wanted to live deep and suck out all the marrow of life, to live so sturdily and Spartan-like as to put to rout all that was not life, to cut a broad swath and shave close, to drive life into a corner, and reduce it to its lowest terms, and, if it proved to be mean, why then to get the whole and genuine meanness of it, and publish its meanness to the world; or if it were sublime, to know it by experience, and be able to give a true account of it in my next excursion.

Thoreau, 1817–1862

☐

The family which takes its mauve and cerise, air-conditioned, power-steered and power-braked automobile out for a tour passes through cities that are badly paved, made hideous by litter, blighted buildings. . . . They pass on into a countryside that has been rendered largely invisible by commercial art. . . . They picnic on exquisitely packaged food from a portable icebox by a polluted stream and go on to spend the night at a park which is a menace to public health and morals. Just before dozing off on an air-mattress, beneath a nylon tent, amid the stench of

decaying refuse, they may reflect vaguely on the curious uneven-
ness of their blessings. Is this, indeed, the American genius?*

John Kenneth Galbraith, 1958

☐

A decline in the quality of life coinciding with an increase in economic affluence symbolizes the trend toward the absurd in technological societies. Present-day countercultures probably are the
expressions of a deep-seated, almost subconscious social wisdom
capable of generating protective responses against this trend.

Throughout history, countercultures have appeared irrational,
at least in their outward manifestation. The prosperous young
men and women who adopted a strictly cloistered monastic life
during the Middle Ages, the nineteenth-century Bohemians who
engaged in antics to protest against the pomposity of bourgeois
life and art, certainly must have looked irrational to the majority
of reasonable people of their times. But in fact, countercultures
have commonly been motivated by a higher kind of rationality
than that of the Establishment. What they express is not ordinary
political dissent but rather the first stirrings of a true revolution
in thought. They represent a soul-searching in quest of values
which once gave zest to living and which are being lost.

René Dubos, 1972

☐

What are the practical means by which we can know our single
lives bound to greater Life and ourselves secure in hope?

From personal experience, I can say that one way is by choosing to be poor, and by refusing to allow validity to the American
standard of living, as an ideal. I am ashamed to write of Poverty,
also as an ideal, because I myself have gone so short a distance
come by such slow, faltering, and partial steps to understand
the relation of voluntary poverty to the religious life, the life of
worship and commitment, the life of wholeness and security; and
because, as a family, we have let our allegiance to the ideal of

poverty and participation in the life of the needy be so much moderated by our own timidity and the solicitude of our friends. Yet what we have learned and experienced is the only thing we have to pass on to others for any help it may be to them.

We started from no specifically religious convictions. I suppose one would say we were then humanists. Probably there was nothing sudden about our change of direction; no doubt we had been slowly veering into that direction throughout our adult lives. We had gradually come to a clear conviction that we ought to work with very poor people, and share in some degree in their hardships by being ourselves poor. In the early thirties, when the great depression was upon the country, we worked for a summer in the Kentucky coal-mining villages.

Meanwhile, we were growing more familiar too with Gandhi's ideas and methods, and his principles of personal discipline. We had always thought of ourselves as pacifists; it was only now that poverty and physical labor began to seem to us an integral part of any total pacifist response to a society in which prosperity depends on war or the preparation for it. [So from 1936–1939, we joined a group of evicted share croppers who had formed a co-operative cotton-growing community in Mississippi. Next we lived with white and Negro tenant farmers in South Carolina. We worked there fifteen years and were ourselves farmers throughout that time.]

The consummation we hoped for, even more than for material improvements, was a close relationship between ourselves and these neighbors. In this we were partly disappointed. After basic necessities, the things we wanted most for them, as for ourselves, were not what they most wanted.

It may be interesting to observe that after a period of prosperity had set in, and after our neighbors bought their own homes, our addiction to Poverty may have widened the cultural gap between some of them and us.

While they were joyfully accumulating for the first time furniture, and good cars, and refrigerators, and beginning to dress as well as the average American, we continued to live in a rather bare way. We wanted to do this, partly because there were still some very poor people around us. . . . But it was also partly because we wanted to make our lives at least a challenge to the ideal of an ever-rising material standard. It seems to us that when we have worked to remedy the condition of any depressed group, we presently come to a point where, if we have succeeded in helping them, we must now try to show them how to be content with their new state without wanting to raise it ever further. We see no possible way to do this except by a steady adherence to a standard of great simplicity for ourselves, even of poverty. Unless we do this, we have but brought them out of a condition of physical need into a condition of mental unrest in the competition for more and more.*

Mildred Binns Young, 1956

☐

In their fundamental aspirations and ideals, the generation of the Wandervögel in the 1920s were not as different from the generation of the Hippies as their external appearance might suggest. The worldly bourgeois society had cut its own throat, and the survivors were free of all moral obligations to their past. It was time to make a fresh start. Redemption would come only through a new austerity, of dress, of manners, of taste, of style. Artistic matters became, for them, matters for moral reflection and judgment, rather than morality a matter of aesthetic taste; *the proper alternative to the arbitrary authoritarianism of society was not anarchism but self-discipline.* All the individual could do was to try to live in his own high-minded way, maintaining and exemplifying in his own life his own exacting standards of humanity, intellectual honesty, craftsmanship and personal integrity.

Young Europeans, among them the young Simone Weil, marched out of the corrupt cities and back into the pine forests where they hoped to recapture the purer and simpler values to which their fathers had been blinded.

Ludwig Wittgenstein was born too early to belong to the Wandervögel generation but he shared many of their values.

The youngest son of Vienna's leading steel magnate and art-patron, he was reared in affluence. Army life brought him in contact with his fellow men and also with the writings of Tolstoy and John Woolman from whom he acquired respect for manual labor, later manifested in his choice of working as a gardener between spells of teaching. When taken prisoner, he had in his rucksack the manuscript of *Tractatus Logico-Philosophicus,* one day to be considered a milestone in Philosophy.

After his father's death, Wittgenstein came into a great fortune and had made large anonymous grants: Rilke was among the recipients. One of his first steps after the war was to give away all his money. Henceforth a great simplicity became characteristic of his life. His Cambridge rooms were austerely furnished: a few deck-chairs and a card-table on which he did his writing, a canvas cot, a few plants, bare walls. Likewise his dress was as simple as possible: gray flannel trousers, shirt open at the throat, a lumberjacket.

What prompted him was an overpowering urge to cast off all encumbrances: his fortune as well as his necktie; all the things, big or small, that he felt to be petty or ludicrous.

What Wittgenstein's life and work shows is the possibility of a new *spiritual attitude.* It is a *lived logic,* because of which he has not been understood. For a new way of life entails a new language and his is the language of wordless faith. Such an attitude adopted by other individuals of the right stature will be the source from which new forms of society will spring. In the future, ideals will not be communicated by attempts to describe them, but by models of an appropriate conduct of life.**

☐

Even if the visionary commonwealth is never more than a relative handful in the city and the wilderness, its role is apt to be like that of the medieval monastics: to exemplify an ideal of life by which the many may judge themselves and the world. The power of such a living example must never be underestimated.

Roszak, 1972

☐

THE NEW POVERTY

Moneytheism is everywhere, in everything we see and read and hear. It is only after a long process of dis-education and re-education that one sees it clearly and sees it whole—the pricewage shell game, the speed-up treadmill: the Save!-Spend! contradictions dinned into our ears night and day. The rat race. A rat race that offers only two alternatives: to run with the hare or hunt with the hounds.

Disaffiliation is a voluntary self-alienation from the family cult, from Moneytheism and all its works and ways.

The New Poverty is the disaffiliate's answer to the New Prosperity.

It is important to make a living, but it is even more important to make a life.

Poverty. The very word is taboo in a society where success is equated with virtue and poverty is a sin. Yet it has an honorable ancestry. St. Francis of Assisi revered Poverty as his bride, with holy fervor and pious rapture.

The poverty of the disaffiliate is not to be confused with the poverty of indigence, intemperance, improvidence or failure.

It is not the poverty of the ill-tempered and embittered, those who wooed the bitch goddess Success with panting breath and came away rebuffed.

It is an independent, voluntary poverty.

It is an art, and like all arts it has to be learned.*

Lawrence Lipton, 1959

☐

From Benedict to Kropotkin there is a profound conviction that the highest possibility of true morality and love is to be found in the life that is as liberated as possible from complexity and overrefinement of function. In the mainstream of the ecological tradition this has never meant stark austerity or abstinence. One of the greatnesses of Benedict's Rule is its insistence upon as normal a life as possible, with ample sleep, rest, good food, and the best of wine, with continuous development of man's mental as well as his spiritual nature. There is, nevertheless, a clear and unwavering emphasis upon simplicity. Precisely the same is true of More's *Utopia*. There is no morbid denial of natural appetites, nor a precious eschewal of the technology that makes a civilized existence possible: none of this. But always, from monk to anarchist, there is an insistence that simplicity should reign in all things.

Robert Nisbet, 1973

□

The true remedy is for men to reduce their wants to the fewest possible, and as much as possible to simplify the mode of supplying them.

William Godwin, 1793

□

Make thyself all simplicity.

Marcus Aurelius, 121–180

□

In proportion as he simplifies his life, the laws of the universe will appear less complex, and solitude will not be solitude, nor poverty poverty, nor weakness weakness.

Why should we be in such desperate haste to succeed, and in such desperate enterprises? If a man does not keep pace with his companions, perhaps it is because he hears a different drummer. Let him step to the music which he hears, however measured or far away.

Thoreau, 1817–1862

□

[Our purpose in going to Vermont] was not to multiply food, housing, fuel and the other necessaries, but to get only enough of these things to meet the requirements of a living standard that would maintain our physical efficiency and at the same time provide us with sufficient leisure to pursue our chosen avocations.

Current practice in United States economy called upon the person who had met his needs for necessaries to turn his attention forthwith to procuring comforts and conveniences, and after that to luxuries and superfluities. Only by such procedures could an economy based on profit accumulation hope to achieve the expansion needed to absorb additional profits and pay a return to those investing in the new industries.

Our practice was almost the exact opposite of the current one. Food from the garden and wood from the forest were the product of our own time and labor. We paid no rent. Taxes were reasonable. We bought no candy, pastries, meats, soft drinks, alcohol, tea, coffee or tobacco. These seemingly minor items mount up and occupy a large place in the ordinary family's budget. We spent little on clothes and knickknacks. We lighted for fifteen years with kerosene and candles. We never had a telephone or radio. Most of our furniture was built in and hand made.

Readers may label such a policy as painfully austere, renunciatory or bordering on deliberate self-punishment. We had no such feeling. We felt as free, in this respect, as a caged wild bird who finds himself once more on the wing. To the extent that we were able to meet our consumer needs in our own way and in our own good time, we had freed ourselves from dependence upon the market economy.*

Helen and Scott Nearing, 1954

□

[Important] is the example of those who have already found the resourcefulness to change their lives and fulfilled themselves in doing so. Nothing counts more heavily against the technocracy than a successful desertion, for there is no underestimating the influence of an authentically happy disaffiliate in a society of affluent self-contempt.*

Theodore Roszak, 1972

☐

All things were ready for us at our birth; it is we that have made everything difficult for ourselves, through our disdain for what is easy. Houses, shelters, creature comforts, food, and all that has now become the source of vast trouble, were ready at hand, free to all, and obtainable for trifling pains. For the limit everywhere corresponded to the need; it is we that have made all those things valuable, we that have made them admired, we that have caused them to be sought for by extensive and manifold devices. . . . For that moderation which nature prescribes, which limits our desires by resources restricted to our needs, has abandoned the field; it has now come to this—that to want only what is enough is a sign both of boorishness and of utter destitution.*

Seneca, 4? B.C.–A.D. 65
Ep. XC

☐

One nearly despairs of the possibility that our entrenched economics of alienation, greed, and anti-sociability will ever lose its authority over people's minds. But there is one way forward: the creation of flesh-and-blood examples of low-consumption, high-quality alternatives to the mainstream pattern of life. This we can see happening already on the counter cultural fringes. And nothing—no amount of argument or research—will take the place of such living proof. What people must see is that ecologically sane, socially responsible living is *good* living; that simplicity, thrift, and reciprocity make for an existence that is free and more self-respecting.

Currently, many well-intentioned ecological propagandists are busy wrapping zero-growth economics in the hair shirt of dismal privation, as if a healthy relationship with nature must mean grim, puritanical self-denial. This is not only politically futile as a stance in public debate, but it is simply untrue. Economy of means and simplicity of life—voluntarily chosen—have always been the secret of fulfillment; while acquisitiveness and extravagance are a despairing waste of life.

Theodore Roszak, 1972

□

I think we can already see the conflict of attitudes which will decide our future. On the one side, I see the people who think they can cope with our . . . crisis by the methods current. . . . I call them the people of the forward stampede. On the other side, there are people in search of a new life-style, who seek to return to certain basic truths about man and his world; I call them home-comers. Let us admit that the people of the forward stampede, like the devil, have all the best tunes or at least the most popular and familiar tunes. You cannot stand still, they say; standing still means going down; you must go forward; there is nothing wrong with modern technology except that it is as yet incomplete; let us complete it.

And what about the other side? This is made up of people who are deeply convinced that technological development has taken a wrong turn and needs to be redirected. The term "home-comer" has, of course, a religious connotation. For it takes a good deal of courage to say "no" to the fashions and fascinations of the age and to question the presuppositions of a civilization which appears destined to conquer the whole world; the requisite strength can be derived only from deep convictions. If it were derived from nothing more than fear of the future, it would be likely to disappear at the decisive moment. The genuine "home-comer" does not have the best tunes, but he has the most exalted text, nothing less than the Gospels. . . .

It may seem daring to connect these beatitudes with matters of technology and economics. But may it not be that we are in trouble precisely because we have failed for so long to make this connection?*

E. F. Schumacher, 1973

☐

That most of us are considered poor is no disgrace, but does us credit; for, as the mind is weakened by luxurious living, so it is strengthened by a frugal life.

Minucius Felix, 3d cent. A.D.

☐

Anticommercial-minded heretics are beginning to unite and speak up. They are willing to undergo official displeasure in order to spread a gospel different from that of the marketplace. They gently urge us to change our lifestyle. . . .

These anticommercial prophets—call them Contrasumers—say, "Take heed, for time is growing short. If we continue to consume at the present rate, the earth has but a decade or two of life before the whirlwind comes. . . ."

The ways in which our citizens desire to qualitatively change their lives should be left to their individual consciences. They should not be required to plod listlessly along on the commercial treadmill when they don't want to. The United States can support a variety of lifestyles and economies. Those desiring to live in an autoless economy should have that right. . . .*

Albert J. Fritsch, 1974

☐

Let us learn to rely upon our limbs and to conform our dress and mode of life, not to the new fashions, but to the customs our ancestors approved; let us learn to increase our self-control, to restrain luxury, to moderate ambition, to soften anger, to view poverty with unprejudiced eyes, to cultivate frugality, even if many shall be ashamed, all the more to apply to the wants of nature the remedies that cost little, and to determine to seek our riches from ourselves rather than from Fortune.

Not only in the race and the contests of the Circus, but also in the arena of life, we must keep to the inner circle.*

Seneca, 4? B.C.–A.D. 65

□

We need not wait for bombs and bullets actually to strike us before we strip our lives of superfluities. . . . We must simplify our daily routine without waiting for ration cards. . . .

More immediately, we must demand: What is the purpose of each new political and economic measure? Does it seek the old goal of expansion or the new one of equilibrium? . . .

If we keep this standard constantly in mind, we shall have both a measure for what must be rejected and a goal for what must be achieved . . . the possibilities of progress will become real again once we lose our blind faith in the external improvements of the machine alone. But the first step is a personal one: a change in direction of interest *towards* the person. Without that change, no great betterment will take place in the social order. Once that change begins, everything is possible.*

Lewis Mumford, 1944

□

The transformation that is coming invites us to reexamine our own lives. It confronts us with a personal and individual choice: are we satisfied with how we have lived; how would we live differently? It offers us a recovery of self. It faces us with the fact that this choice cannot be evaded, for as the freedom is already there, so must the responsibility be there.

At the heart of everything is what we shall call a change of consciousness. This means a "new head"—a new way of living

—a new man. This is what the new generation has been searching for, and what it has started achieving. Industrialism produced a new man, too—one adapted to the demands of the machine. In contrast, today's emerging consciousness seeks a new knowledge of what it means to be human, in order that the machine, having been built, may now be turned to human ends. . . .

Charles Reich, 1970

12

CREATIVE POVERTY:
THE ASCETIC AESTHETIC

VOLUNTARY POVERTY AND THE ARTIST

Man's cry is to reach his fullest expression. It is the desire for self-expression that leads him to seek wealth and power. But he has to discover that accumulation is not realization.

Tagore, 1913

□

At the present time, the closest thing we have to the traditional ideology of the leisure class is a group of artists and intellectuals who regard their work as play and their play as work. For such people . . . work frequently provides the central focus of life without necessarily being compartmentalized from the rest of life either by its drudgery and severity or by its precariousness.*

David Riesman, 1964

□

Things being as they are, the life of an artist is a battle wherein great economy must be exercised. The kind of economy which will result in moments of the purest freedom in spite of the world's exactions.

If one is a painter this purest freedom must exist at the time of painting. This is as much to say that a painter may give up his hope of making a living as a painter but must make it some other way. This is generally true, although some do, by a freak of appreciation, make enough while going their way to live sufficiently well. Perhaps this happens, but I am not sure but that there is some curtailing of the purity of the freedom.

Robert Henri, 1923

☐

Gauguin, like any Desert fanatic, left his Paris banking house and his comfortable wife, and watched his small son starve and himself died in nakedness and ecstasy, because he had discovered paint as the Desert discovered God. Van Gogh went mad in struggling to paint light: they found a fragment of a letter in his pocket after he had shot himself. "Well, my own work, I am risking my life for it, and my reason has half foundered in it— that's all Right." It is not that these are not grieved for: but they are not grudged. No generous spirit will shirk the arduous, provided it be unknown. A man must follow his star.

Helen Waddell, 1889–1965

☐

The only sensible way to regard the art life is that it is a privilege you are willing to pay for.

Robert Henri, 1923

☐

We are all poor in Ireland . . . so many artists want a motor car, a house, to give parties, etc., that they sell their genius for cash. They should take the vow of poverty that is *an inside vow.*

"A. E.," 1934

☐

Hasn't the artist always kept the true balance between the poverty
of riches and the riches of poverty?

Honoré de Balzac, 1799–1850

☐

[I think] that if a man find in himself any strong bias to poetry,
to art, to the contemplative life, drawing him to see these things
with a devotion incompatible with good husbandry, that a man
ought to reckon early with himself, and, respecting the compen-
sations of the Universe, ought to ransom himself from the
duties of economy by a certain rigor and privation in his habits.
For privileges so rare and grand, let him not stint to pay a great
tax. Let him be a cenobite, a pauper, and if need be, a celibate
also. Let him learn to eat his meals standing and to relish the
taste of fair water and black bread. He may leave to others the
costly conveniences of housekeeping and large hospitality, and
the possession of works of art. Let him feel that genius is a hospitality, and that he who can create works of art need not collect
them. He must live in a chamber and postpone his self-indulgence
forewarned and forearmed against that frequent misfortune of
men of genius,—the taste for luxury.

Milton says, that the lyric poet may drink wine and live generously but the epic poet, he who shall sing of the gods and their
descent unto men, must drink water out of a wooden bowl.

So the poet's habit of living should be set on a key so low
and plain that the common influences shall delight him. His
cheerfulness should be the gift of the sunlight; the air should
suffice for his inspiration, and he should be tipsy with water.*

Emerson, 1803–1882

☐

I never have sought wealth, I have been too much absorbed in
enjoying the world about me. I had no talent for business any-
how—for the cutthroat competition that modern business for
the most part is—and probably could not have attained wealth

had I desired it. I dare not aver that I had really rather be
cheated than to cheat, but I am quite sure I could never know-
ingly overreach a man, and what chance of success could such a
tenderfoot have in the conscienceless struggle for money that goes
on in the business world? I am a fairly successful farmer and
fruit-grower. I love the soil, I love to see the crops grow and
mature, but the marketing of them, the turning of them into
money, grinds my soul because of the sense of strife and competition that pervades the air of the market-place. If one could afford
to give one's fruit away, after he had grown it to perfection, to
people who would be sure to appreciate it, that would be worth
while, and would leave no wounds. But that is what I have in a
sense done with my intellectual products. I have not written one
book for money (yes, one, and that was a failure); I have written
them for love, and the modest sum they have brought me has left
no sting.

John Burroughs, 1908

☐

If there's no money in poetry, neither is there poetry in money.

Robert Graves, 1965

☐

The poets of the kosmos advance through all interpositions and
coverings and turmoils and stratagems to first principles. They
are of use . . . they dissolve poverty from its need and riches from
its conceit. . . . It has been thought that the prudent citizen
was the citizen who applied himself to solid gains and did well
for his family and completed a lawful life without debt or crime.
The greatest poet sees and admits these economies as he sees the
economies of food and sleep, but has higher notions of prudence
than to think he gives much when he gives a few slight atten-
tions at the latch of the gate. . . . Beyond the independence of a
little sum laid aside for burial-money, and of a few clapboards
around and shingles overhead on a lot of American soil owned,

and the easy dollars that supply the year's plain clothing and meals, the melancholy prudence of the abandonment of such a great being as a man is to the toss and pallor of years of money-making with all their scorching days and icy nights and all their stifling deceits and underhanded dodgings, or infinitesimals of parlors, or shameless stuffing while others starve. . . . The prudence of the greatest poet . . . knows that the young man who composedly perilled his life and lost it has done exceedingly well for himself, while the man who has not perilled his life and retains the old age in riches and ease has perhaps achieved nothing for himself worth mentioning. . . .

Walt Whitman, 1819–1892

☐

My life has been too simple and stern to embarrass any.

Emily Dickinson, 1830–1886

☐

SHELTER

Less is more.

Mies Van der Rohe,
Twentieth-Century Architect

☐

Beauty rides on a lion. Beauty rests on necessities. The line of beauty is the result of perfect economy. The cell of the bee is built at that angle which gives the most strength with the least wax; the bone or the quill of the bird gives the most alar strength, with the least weight. "It is the purgation of super-fluities," said Michelangelo. There is not a particle to spare in natural structures. There is a compelling reason in the uses of

244

the plant, for every novelty of color or form: and our art saves material, by more skillful arrangement, and reaches beauty by taking every superfluous ounce that can be spared from a wall, and keeping all its strength in the poetry of columns. In rhetoric, this art of omission is a chief secret of power, and, in general, it is proof of high culture, to say the greatest matters in the simplest way. . . . [If] a man can build a plain cottage with such symmetry, as to make all the fine palaces look cheap and vulgar; can take such advantage of Nature, that all her powers serve him; making use of geometry, instead of expense; tapping a mountain for his water-jet; causing the sun and moon to seem only the decorations of his estate; this is still the legitimate dominion of beauty.*

Emerson, 1803–1882

☐

There is no artifice as good and desirable as simplicity.

St. François de Sales, 1567–1622

☐

Most men appear never to have considered what a house is, and are actually though needlessly poor all their lives because they think that they must have such a one as their neighbors have.

It is possible to invent a house still more convenient and luxurious than we have, which yet all would admit that man could not afford to pay for. Shall we always study to obtain more of these things, and not sometimes to be content with less? Why should not our furniture be as simple as the Arab's or the Indian's?

At present our houses are cluttered and defiled with it, and a good housewife would sweep out the greater part into the dust hole, and not leave her morning's work undone. Morning work! By the blushes of Aurora and the music of Memnon, what should be man's *morning work* in this world? I had three pieces of limestone on my desk, but I was terrified to find that they required to be dusted daily, when the furniture of my mind was all undusted still, and I threw them out the window in disgust. How, then, could I have a furnished house?

The cart before the horse is neither beautiful nor useful. Before we can adorn our houses with beautiful objects the walls must be stripped, and our lives must be stripped, and beautiful house-keeping and beautiful living be laid for a foundation: now, a taste for the beautiful is most cultivated out of doors, where there is no house and no housekeeper.*

Thoreau, 1817–1862

□

Before I was aware, I had become heavy with years, and with each remove my dwelling grew smaller. The present hut is of no ordinary appearance. It is a bare ten feet square and less than seven feet high.

I laid a foundation and roughly thatched a roof. I fastened hinges to the joints of the beams, the easier to move elsewhere should anything displease me. What difficulty would there be in changing my dwelling? A bare two carts would suffice to carry off the whole house, and except for the carter's fee there will be no expenses at all.

Since first I hid my traces here in the heart of Mount Hino, I have added a lean-to on the south and a porch of bamboo. On the west I have built a shelf for holy water, and inside the hut, along the west wall, I have installed an image of Amida. The light of the setting sun shines between its eyebrows. Above the sliding door that faces north I have built a little shelf on which I keep three or four black leather baskets that contain books of poetry and music and extracts from the sacred writings. Beside them stand a folding koto and a lute.

Along the east wall I have spread long fern fronds and mats of straw which serve as my bed for the night. I have cut open a window in the eastern wall, and beneath it have made a desk. Near my pillow is a square brazier in which I burn brushwood.

My clothing and food are as simple as my lodgings. I cover

my nakedness with whatever clothes woven of wistaria fiber and quilts of hempen cloth come to hand, and I eke out my life with berries of the fields and nuts from the trees on the peaks. I need not feel ashamed of my appearance, for I do not mix in society and the very scantiness of the food gives it additional savor, simple though it is. My body is like a drifting cloud—I ask for nothing, I want nothing. My greatest joy is a quiet nap; my only desire for this life is to see the beauties of the seasons.

The Three Worlds are joined by one mind. If the mind is not at peace, neither beasts of burden nor possessions are of service, neither palaces nor pavilions bring any cheer. This lonely house is but a tiny hut, but I somehow love it. The essence of the Buddha's teaching to man is that we must not have attachment for any object. It is a sin for me now to love my little hut, and my attachment to its solitude may also be a hindrance to salvation. Why should I waste more precious time in relating such trifling pleasures?*

Kamo no Chomei, 1153–1216

□

Special care should be taken, if you build yourself, not to go beyond reasonable limits in costliness and splendor. In such extravagance great mischief is done by mere example; for very many are anxious, especially in this direction, to follow the example of distinguished men. . . . Here there certainly is need of a limit, and of a return to a moderate standard. The same standard ought to be applied to the entire habit and style of living.*

Cicero, 106–43 B.C.

□

My furniture, part of which I made myself, and the rest cost me nothing of which I have not rendered an account, consisted of a bed, a table, a desk, three chairs, a looking-glass three inches in diameter, a pair of tongs and andirons, a kettle, a skillet, and a frying pan, a dipper, a wash-bowl, two knives and forks, three plates, one cup, one spoon, a jug for oil, a jug for molasses, and a japanned lamp. None is so poor that he need sit on a pumpkin. That is shiftlessness. There is a plenty of such chairs as I like best in the village garrets to be had for taking them away. Furniture! Thank God, I can sit and I can stand without the aid of a furniture warehouse.

Thoreau, 1817–1862

☐

In my hut this spring
there is nothing—
there is everything.

Sodō, 1641–1716

☐

Small rooms or dwellings set the mind in the right path, large ones cause it to go astray.

Leonardo da Vinci, 1452–1519

☐

When the dwelling is cramped, the purse limited, the table modest, a woman who has the gift, finds a way to make order, fitness and convenience reign in her house. She puts care and art into everything she undertakes. To do well what one has to do is not in her eyes the privilege of the rich, but the right of all. That is her aim, and she knows how to give her home a dignity and an attractiveness that the dwellings of princes, if everything is left to mercenaries, cannot possess.

Charles Wagner, 1895

☐

CREATIVE POVERTY: THE ASCETIC AESTHETIC

Even small spaces by skillful planning often reveal many uses; and arrangement will make habitable a place of ever so small dimensions.

Seneca, 4? B.C.–A.D. 65

☐

One of the surprising features that strikes a foreigner as he becomes acquainted with the Japanese house is the entire absence of so many things that with us clutter the closets, or make squirrel-nests of the attic. . . . The reason of this is that the people have never developed the miserly spirit of hoarding truck and rubbish with the idea that some day it may come into use: this spirit when developed into a mania converts a man's attic and shed into a junkshop. The few necessary articles kept by the Japanese are stowed away in boxes, cupboards, or inter-spaces beneath the floors. . . .

The general nakedness, or rather emptiness, of the apartments would be the first thing noticed. . . . The reader must not imagine that the family are constrained for want of room, or stinted in the necessary furniture; on the contrary, they are enabled to live in the most comfortable manner. Their wants are few, and their tastes are simple and refined. They live without the slightest ostentation; no false display leads them into criminal debt. The monstrous bills for carpets, curtains, furniture, silver, dishes, etc., often entailed by young housekeepers at home in any attempt at housekeeping,—the premonition even of such bills often preventing marriage,—are social miseries that the Japanese happily know but little about. . . .

After living in Japan for a time one realizes how few are the essentials necessary for personal comfort. He further realizes that his personal comfort is enhanced by the absence of many things deemed indispensable at home.

I do not expect to do much good in thus pointing out what I believe to be better methods, resting on more refined standards. There are some, I am sure, who will approve; but the throng— who are won by tawdry glint and tinsel; who make possible, by admiration and purchase, the horrors of much that is made for house-furnishing and adornment—will, with characteristic obtuseness, call all else but themselves and their own ways heathen and barbarous.*

Edward S. Morse, 1838–1925

□

Zennism, with the Buddhist theory of evanescence and its demands for the mastery of spirit over matter, recognized the house only as the temporary refuge for the body. The body itself was but as a hut in the wilderness, a flimsy shelter made by tying together the grasses that grew around,—when these ceased to be bound together they again became resolved into the original waste. In the tea-room fugitiveness is suggested in the thatched roof, frailty in the slender pillars, lightness in the bamboo support, apparent carelessness in the use of commonplace materials. The eternal is to be found only in the spirit which, embodied in these simple surroundings, beautifies them with the subtle light of its refinement. The simplicity of the tea-room and its freedom from vulgarity make it truly a sanctuary from the vexations of the outer world. There and there alone can one consecrate himself to undisturbed adoration of the beautiful. Nowadays industrialism is making true refinement more and more difficult all the world over. Do we not need the tea-room more than ever?*

Okakura Kakuzo, 1906

□

[An appreciation of transcendental aloofness in the midst of multiplicities is known as *wabi* in the dictionary of Japanese cultural terms.] *Wabi* really means "poverty," or, negatively, "not to be in the fashionable society of the time." To be poor, that is, not to be dependent on things worldly—wealth, power, and reputation—and yet to feel inwardly the presence of something of the highest value, above time and social position: this is what essentially constitutes *wabi*. Stated in terms of practical everyday life, *wabi* is to be satisfied with a little hut, a room of two or three *tatami* (mats), like the log cabin of Thoreau, and with a dish of vegetables picked in the neighboring fields, and perhaps to be listening to the pattering of a gentle spring rainfall. . . . It is in truth the worshiping of poverty. . . .

And *wabi* is not merely a psychological reaction to a certain pattern of environment. There is an active principle of aestheticism in it; when this is lacking poverty becomes indigence. . . . *Wabi* may be defined as an active aesthetical appreciation of poverty. . . .

D. T. Suzuki, 1959

□

The blessed Francis taught his friars to make their huts poor and their little cabins of wood, not stone, and he would have them be constructed and built of mean appearance, and not only did he hate pride in dwellings but also he did much abhor many or choice utensils. He loved that they should preserve in their tables or in their vessels nothing of worldly seeming, by which they should recall the world, so that all things should end in poverty, should sing out to them of their pilgrimage and exile.

Leo of Assisi, 13th cent.

□

For years the public resisted the "less is more" school of design, believing that if you had less it was only because you couldn't afford more. . . .

Karen Fisher, 1972

□

One of the curses of art is "Art." This filling up of things with "decorations," with by-play, to make them "beautiful." When art has attained its place, surfaces will be infinitely less broken. There will be millions less of *things,* less words, less gesture, less of everything. But each word and each gesture and everything will count in a fuller value. When we have attained a sense of the relative value of things, we will need fewer things. . . .

The most furnished rooms have very little in them. The mere proportions of a room act on our sensibilities much more than is declared by our present consciousness. . . .

It is not the barrenness of an empty room, or an empty life that we seek, we would get rid of clutter, and thus get room for fullness.*

Robert Henri, 1923

☐

He who always dwells within himself becomes possessed of very ample means.

Blessed Henry Suso, 1295–1365

☐

GARB

And why take ye thought for raiment? Consider the lilies of the field, how they grow; they toil not, neither do they spin: And yet I say unto you, That even Solomon in all his glory was not arrayed like one of these.

Matthew 6:28–9

☐

Cultivate poverty like a garden herb, like sage. Do not trouble yourself much to get new things, whether clothes or friends.

Thoreau, 1817–1862

CREATIVE POVERTY: THE ASCETIC AESTHETIC

□

And let all the brothers be dressed in shabby clothes and let them
patch them with sackcloth or other rags with the blessing of God.

The Rule, ca. 1210
Order of the Friars Minor

□

A sainted soul is always elegant.

Emerson, 1803–1882

□

There is another branch of decorative art in which I am sorry
to say we cannot, at least under existing circumstances, indulge
ourselves, with the hope of doing good to anybody, I mean the
great and subtle art of dress. . . .
    There can be no question, that all the money we spend on the
forms of dress at present worn, is, so far as any good purpose is
concerned, wholly lost.*

Ruskin, 1819–1900

□

As for Clothing, to come at once to the practical part of the question, perhaps we are led oftener by the love of novelty, and a
regard for the opinions of men, in procuring it, than by a true
utility. Let him who has work to do recollect that the object of
clothing, is, first, to retain the vital heat, and secondly, in this state
of society, to cover nakedness, and he may judge how much of
any necessary or important work may be accomplished without
adding to his wardrobe. A man who has at length found something to do will not need to get a new suit to do it in. . . . Only
they who go to soirées and legislative halls must have new coats,

253

coats to change as often as the man changes in them. We know but few men, a great many coats and breeches.

Thoreau, 1817–1862

☐

Through a too common illusion, simplicity and beauty are considered as rivals. But simple is not synonymous with ugly, any more than sumptuous, stylish and costly are synonymous with beautiful. Our eyes are wounded by the crying spectacle of gaudy ornament, venal art and senseless and graceless luxury. Wealth coupled with bad taste sometimes makes us regret that so much money is in circulation to provoke the creation of such a prodigality of horrors.

Yet what we now have most at heart is to speak of the ordinary esthetics of life, of the care one should bestow upon the adornment of his dwelling and his person, giving to existence that luster without which it lacks charm.

The beauty and poetry of existence lie in the understanding we have of it. Our home, our table, our dress should be the interpreters of intentions. That these intentions be so expressed, it is first necessary to have them, and he who possesses them makes them evident through the simplest means. One need not be rich to give grace and charm to his habit and his habitation: it suffices to have good taste and good-will.*

Charles Wagner, 1895

☐

When I get dressed I don't want to look simply elegant, I want to look elegantly simple.

Anita A. Novak, 1976

☐

[The modern economist] is used to measuring the "standard of living" by the amount of annual consumption, assuming all the time that a man who consumes more is "better off" than a man who consumes less. A Buddhist economist would consider this approach excessively irrational: since consumption is merely a means to human well-being, the aim should be to obtain the maximum of well-being with the minimum of consumption. Thus, if the purpose of clothing is a certain amount of temperature comfort and an attractive appearance, the task is to attain this purpose with smallest possible effort, that is, with the smallest annual destruction of cloth and with the help of designs that involve the smallest possible input of toil. The less toil there is, the more time and strength is left for artistic creativity. It would be highly uneconomic, for instance, to go in for complicated tailoring, like the modern West, when a much more beautiful effect can be achieved by the skilful draping of uncut material. It would be the height of folly to make material so that it would wear out quickly and the height of barbarity to make anything ugly, shabby or mean.

E. F. Schumacher, 1973

□

The sage wears clothes coarse of cloth but carries jewels in his heart.

Tao Te Ching

□

Excess in Apparel is another costly Folly. The very Trimming of the vain World would cloath all the naked one.

Chuse thy Cloaths by thine own Eyes, not another's. The more plain and simple they are, the better. Neither unshapely, nor fantastical; and for Use and Decency, and not for Pride.

If thou art clean and warm, it is sufficient; for more doth but rob the Poor, and please the Wanton.

We are told with Truth, that Meekness and Modesty are the Rich and Charming Attire of the Soul: And the plainer the Dress, the more Distinctly, and with greater Lustre, their Beauty shines.

William Penn, 1644–1718

LESS IS MORE

☐

Clothes, which began in foolishest love of Ornament, what have they not become! Increased Security and pleasurable Heat soon followed: but what of these? Shame, divine Shame as yet a stranger to the Anthropophagous bosom, arose there mysteriously under Clothes; a mystic grove-encircled shrine for the Holy in man. Clothes gave us individuality, distinctions, social polity; Clothes have made Men of us; they are threatening to make Clothes-screens of us.

Thomas Carlyle, 1795–1881

☐

Oh, how much cost is bestowed nowadays upon our bodies, and how little upon our souls! How many suits of apparel hath the one, and how little furniture hath the other! How long time is asked in decking up of the first, and how little space left wherein to feed the latter!

Holinshed's Chronicles, 1577

☐

Fashion is a poor vocation. Its creed, that idleness is a privilege, and work a disgrace, is among the deadliest errors. Without depth of thought, or earnestness of feeling, or strength of purpose, living an unreal life, sacrificing substance to show, substituting the factitious for the natural, mistaking a crowd for society, finding its chief pleasure in ridicule, and exhausting its ingenuity in expedients for killing time, fashion is among the last influences under which a human being, who respects himself or who comprehends the great end of life, would desire to be placed. I use strong language, because I would combat the disposition, too common in the laboring mass, to regard what is called the upper class with envy or admiration.

Channing, 1780–1842

CREATIVE POVERTY: THE ASCETIC AESTHETIC

☐

When I ask for a garment of a particular form, my tailoress tells
me gravely, "They do not make them so now," not emphasizing
the "They" at all, as if she quoted an authority as impersonal
as the Fates, and I find it difficult to get made what I want, simply because she cannot believe that I mean what I say, that I am
so rash. We worship not the Graces, nor the Parcæ, but Fashion.
She spins and weaves and cuts with full authority. The head
monkey at Paris puts on a traveller's cap, and all the monkeys
in America do the same. I sometimes despair of getting any thing
quite simple and honest done in this world by the help of men.*

Thoreau, 1817–1862

☐

The choice of the pace of fashion, surely a crucial choice, is not
open to the individual, only to society as a whole where, at present, it is left entirely to commercial interests to exploit to the
limit of technical feasibility. The fashion industry is the prime
example of an activity dedicated to using up resources, not to
create satisfactions, but to create dissatisfactions with what people
possess—in effect to create obsolescence in otherwise perfectly
satisfactory goods. Though it has been doing this for ages, it is the
increasing frequency of fashion change, and its extension to many
articles other than clothes, that is disturbing. Following the lead
of United States manufacturers, we are extending the pace of
fashion to automobiles, furniture, hardware and electrical goods.
Any practical proposals to regulate the rate of change of fashion
in clothes and in durable goods may attract a great deal of public support. The would-be pace-setters would, of course, be
deprived of approved opportunities for self-display, but the
potential saving in national resources should more than suffice
to compensate them.**

E. J. Mishan, 1967

☐

LESS IS MORE

A frugal wife should not neglect neatness, for untidiness disgusts
one with parsimonious living.

Plutarch, 46 B.C.–120 A.D.

☐

Of course, you must not infer from these suggestions that we
should approve of an uncouth roughness in dress. We do not urge
that squalor and slovenliness are good things. We merely set forth
the limit and bounds and just measure of bodily adornment. You
must not overstep the line to which simple and sufficient elegance
limits its desires. . . . Clothe yourselves with the silk of honesty,
the fine linen of righteousness, and the purple of chastity. Thus
painted you will have God for your lover.*

Tertullian, 160?–230?

☐

Repellent attire, unkempt hair, slovenly beard, open scorn of
silver dishes, a couch on the bare earth, and any other perverted
forms of self-display, are to be avoided. . . . Inwardly, we ought
to be different in all respects, but our exterior should conform
to society. Do not wear too fine, nor yet too frowsy, a toga. One
needs no silver plate, encrusted and embossed in solid gold; but
we should not believe the lack of silver and gold to be proof of
the simple life. Let us try to maintain a higher standard of life
than that of the multitude, but not a contrary standard; otherwise, we shall frighten away and repel the very persons whom we
are trying to improve. We also bring it about that they are unwilling to imitate us in anything, because they are afraid lest
they might be compelled to imitate us in everything. . . .

Philosophy calls for plain living, but not for penance; and we
may perfectly well be plain and neat at the same time. This is
the mean of which I approve; our life should observe a happy
medium between the ways of a sage and the ways of the world at

large; all men should admire it, but they should understand it
also.*

Seneca, 4? B.C.–A.D. 65

Ep. V

☐

FEASTING AND FASTING

Two things have I required of thee; deny me them not before I
die: Remove far from me vanity and lies: give me neither poverty nor riches; feed me with food convenient for me lest I be
full. . . .

Proverbs 30:7–9

☐

One man is found eating much and yet refraining while he is
still hungry, lest he be filled: and another eats little, and is filled.
He who eats much and refrains while he is still hungry hath
more merit than he who eats little and is full fed.

Sayings of the Fathers

☐

Voluntary meagre eating is one of the most difficult things in
the world. Meagre food voluntarily taken *must* lead to perfect
poise, i.e., perfect health of body and mind. We can but make
the attempt.

Gandhi, 1869–1948

☐

I came quickly upon the road to happiness. Arriving at the place where Happiness resided, I said, "I remain, O Happiness, on account of you and drink water and eat water cress and sleep on the ground." She answered me and said, "I will make hardships more pleasant for you than the, benefits to be obtained from wealth, which men prefer and ask of me, not perceiving that they are entrusting themselves to a tyrant." When I heard Happiness say that eating and drinking these things was not training but pleasure, it impelled me to this way of living.

Diogenes, 412?–323 B.C.

□

Therefore I say unto you, Take no thought for your life, what ye shall eat, or what ye shall drink; nor yet for your body, what ye shall put on. Is not the life more than meat, and the body than raiment?

Matthew 6:25

□

Wherefore also there is discrimination to be employed with reference to food. And it is to be simple, truly plain, suiting precisely simple and artless children—as ministering to life, not to luxury.

We must therefore reject different varieties, which engender various mischiefs, such as a depraved habit of body and disorders of the stomach, the taste being vitiated by an unhappy art—that of cookery, and the useless art of making pastry. For people dare to call by the name of food their dabbling in luxuries, which glides into mischievous pleasures.

Clement of Alexandria, 150?–220?

□

If my young master must needs have flesh, let it be but once a day, and of one sort at a meal. Plain beef, mutton, veal, &c, without other sauce than hunger, is best; and great care should be used, that he eat *bread* plentifully, both alone and with everything else; and whatever he eats that is solid, make him chew it well. . . . If he at any time calls for victuals between meals, use him to nothing but *dry bread.* If he be hungry more than wanton, *bread* alone will down; and if he be not hungry, 'tis not fit he should eat. By this you will obtain two good effects: 1. That by custom he will come to be in love with *bread;* for as I said, our palates and stomachs too are pleased with the things we are used to. 2. Another good you will gain hereby is, that you will not teach him to eat more nor oftener than nature requires.*

John Locke, 1632–1704

☐

If you are entertaining a dervish, remember that dry bread is enough for him.

Al-Muhasibi, d. 857 A.D.

☐

The women of old Rome were satisfied
With water for their beverage. Daniel fed
On pulse, and wisdom gained. The primal age
Was beautiful as gold: and hunger then
Made acorns tasteful; thirst, each rivulet
Run nectar. Honey and locust were the food,
Whereon the Baptist in the wilderness
Fed, and that eminence of glory reached,
And greatness, which the Evangelist records.

Dante, 1265–1321

☐

What has become of those laws which restrained extravagance and bribery? which forbade the spending of more than a hundred

asses on a supper, or the serving of more than one hen—and
that an unfattened one?

Tertullian, 160?–230?

☐

"There is," said Michael, "if thou well observe
The rule of *Not too much,* by temperance taught
In what thou eat'st and drink'st, seeking from thence
Due nourishment, not gluttonous delight. . . .

John Milton, 1608–1674

☐

The *Gita* enjoins not temperance in food but "meagerness."
Meagerness is a perpetual fast.

Meagerness means just enough to sustain the body for the
service for which it is made. The test is again supplied by saying that food should be taken as one takes medicine in measured
doses, at measured times and as required, not for taste, but for the
welfare of the body.

'Spare diet' is a good expression . . . meaning less than enough.
What is enough is a matter of conjecture, therefore, our own
mental picture. The man of truth, knowing that man is always
indulgent to the body, said, in order to counteract the indulgence,
that he should take less food than what he would think was
enough. So, what we often think is spare or meager, is likely even
to be more than enough. . . . It is wonderful, if we chose the right
diet, what an extraordinarily small quantity would suffice.*

Gandhi, 1869–1948

☐

It is a cruel Folly to offer up to Ostentation so many Lives of
Creatures, as to make up the State of our Treats; as it is a prodigal one to spend more in Sawce than in Meat.

CREATIVE POVERTY: THE ASCETIC AESTHETIC

The Proverb says, That enough is as good as a Feast: But it is certainly better, if Superfluity be a Fault, which never fails to be at Festivals.

If thou rise with an Appetite, thou art sure never to sit down without one.

William Penn, 1644–1718

☐

In the refectory, guard against eating in excess, even though you should feel great hunger, and a great desire to drink or eat. . . . Consider neither your taste, pleasure nor convenience, but rather be content with coarse food and with what others leave. . . .

Jan Van Ruysbroeck, 1293–1381

☐

Yes, I did eat $8.74, all told; but I should not thus unblushingly publish my guilt, if I did not know that most of my readers were equally guilty with myself, and that their deeds would look no better in print.

My food alone cost me in money about twenty-seven cents a week. It was, for nearly two years after this, rye and Indian meal without yeast, potatoes, rice, a very little salt pork, molasses and salt, and my drink water. It was fit that I should live on rice, mainly, who loved so well the philosophy of India.*

Thoreau, 1817–1862

☐

Night and day, for over three years, I continued to meditate unceasingly and felt my spiritual knowledge expanding and improving greatly. I had resolved on a diet of twenty measures of barley flour per year, but now even that had run out. I might have died without being able to attain Buddhahood; this would have been a deplorable interruption in mine eternal career. I

263

considered how worldly people rejoiced over a bit of gold and felt unhappy at losing it. Compared to that, my life, devoted as it was to the attainment of Buddhahood, was infinitely more precious. At the same time, it would be preferable to die in the course of my devotional life rather than break my vows. What should I do? It occurred to me that if I found some food without descending to human habitations to beg, I should not be breaking my vows. Accordingly, I strolled beyond my cave and discovering a sunny spot with good springs of water, with plenty of nettles growing round about, I removed to it.

Living on nettle broth alone, I persevered in my devotions in a most joyous mood, obtaining infinite phenomenal powers until, finally, I actually could fly. But having been seen flying by human beings, if I continued here, people would flock to me in crowds. Worldly fame might retard the progress of my devotion, so I resolved to go and carry on my meditation in the solitudes of Lapchi-Chubar. Accordingly, I started forth, carrying on my back the earthen vessel in which I had been cooking my nettle-food. But as I had long practiced meditation nourished only on this meagre diet, and having gone barefoot most of the time, my soles becoming hard and calloused, I slipped on a rock beside my cave and fell. The handle of the clay pot breaking, the pot itself rolled away and shattered, despite mine attempts to catch it. From within the broken bowl there rolled a perfect green image of it, this being the hardened encrustation of the froth of the nettle broth which had assumed the shape of the outer vessel. This mishap vividly reminded me of the fleetingness of all things and I also took it as a sort of exhortation to persevere in my devotions.

Milarepa, 1052–1135

□

I am thrilled with pleasure in the body, when I live on bread and water, and I spit upon luxurious pleasures not for their own sake, but because of the inconveniences that follow them.

Epicurus, 342?–270? B.C.

CREATIVE POVERTY: THE ASCETIC AESTHETIC

☐

We think it sufficient for the daily meal that there be at all the tables two dishes of cooked food because of the weaknesses of different persons; so that he who perhaps cannot eat of the one may make his meal of the other. Therefore, let two cooked dishes suffice for the brethren; and if there be any fruit or fresh vegetables, let a third dish be added. Let a full pound of bread suffice for each day. But if the work has been rather heavy, it shall be in the discretion and power of the abbot to make some addition, if he think it expedient, provided that excess be avoided above all things, that no monk be ever guilty of surfeiting.

St. Benedict of Nursia, 480–543?
The Rule

☐

Simplify, simplify. Instead of three meals a day, if it be necessary eat but one; instead of a hundred dishes, five; and reduce other things in proportion.

Thoreau, 1817–1862

☐

Send me some preserved cheese, that when I like I may have a feast.

Epicurus, 342?–270? B.C.

☐

Remember that in life thou shouldst order thy conduct as at a banquet. Has any dish that is being served reached thee? Stretch forth thy hand and help thyself modestly. Doth it pass thee by? Seek not to detain it. Has it not yet come? Send not forth thy desire to meet it, but wait until it reaches thee. Deal thus with children, thus with wife; thus with office, thus with wealth—and one day thou wilt be meet to share the Banquets of the Gods. But if thou dost not so much as touch that which is placed before thee, but despisest it, then thou shalt not only share the Banquets of the Gods, but their Empire also. For by so doing, Diogenes and Heraclitus and men like them were called divine and deserved the name.

Epictetus, 60?–100? B.C.

☐

For it is the mark of a silly mind to be amazed and stupefied at what is presented at vulgar banquets, after the rich fare which is in the Word; and much sillier to make one's eyes the slaves of delicacies, so that one's greed is, so to speak, carried round by the servants. For you may see such people in such a hurry to feed themselves full, that both jaws are stuffed out at once, the veins about the face raised . . . the food pushed with unsocial eagerness into their stomach, as if they were stowing away their victuals for provision for a journey, not for digestion. Excess, which in all things is an evil, is very highly reprehensible in the matter of food.

Clement of Alexandria, 150?–220

☐

What, then, do I not encourage you to do? Nothing new—we are not trying to find cures for new evils—but this first of all; namely, to see clearly for yourself what is necessary and what is superfluous. What is necessary will meet you everywhere; what is superfluous has always to be hunted out—and with great endeavor. But there is no reason why you should flatter yourself over-much if you despise gilded couches and jewelled furniture. For what virtue lies in despising useless things? The time to admire your own conduct is when you have come to despise the necessities. You are doing no great thing if you can live without royal pomp, if you feel no craving for boars which weigh a thousand pounds, or for flamingo tongues. . . . I shall admire you only when you have learned to scorn even the common sort of bread, when you have made yourself believe that grass grows for the needs of men as well as of cattle.**

Seneca, 4? B.C.–A.D. 65
Ep. CX

□

Although human beings do not generally think of eating grass, this simple plant is actually the basis for much of what we do eat. We eat the steak or drink the milk that comes from the cow that eats the grass. But there is a direct way to obtain high nutrition and stay healthy for very little money and effort. History shows that wheat has always been a prime source of food, and through use of its many forms, one can keep alive and in excellent health for as little as 6¢ a day. One pound of dry wheat can be converted into four pounds of grass or two pounds of sprouts or 42 ounces of wheat juice. Using earth as a medium, even in an indoor window garden, the wheat berry will produce a 7-inch growth in 8 days. When put through a special press, a small amount will produce a cup of pure chlorophyll which can serve as a soup stock, providing all the nourishment you need even when you are poor or snowbound.

Dr. Ann Wigmore, 1976

□

We think highly of frugality not that we may always keep to a cheap and simple diet, but that we may be free from desire regarding it.

Epicurus, 342?–270? B.C.

□

LESS IS MORE

I who from midnoon with convivial souls
Would sit carousing o'er Falernian bowls,—
Now praise the frugal meal and sober glass,
With slumbers near a fountain, on the grass.

Horace, 65–8 B.C.

☐

When you have brought yourself to supply the needs of the body
at small cost, do not pique yourself on that, nor if you drink
only water, keep saying on each occasion, *I drink water!*

Epictetus, 60?–100?

☐

The foods which Nature has placed in every region lie all about
us, but men, just as if blind, pass these by and roam through
every region, they cross the seas and at great cost excite their
hunger when at little cost they might allay it. Is it not madness
and the wildest lunacy to desire so much when you can hold so
little? And so you may swell your incomes, and extend your
boundaries; yet you will never enlarge the capacity of your bellies.

Seneca, 4? B.C.–A.D. 65
Ep. V

☐

Only we must remember, that our portion of temporal things is
but *food and raiment*. God hath not promised us coaches and
horses, rich houses and jewels, Tyrian silks and Persian carpets. . . . But if [God] takes away the flesh-pots from thee, he
can also alter the appetite and he hath given thee power and
commandment to restrain it; and if he lessens the revenue, he
will also shrink the necessity; or if he gives but a very little, he
will make it go a great way; or if he sends thee but a coarse diet,
he will bless it and make it healthful . . . and if a thin table be
apt to enfeeble the spirits of one used to feed better, yet the

cheerfulness of a spirit that is blessed will make a thin table become a delicacy. . . . Poverty therefore is in some senses eligible, and to be preferred before riches; but in all senses it is very tolerable.*

Jeremy Taylor, 1840

☐

Even Epicurus, the teacher of pleasure, used to observe stated intervals, during which he satisfied his hunger in niggardly fashion; he wished to see whether he thereby fell short of full and complete happiness, and, if so, by what amount he fell short, and whether this amount was worth purchasing at the price of great effort.

For although water, barley-meal, and crusts of barley-bread, are not a cheerful diet, yet it is the highest kind of pleasure to be able to derive pleasure from this sort of food, and to have reduced one's needs to that modicum which no unfairness of Fortune can snatch away.

So begin to follow this custom, and set apart certain days on which you shall withdraw from your business and make yourself at home with the scantiest fare. Establish business relations with poverty.

Seneca, 4? B.C.–A.D. 65
Ep. XVIII

☐

THE SUPERMARKET MEDITATION

Those who anguish over a starving mankind on the easy assumption that there just is not enough land and resources to feed the hungry might do well to pay a special kind of visit to their local supermarket. Not to shop, but to observe and to meditate on what they see before them and have always taken for granted. How much of the world's land and labor was wasted producing the tobacco, the coffee, the tea, the refined cane sugars, the polished rice, the ice creams, the candies, the cookies, the soft drinks, the thousand and one non-nutritional luxuries one finds there? The grains that become liquor, the fruits and vegetables that lost all their food value going into cans and jars full of syrups and condiments, the potatoes and corn that became various kinds of chips, crackles, crunchies, and yum-yums, the cereals that became breakfast novelties less nourishing (as a matter of scientific fact) than the boxes they are packed in, the wheat that became white breads and pastry flours. . . . How many forests perished to package these non-foods? How many resources went into transporting and processing them? (And the less nutrition, the more processing.) How much skilled energy went into advertising and merchandising them? There they stand in our markets, row upon row, aisle upon aisle of nutritional zero, gaily boxed and packed, and costing those fancy prices we then gripe about as the high cost of living.

It is out of such routine extravagances that the technocracy weaves its spell over our allegiance . . . and then assures us we are the hope of the world.*

Theodore Roszak, 1972

☐

Fools! they know not how much the half is greater than the whole, and what blessings there are in the cheapest herbs man can eat, mallow and asphodel.

Hesiod, 8th cent. B.C.

☐

And having food and raiment let us be therewith content.

I Timothy 6:8

13

APPLIED POVERTY:
EDUCATION

CRYLESS BABIES: *PLAYING WITHOUT TOYS*

It seems plain to me, that the principle of all virtue and excellence lies in a power of denying ourselves the satisfaction of our own desires, where reason does not authorize them. This power is to be got and improv'd by custom, made easy and familiar by an *early* practice. If therefore I might be heard, I would advise, that, contrary to the ordinary way, children should be us'd to submit their desires, and go without their longings, even *from their very cradles*. The first thing they should learn to know, should be, that they were not to have anything because it pleas'd them, but because it was thought fit for them. If things suitable to their wants were supply'd to them, so that they were never suffer'd to have what they once cry'd for, they would learn to be content without it, would never, with bawling and peevishness, contend for mastery, nor be half so uneasy to themselves and others as they are because *from the first* beginning they are not thus handled. If they were never suffer'd to obtain their desire by the impatience they express'd for it, they would no more cry for another thing, than they do for the moon.

John Locke, 1632–1704

□

271

LESS IS MORE

If you must have babies, let them be cryless babies.

Kanya KeKumba, 1974

□

Children live at the beck and call of appetite, and it is in them that the desire for what is pleasant is strongest. If, then, [the child] is not going to be obedient and subject to the ruling principle, it will go to great lengths; for in an irrational being the desire for pleasure is insatiable even if it tries every source of gratification, and the exercise of appetite increases its innate force, and if appetites are strong and violent they even expel the power of calculation. Hence they should be moderate and few, and as the child should live according to the direction of his tutor, so the appetitive element should live according to the rational principle.

Aristotle, 384–322 B.C.

□

In contemporary America children must be trained to *insatiable* consumption of *impulsive* choice and *infinite variety*. These attributes, once instilled, are converted into cash by advertising directed at children. . . . The argument that advertising campaigns beamed at young children are somehow sickening because such campaigns take advantage of the impulsiveness and the unformed judgment of the child is old-fashioned squeamishness, somehow reminiscent of the fight against vivisection. Time and again we have had to fight off crackpots who do not understand that animals must be sacrificed to human welfare, and that because of anesthetics vivisection is now painless. So it is with the child versus the gross national product: what individual child is more important than the gross national product? And is it not true that TV is an anesthetic?*

Jules Henry, 1963

☐

Play-things, I think, children should have, and of divers sorts; but still to be in the custody of their tutors or some body else, whereof the child should have in his power but one at once, and should not be suffered to have another but when he restored that. This teaches them betimes to be careful of not losing or spoiling the things they have; whereas plenty and variety in their own keeping, makes them wanton and careless, and teaches them from the beginning to be squanderers and wasters.

Though it be agreed they should have of several sorts, yet, I think, they should have none bought for them.

"How then shall they have the play-games you allow them, if none must be bought for them?" I answer, they should make them themselves, or at least endeavour it, and set themselves about it; till then they should have none, and till then they will want none of any great artifice.

Play-things which are above their skill to make, as tops, gigs, battledores, and the like, which are to be used with labour, should indeed be procured them. These 'tis convenient they should have, not for variety but exercise; but these too should be given them as bare as might be. If they had a top, the scourge-stick and leather-strap should be left to their own making and fitting. If they sit gaping to have such things drop into their mouths, they should go without them. This will accustom them to seek for what they want, in themselves and in their own endeavours; whereby they will be taught moderation in their desires, application, industry, thought, contrivance, and good husbandry; qualities that will be useful to them when they are men, and therefore cannot be learned too soon, nor fixed too deep.*

John Locke, 1632–1704

☐

We fill the hands and nurseries of our children with all manner of dolls, drums, and horses, withdrawing their eyes from the plain face and sufficing object of nature, the sun and moon, the animals, the water, and stones, which should be their toys.

Emerson, 1803–1882

☐

By this let nurses, and those parents that desire Holy Children learn to make them possessors of Heaven and Earth betimes; to remove silly objects from before them, to magnify nothing but what is great indeed, and to talk of God to them, and of His works and ways before they can either speak or go. For nothing is so easy as to teach the truth because the nature of the thing confirms the doctrine: As when we say the sun is glorious, a man is a beautiful creature, sovereign over beasts and fowls and fishes, the stars minister unto us, the world was made for you, &c. But to say this house is yours, and these lands are another man's, and this bauble is a jewel and this gew-gaw a fine thing, this rattle makes music, &c., is deadly barbarous and uncouth to a little child; and makes him suspect all you say, because the nature of the thing contradicts your words.

Thomas Traherne, 1638–1674

☐

Is not the exclusively sympathetic and facetious way in which most children are brought up today in danger, in spite of its many advantages, of developing a certain trashiness of fibre? Are there not hereabout some points of application for a renovated and revised ascetic discipline?*

William James, 1842–1910

☐

Teach children to want little while they *are* little.

Surya Prem, 1965

☐

The coverings of our bodies which are for modesty, warmth and defence, are by the folly or vice of parents recommended to their children for other uses. They are made matters of vanity and emulation. A child is set a-longing after a new suit, for the finery of it; and when the little girl is trick'd up in her new gown and commode, how can her mother do less than teach her to admire herself, by calling her, *her little queen* and *her princess?* Thus the little ones are taught to be *proud* of their clothes before they can put them on. And why should they not continue to value themselves for their outside fashionableness of the taylor or tire-woman's making, when their parents have so early instructed them to do so?

Whatever compliance the necessities of nature may require, the wants of fancy children should never be gratify'd in, nor suffered to *mention*. The very *speaking* for any such thing should make them lose it. Clothes, when they need, they must have; but if they *speak* for this stuff or that colour, they should be sure to go without it.

'Tis a great step towards the mastery of our desires, to give this stop to them, and shut them up in silence. This habit got by children, of staying the forwardness of their fancies, and deliberating whether it be fit or no, before they *speak*, will be of no small advantage to them in matters of greater consequence, in the future course of their lives. But as they should never be heard, when they speak for any particular thing they would *have*, unless it be first propos'd to them; so they should always be heard, and fairly and kindly answer'd, when they ask for any thing they would *know*, and desire to be inform'd about. *Curiosity* should be as carefully *cherish'd* in children, as other appetites suppress'd.*

John Locke, 1632–1704

☐

DESCHOOLING THE SELF

It is the function of the teacher to arrange the right operation of the answer to needs, not wants. Wants belong to the sphere of Lesser Understanding.

Rais Tchaqmaqzade

☐

Among the liberall Sciences, let us begin with that which makes us free: If we could restraine and adapt the appurtenances of our life to their right byase and naturall limits, we should find the best part of the Sciences that are now in use, cleane out of fashion with us: yea, and in those that are most in use, there are certaine by-wayes and deep-flows most profitable, which we should do well to leave, and according to the institution of Socrates, limit the course of our studies in those where profit is wanting.*

Montaigne, 1533–1592

☐

I respect no study, and deem no study good, which results in money-making. Such studies are profit-bringing occupations, useful only in so far as they give the mind a preparation and do not engage it permanently. One should linger upon them only so long as the mind can occupy itself with nothing greater; they are our apprenticeship, not our real work. Hence you see why "liberal studies" are so called; it is because they are studies worthy of a free-born gentleman. But there is only one really liberal study,—that which gives a man his liberty.

Seneca, 4? B.C.–A.D. 65
Ep. LXXXVIII

APPLIED POVERTY: EDUCATION

□

The science which teacheth arts and handicrafts
Is merely science for the gaining of a living;
But the science which teacheth deliverance from worldly existence,
Is not that the true science?

Nagarjuna, 1st cent. B.C.

□

Survival University will not be a multiversity offering courses in every conceivable field. Its motto—emblazoned on a life jacket rampant—will be: "What must we do to be saved?" If a course does not help to answer that question, it will not be taught here. Neither will our professors be detached, dispassionate scholars. To get hired, each will have to demonstrate an emotional commitment to our cause. Moreover, he will be expected to be a moralist; for this generation of students, like no other in my lifetime, is hungering and thirsting after righteousness. What it wants is a moral system it can believe in—and that is what our university will try to provide. In every class it will preach the primordial ethic of survival. Survival University, therefore, will prepare its students to consume less. This does not necessarily mean an immediate drop in living standards—perhaps only a change in the yardstick by which we measure them. Conceivably Americans might be happier with fewer automobiles, neon signs, beer cans, supersonic jets, barbecue grills, and similar metallic fluff. But happy or not, our students had better learn how to live the Simpler Life, because that is what most of them are likely to have before they reach middle age.

John Fischer, 1969

□

Strive toward a sound mind at top speed and with your whole strength. If any bond holds you back, untie it or sever it. "But,"

you say, "my estate delays me; I wish to make such disposition
of it that it may suffice for me when I have nothing to do, lest
either poverty be a burden to me, or I myself a burden to others."
. . . Doubtless, your object, what you wish to attain by such post-
ponement of your studies, is that poverty may not have to be
feared by you. But what if it is something to be desired? Riches
have shut off many a man from the attainment of wisdom.

Why, then, should you reject Philosophy as a comrade? Even
the rich man copies her ways when he is in his senses. If you wish
to have leisure for your mind, either be a poor man, or resemble
a poor man. Study cannot be helpful unless you take pains to
live simply; and living simply is voluntary poverty. . . . Therefore one should not seek to lay up riches first.*

Seneca, 4? B.C.–A.D. 65
Ep. LXXXVIII

□

I have one more thing to add, which as soon as I mention I shall
run the danger of being suspected to have forgotten what I am
about, and what I have written concerning education all tending
towards a gentleman's calling, with which a trade seems wholly
inconsistent. And yet I cannot forbear to say, I would have him
learn a trade, a manual trade, nay two or three, but one more
particularly.

John Locke, 1632–1704

□

He that is taught to live upon a little owes more to his Father's
Wisdom than he that has a great deal left him does to his Father's
Care.

William Penn, 1644–1718

□

APPLIED POVERTY: EDUCATION

From my mother [I learned] piety and beneficence, and simplicity in my way of living, far removed from the habits of the rich. From my governor, I learned endurance of labor, and to want little, and to work with my own hands. From Diognetus, not to busy myself about trifling things, and to have desired a plank bed and skin, and whatever else of the kind belongs to the Grecian discipline.

Marcus Aurelius, 121–180

☐

Worldly people value those who help them more than those who harm them; we must do the opposite. Why? In this world, parents are considered to be the greatest help, for they give their children servants, wives, herds of horses, palaces, gold, turquoise, and land. Yet, according to the Dharma, there is no greater harm than that, because, desiring these gifts, children accumulate and extend bad karma and fettering passions, and by this they may finally fall into hell. What appears now to be help has a final result of misery, and the kind fathers and mothers of this life can thus be considered our greatest enemies.

Geshé Chen-na-wa, 11th cent. A.D.

☐

Our parents have instilled into us a respect for gold and silver; in our early years the craving has been implanted, settling deep within us and growing with our growth, and finally, public opinion has come to such a pass that poverty is a hissing and a reproach.

Seneca, 4? B.C.–A.D. 65
Ep. CXV

☐

Dad looked at his house and car and manicured lawn, and he was proud. All of his material possessions justified his life. He tried to teach his kids: he told us not to do anything that would lead us away from the path of Success. We were conditioned in self-denial. And we were confused. We didn't dig why we needed to work toward owning bigger houses? bigger cars? bigger manicured lawns? We went crazy. We couldn't hold it back any more. . . .*

Jerry Rubin, 1970

☐

Our life must be converted into its contrary. We must unlearn those things which we have learned; by learning them we have hitherto not known ourselves. We must learn those things we have neglected: without knowing them we cannot know ourselves. We must like what we neglect, neglect what we like, tolerate what we flee, flee what we follow.

Marsilio Ficino, 1433–1499

☐

Self-taught poverty is a help toward philosophy for the things which philosophy attempts to teach by reasoning, poverty forces us to practice.

Diogenes, 412?–323 B.C.

☐

People must learn to live within bounds. This cannot be *taught*. Survival depends on people *learning* fast what they *cannot* do. They must *learn* to abstain from unlimited progeny, consumption, and use. It is impossible to *educate* people for voluntary poverty or to manipulate them into self-control. It is impossible to *teach* joyful renunciation in a world totally structured for higher output and the illusion of declining costs.

Ivan Illich, 1973

APPLIED POVERTY: EDUCATION

□

I think I have said enough of the spirit and manifestations of the simple life, to make it evident that there is here a whole forgotten world of strength and beauty. He can make conquest of it who has sufficient energy to detach himself from the fatal rubbish that trammels our days. It will not take him long to perceive that in renouncing some surface satisfactions and childish ambitions, he increases his faculty of happiness and his possibilities of right judgment.

These results concern as much the private as the public life. It is incontestable that in striving against the feverish will to shine, in ceasing to make the satisfaction of our desires the end of our activity, in returning to modest tastes, to the true life, we shall labor for the unity of the family. Another spirit will breath in our homes, creating new customs and an atmosphere more favorable to the education of children.

Charles Wagner, 1895

14

VOLUNTARY POVERTY
AND THE U.S.A.

AMERICA IN THE ALEMBIC

Americans, admit that a superfluity lightens the soul. Luxury is a noble virtue that must not be confused with comfort. You have comfort. You lack luxury. And don't tell me that money plays a part. The luxury that I advocate has nothing to do with money. It cannot be bought. It is the reward of those who have no fear of discomfort. It is a pledge to our own selves. It is food for the soul.

Jean Cocteau, 1949

☐

In America, every one finds facilities unknown elsewhere for making or increasing his fortune. The spirit of gain is always on the stretch, and the human mind, constantly diverted from the pleasures of imagination and the labors of the intellect, is there swayed by no impulse but the pursuit of wealth.

What chiefly diverts men of the democracies from lofty ambition is not the scantiness of their fortunes but the vehemence of the exertions they daily make to improve them. They strain their faculties to the utmost to achieve paltry results and this cannot fail speedily to limit their range of view, and to circumscribe their powers. They might be much poorer and still be greater.

Alexis de Tocqueville, 1835

VOLUNTARY POVERTY AND THE U.S.A.

☐

The course that a free nation runs is from virtuous industry
to wealth; from wealth to luxury; from luxury to an impatience
of discipline and corruption of morals; till by a total degeneracy
and loss of virtue, being grown ripe for destruction, it falls at last
prey to some hardy oppressor, and with the loss of liberty, loses
everything else that is valuable.

Ezra Sampson, 1818

☐

Luxury enters into cities in the first place, afterwards satiety,
then lascivious insolence, and after all these, destruction.

Pythagoras, 6th cent. B.C.

☐

The nation itself, with all its so called internal improvements,
which, by the way, are all external and superficial, is an unwieldy
and overgrown establishment, cluttered with furniture and
tripped up by its own traps, ruined by luxury and heedless
expense, by want of calculation and a worthy aim, as the million
households in the land; and the only cure for it as for them is in
a rigid economy, a stern and more than Spartan simplicity of life
and elevation of purpose.*

Thoreau, 1817–1862

☐

To furnish a barren room is one thing. To continue to crowd in
furniture until the foundation buckles is quite another. To have
failed to solve the problem of producing goods would have been
to continue man in his oldest and most grievous misfortune.

But to fail to see that we have solved it and to fail to proceed thence to the next task, would be fully as tragic.

Galbraith, 1958

☐

The level above which a man's goods become superfluous and burn the hand he holds them in goes up and down according to the needs of the poor. The presence of the poor in any society is a call to it to lower its standard of living.

Pie-Raymond Régamey, 1954

☐

Surely there can be no question that much of the dangerous strain between our country and other countries comes from our rich standard, which we are not willing to share except piece-meal. So, as a nation, we give and give, and yet, because we give not "of our substance" but only of our surplus, we remain a powerful, feared, and even hated pariah among nations. If every last and least solvent American could show himself willing to do with less household machines and cars, simpler food, less paper, less clothing and ornaments, in order that the poorer nations may have necessities, our country might become the leader of a peaceful world. . . .

Mildred Binns Young, 1956

☐

No other society has ever been in the same position as ours, of coming close to fulfilling the age-old dream of freedom from want, the dream of plenty. Millions of Americans, perhaps still the great majority, find sufficient vitality in pursuit of that dream: the trip to the end of the consumer rainbow retains its magic for the previously deprived. Yet, by concentrating all energies on preserving freedom from want and pressing for consumer satia-tion at ever more opulent levels, we jeopardize this achievement in a world where there are many more poor nations than rich ones and in which there are many more desires, even among ourselves, for things other than abundance.*

David Riesman, 1964

□

We are so blinded by the perspectives of our own society that we can not realize that complex material achievements of the type which we possess, or rather by which we are often possessed, are usually had at the expense of human and spiritual values. But a minimum of material possessions does not necessarily mean a corresponding poverty in mental and spiritual achievements. The nomadic type of culture offers valuable lessons to the contemporary industrial man who is in danger of being crushed by the sheer weight of his civilization, and who therefore often sacrifices the deepest and most meaningful values of life by identifying himself with an endless series of distracting and often destructive gadgets.

Joseph Epes Brown, 1964

□

The West wants the people of the poor countries to live as we do ourselves. We pity the nomad who is clearly "poverty-stricken." We fail to understand that his life can be more satisfying than our own.

Robert Theobald, 1961

□

The Great Society asks not only how much, but how good; not only how to create wealth, but how to use it.

Lyndon Johnson, 1965
State of the Union Address

LESS IS MORE

□

The War Against Poverty is a call to action, to introspection, and to change for those who dwell in comfort as well as for those who dwell in misery and privation.

The real test of the spirit and success of this program will be not simply what happens to the twenty percent of this nation who are poor, but what happens to the eighty percent who are not. If nothing happens to that eighty percent, if there is no inter-action, dedication, and fulfillment in meaningful social en-deavors, then there will have been no real dialogue. The Volun-teers are a symbol of this outreaching effort. But they will provide only the vanguard of a larger movement to enlist the spirit, the conscience, the altruism, the dedication, and the ideal-ism which we know from our experience with the Peace Corps is latent in all Americans.

Sargent Shriver, 1964

□

The American people cannot continue their accelerating growth binge. Sooner or later, even without our intervention, limiting factors will halt the growth. The major question is whether or not control of the growth syndrome will be the result of rational, carefully planned human action or of chaos.

What has happened? I suggest to you that the American dream, based as it is on the concept of unlimited space and re-sources, has run aground on the natural limits of the earth. . . .

Given the staggering growth rates of technological- and popu-lation-based problems, I suspect that within a decade all will realize that the main problems of the environment do not arise from temporary and accidental malfunctions of existing eco-nomic and social systems.

On the contrary, they will probably be seen as warning signs of a profound incompatibility between deep-rooted beliefs in continuous accelerated growth and the dawning recognition that the earth is limited in its resources and vulnerable to thought-less mishandling.

Will we be able to vastly scale down or redirect our commitment to growth and effect fundamental changes in our economy? The implications of such changes are huge. Not only will they affect industry, labor, business, government, all income groups, minority groups and international relations, they will affect the very way we think, the way we relate to each other, and the way we relate to the finite resources of Mother Earth.

Nathaniel P. Reed, 1974
[Ass't Secretary of the Interior
for Fish and Wildlife and Parks]

□

Though I can see no way to defend the economy, I recognize the need to be concerned for the suffering that would be produced by its failure. But I ask if it is necessary for it to fail in order to change; I am assuming that if it does not change it must sooner or later fail, and that a great deal that is more valuable will fail with it.

It apparently can see no alternative to itself except chaos, and perhaps that is its chief weakness. For, of course, chaos is not the only alternative to it. A better alternative is a better economy. But we will not conceive the possibility of a better economy, and therefore will not begin to change, until we quit deifying the present one.

The change I am talking about appeals to me precisely because it need not wait upon "other people." Anybody who wants to can begin it in himself and in his household as soon as he is ready—by becoming answerable to at least some of his own needs, by acquiring skills and tools, by learning what his real needs are, by refusing the merely glamorous and frivolous. When a person learns to *act* on his best hopes he enfranchises and validates them as no government or public policy ever will.*

Wendell Berry, 1970

□

Ideas that seem, at first, to be doomed to political impotence may strike roots in the imagination of ordinary men and women, spreading and growing in strength until ready to emerge in political form.

E. J. Mishan, 1969

□

DO-IT-THYSELF ECONOMICS

One does not fight a machine head-on, one pulls the plug. . . .

[The] motivating power of the machine is found *within each of us*. More specifically, the motivating power is that portion of each individual's life in which he acts as a machine-part, namely, when he acts as a motivated producer or consumer. Revolution by consciousness can be accomplished when enough individuals change that part of their lives.

The machine can be controlled at the "consumer" level only by people who change their whole value system, their whole world view, their whole way of life.

Outside efforts have little effectiveness; the machine rolls on. Inside efforts—"consumer" or "producer"—*are* effective. The maxim is, act where you have power. When Americans refuse to buy what the [corporate] State wants to sell—economically or politically—and refuse to produce by striving for the goals set by the State's organizations, the wheel will have no power to turn, and revolution by consciousness will have become a reality. A change in one's own way of life is an "inside" change.*

Charles Reich, 1970

□

VOLUNTARY POVERTY AND THE U.S.A.

The inner crisis of our civilization must be resolved if the outer crisis is to be effectively met. Our first duty is to revamp our ideas and values and to reorganize the human personality around its highest and most central needs. . . .

Only in one place can an immediate renewal begin: that is, within the person; and a remolding of the self and the super-ego is an inescapable preliminary to the great changes that must be made throughout every community, in every part of the world. Each one, within his or her own field of action . . . must carry into his immediate day's work a changed attitude toward all his functions and obligations.*

Lewis Mumford, 1944

□

The old-fashioned economic law of eventually diminishing marginal utility was founded on the supposed satiation of human wants, whether the wants were physical, intellectual, aesthetic or emotional. No matter how rich he becomes a man has still but one pair of eyes, one pair of ears, one stomach, one sexual organ, a single brain and a single nervous system. In the face of this unremarkable fact of life, continuous material growth cannot be sustained by a system geared simply to produce ever larger quantities of the same goods.

Today no refuge remains from the desperate universal clamor for more efficiency, more excitement and more novelty that goads us furiously onward, competing, accumulating, innovating,—and inevitably destroying. The more affluent a society the more covetous it needs to be. What conceivable alternative could there be to economic growth? [To] be tediously logical about it, there is an alternative to the post-war growth-rush as an overriding objective of economic policy: the simple alternative, that is, of not rushing for growth. The alternative is intended to be taken seriously.

E. J. Mishan, 1967

□

THE POWER OF THE INDIVIDUAL

Each one of us, as long as life stirs in him, may play a part in extricating himself from the power system by asserting his primacy as a person in quiet acts of mental or physical withdrawal—in gestures of non-comformity, in abstentions, restrictions, inhibitions, which will liberate him from the domination of the pentagon of power.

Lewis Mumford, 1964

□

I have no doubt that it is possible to give a new direction to technological development, a direction that shall lead it back to the real needs of man, and that also means: *to the actual size of man.* Man is small, and, therefore, small is beautiful. To go for giantism is to go for self-destruction.

E. F. Schumacher, 1973

□

While the government is "studying" and funding and organizing its Big Thought, nothing is being done. But the citizen who is willing to Think Little, and, accepting the discipline of that, to go ahead on his own, is already solving the problem.

A man who is willing to undertake the discipline and the difficulty of mending his own ways is worth more to the conservation movement than a hundred who are insisting merely that the government and industries mend *their* ways.

We need persons and households that do not have to wait upon organizations, but can make necessary changes in themselves, on their own.*

Wendell Berry, 1970

VOLUNTARY POVERTY AND THE U.S.A.

□

The discipline of slavery is unknown
Amongst us; hence the more do we require
The discipline of virtue.

Wordsworth, 1770–1850

□

There will be *less* external discipline, the *more* internal discipline there is.

Simone Weil, 1909–1943

□

CHANGE YOUR LIFESTYLE NOW AND AVOID THE RUSH LATER

The high-energy, waste-happy growthmanic way of life is on its way out. This is going to be *the central fact* in everyone's future that must be considered as major personal decisions are made. . . .

Clearly, the people who are going to be best able to survive and prosper in the time of crises that we are now entering will be those who have anticipated changes. They will have made their personal adjustments gradually and sensibly, rather than in shocked response to events as they unfold.*

Paul and Anne Ehrlich, 1974

□

This is the supreme instant, the turning point in history at which man either vanquishes the processes of change or vanishes, at which, from being the unconscious puppet of evolution he becomes either its victim or its master.

A challenge of such proportions demands of us a dramatically new, a more deeply rational response toward change.

Our first and most pressing need, therefore, before we can begin to gently guide our evolutionary destiny, before we can build a humane future, is to halt the runaway acceleration that is subjecting multitudes to the threat of future shock while, at the very same moment, intensifying all the problems they must deal with—war, ecological incursions, racism, the obscene contrast between rich and poor, the revolt of the young, and the rise of a potentially deadly mass irrationalism.*

Alvin Toffler, 1970

☐

The deadline is for real.

Dr. John Moore, 1976

☐

Material simplicity, visionary abundance. Who can say what gifts and wonders such a cultural style might not bring?

Now this ancient style of experience returns to us as a new celebration of the common, the humble, the unadorned. It is a teaching which a material simplicity of life . . . clearly demands. For in this transcendent awareness, we discover a *new wealth* of a new culture: a wealth that cannot be stolen, exploited, or counterfeited.

It should be obvious that the more widely this new wealth comes to be honored, the less we will covet conventional affluence: the merchandise, the material plenty, the cash hoards and capitals which nations now kill and connive to gain. The result need not be an austere and ascetic regimen of life (though we seem to be gaining a new respect for the disciplines that have always been part of spiritual culture) but only a taste for plenitude—the sufficiency that liberates from need and greed.

Perhaps the saints have always been in touch with such truths; but when have so many ordinary mortals, having enjoyed and outgrown the charms of material abundance, been so open to the great teaching? When has it been more imperative for all the world's people to learn the limits of economic growth, the treacheries of affluence?*

Theodore Roszak, 1975

□

This is a hymn of thanksgiving from the people of the United States to their gods: the god of plenty, the god of profit, and the goddess of convenience:

Lords of Affluence and Avarice, Holy Creators of the Gross National Product, accept herewith these sacrifices in gratitude for the American continent which you bestowed on us, with all its mountains, rivers, lakes, seas, and valleys, and with the liberty given to each of us to do with them what we pleased.

In boundless gratitude for all this wealth, O gods of plenty, profit, and convenience, we lay at your feet a hundred billion cans of beer and bottles of Coke, sixty billion plastic containers and paper wrappings, ninety billion tons of raw sewage, and enough lethal chemicals in air and water to kill legions of animals and to invade our lungs with deadly gases and our blood with deadly poisons.

O lords of affluence and avarice, we repay this infinite generosity of the Gross National Product with Gross National Pollution: seas of oil, rivers of cars, the ugliest cities in the world, and all the sick and poor and criminal human waste produced by them.

These we have made in your name from the boundless beauties you stole from the Creator of all living things. May we now expiate these massive crimes by repudiating you and by restoring the beauty of life on Earth before its death claims us all.

Amen.

Marya Mannes
Bryant Park
NYC Earth Day
April 22, 1970

□

Voluntary Poverty is the only creative poverty, achieved, not suffered, necessary to freedom, the poverty of saints. It is a sure antidote to a valorized future, to striving against being, to ambition, root of power; to loss of love and fatalism for others at the expense of self.

Voluntary Poverty must be a deduction from wealth, from lack of necessity. It is precisely this lack which voluntary poverty will satisfy: it will replace all needs of wealth by a necessary minimum, a mere structure of being. This is not an event but rather a process, a genesis, an achievement.

Voluntary Poverty vanquishes Ego. Wherefore it becomes a tool of spirituality.

It can be logically and physically shown to be the conduct within materiality which reduces pain, thus furthering health and happiness.

It has a constant philosophical attitude, and it is perfectly adaptable to experience.

It carries a strong social commitment, recognizing institutionalized poverty as a deprivation of the right to voluntary poverty.

The pride of poverty, as the only creative pride, is an attribute of voluntary poverty only.

Voluntary Poverty is peace of mind.

André VandenBroeck

SOURCES

The gist of this anthology is its message rather than the scholarly minutia of its sources, many of which appear in the course of the book; others are not given because they seemed self-evident. Some fragments are as sourceless as the Nile, which is not sufficient reason to exclude them from the collection. For any inadvertent errors or omissions, apologies are extended and they will be corrected in future editions after notification to the editor.

In abridging material every effort has been made to retain the author's intention. Deletions and slight rearrangements were made at all times with an eye to the needs of a general audience, rather than one specialized or academic, and also to space requirements.

□

" 'He who needs riches least, enjoys riches most.' 'Author's name, please!' you say. . . . The phrase belongs to Epicurus, or Metrodorus, or some one of that particular thinking-shop. But what difference does it make who spoke the words? They were uttered for the world."

Seneca

The following sources reappear throughout the book:

All St. Augustine's *Confessions* tr. E. B. Pusey
All quotations from Sri Baba Hari Dass are from The Yellow Book:
  The Sayings of Baba Hari Dass, Lama Foundation Publications, 1973,
  or from secondary sources.
All Bacon from *Essays*
Bruce Barton of Batten, Barton, Durstine & Osborn Advertising Agency
All Bennett from *The Human Machine*
All Berrill from *Man's Emerging Mind*
All Berry from *A Continuous Harmony*
Bhagavad-Gita. The "Gita," the "New Testament" of Hindu Scriptures,
  dates from the first century B.C.
All Carlyle from *Sartor Resartus*
All Channing from *On the Elevation of the Laboring Classes*
All Confucius tr. Lin Yutang
All Dorothy Day from *Loaves and Fishes* unless otherwise stated
All DeBell from *The Environmental Handbook,* ed. DeBell
All *Dhammapada* tr. Irving Babbitt, 1936
All Dubos from *A God Within*
All *Ecclesiasticus,* or *The Wisdom of Jesus, Ben Sirach,* 190 B.C. edited
  by John G. Snaith
All Ehrlich from *The End of Affluence*
All Emerson from *Essays*
All Epictetus from *Golden Sayings,* tr. Hastings Crossley
All Epicurus tr. Cyril Bailey
All St. François de Sales from *Introduction to the Devout Life*

All Galbraith from *The Affluent Society*
All Hazrat Inayat Khan from *The Smiling Forehead*
All Heilbroner from *The Quest for Wealth*
All Hesiod from *Works and Days,* tr. Hugh G. Evelyn-White
All Robert Henri from *The Art Spirit*
All Jules Henry from *Culture Against Man*
All *I Ching* (which dates from mythical antiquity) tr. by Richard
   Wilhelm
All Illich from *Tools for Conviviality*
All William James from *The Varieties of Religious Experience*
All Kakuzo from *The Book of Tea*
All Kenko from *Tzurezure-Gusa (Essays in Idleness)* tr. G. B. Sansom
All Korzybski from *The Manhood of Humanity*
All Law from *A Serious Call to a Devout and Holy Life*
All Longinus from *On the Sublime,* tr. T. S. Dorsch
All Mandeville from *The Fable of the Bees*
All Marcus Aurelius from his *Meditations,* tr. George Long
All Milarepa from *One Hundred Thousand Songs of Milarepa,* tr.
   Garma C. C. Chang, unless otherwise stated
All Minucius Felix from Octavius, tr. Rudolph Arbesmann, OSA
All Montaigne from his *Essays,* tr. George B. Ives
All More from *Utopia*
All Keith Murray from "Suggestions toward an Ecologic Platform" in
   The Environmental Handbook
All Pascal from his *Thoughts,* tr. W. I. Trotter
All Patanjali from his *Yoga Aphorisms,* tr. Swami Vivekananda
All Péguy from *Basic Verities,* tr. Ann and Julian Green
All William Penn from *Fruits of Solitude*
All Plutarch's *Essays* tr. Louise Roper Loomis
All Pope from *Epistle to Bathurst, Of the Use of Riches* unless
   otherwise stated
All Ramakrishna from *The Gospel of Ramakrishna,* tr. Nikhilananda
All Regamey, *The Cross and the Christian*
All Reich from *The Greening of America*
All Reisman from *Abundance for What?*
All *Roman de la Rose* from Charles Dahlberg's tr. from the French by
   Guillaume de Lorris and Jean de Meun
All Roszak from *Where the Wasteland Ends* unless otherwise stated
All Rousseau from *Discourse on Inequality*
All *Sayings of the Fathers* dated approximately between 4th and 5th
   centuries, tr. Helen Waddell in *The Desert Fathers*

SOURCES

All Schopenhauer from *The World as Will*
All Schumacher from *Small Is Beautiful*
All Seneca's *Epistles* tr. Richard M. Gummere
All Seneca's *Essays* tr. John W. Basore unless stated otherwise
All Tagore from *Sadhana*
All *Tao Te Ching* (by Lao Tsu, 6th century B.C.?) tr. Gia-Fu Feng and Jane English unless otherwise stated
All Tawney from *The Acquisitive Society*
All Taylor from *The Rule and Exercises of Holy Living*
All St. Teresa from *The Way of Perfection,* tr. E. Allison Peers
All Theobald from *The Challenge of Abundance*
All Thoreau from *Walden* unless otherwise stated
All Tocqueville from *Democracy in America,* tr. Reeve and Brown
All Toffler from *Future Shock*
All Tolstoy from *My Religion*
All Traherne from *Centuries of Meditation*
All Underhill from *Mysticism*
All Veblen from *The Theory of the Leisure Class*
All Wagner from *The Simple Life,* (Paris, 1895), tr. Mary Louise Hendee
All Woolman from his *Journal* and *Major Essays*

The following sources refer to individual entries:

CHAPTER 2—IN PRAISE OF POVERTY

page
9–10　Fu Hsüan tr. Arthur Waley in *A Hundred and Seventy Chinese Poems*
11　Eckhart tr. Clark and Skinner
15　Zengetzu cited by Paul Reps in *Zen Flesh, Zen Bones*
16　Rilke from *The Book of Hours,* tr. A. VandenBroeck
17–18　Clement of Alexandria: *Can a Rich Man Be Saved,* tr. G. W. Butterworth
18　Young: *Insured by Hope*
19　Solon from Herodotus, tr. George Rawlinson
19　Plutarch from his *Lives,* tr. John Dryden
21　Gandhi in *Yeravda Mandir*
21　Bossuet's *Panegyrics of the Saints*
22　Eckhart tr. Jeanne Ancelet-Hustache

SOURCES

CHAPTER 3—LADY POVERTY

CHAPTER 4—LADY PECUNIA

page
46–47   Black Elk (John G. Neihardt) : *Black Elk Speaks*
47   Ovid's *Metamorphosis,* tr. Frank Justus Miller
47   Seneca's Essay: *Of Benefits*
48–49   Keynes: first paragraph from *Laissez-Faire and Communism,* second paragraph from *General Theory of Employment, Interest and Money*
49   St. Augustine's *Free Choice of the Will,* tr. Anna S. Benjamin
50   Plowman's *Bridge into the Future*
50   Weil's *Pre-War Notebooks,* tr. Richard Rees
50–51   A. VandenBroeck from a pamphlet written for the *America Center Project in Auroville, India,* 1965
53   Ruskin's *Crown of Wild Olive*
54   Aquinas: *Summa Theologica,* tr. Thomas Gilby
54   Weil's *Gravity and Grace,* tr. Arthur Wills
54–55   Young's *Functional Poverty*
56   Horace tr. Alexander Falconer Murison
58   Freud's *Future of an Illusion*
58–59   Einstein: *The World as I See It*
59   Carnegie: *The Gospel of Wealth*
59   Gandhi in *The Modern Review,* October 1935
60   Gandhi in *Yeravda Mandir*
61   D. Day quoted by Pete Hamill in the *New York Post,* 8–8–73
61–62   Bossuet's *Apostrophe to the Rich*
62   Peter Martyr was a royal Italian chronicler
63   Seneca's Essay: *On Tranquility of Mind*
63   Ruskin: *Morals and Religion*
63–64   Eckhart: *Sequere Me,* tr. Clark and Skinner

CHAPTER 5—THE RIGHT THING

64   Coriolanus from Plutarch's *Lives,* tr. John Dryden
65   Gampopa from "Precepts of the Gurus" in *Tibetan Yoga and Secret Doctrines,* ed. Evans-Wentz
66   Boehme's *Principles XXV, 74*
66   Burroughs' *Leaf and Tendril*
67   St. Augustine: *To the Nuns*
67   Seneca Essay: *To Helvia*
68–69   Seneca: conflation of *Epistles XVIII* and *XX*
71–72   Gandhi from *Speeches and Writings,* Madras, India
72   Seneca Essay: *On Tranquility of Mind*

SOURCES

page
110 Shakespeare's *Cymbeline*, I.vi.47
111 Newfield in *The Village Voice*, 11–8–75
111 Horace tr. Francis Howes
113 Roszak's *Unfinished Animal*
114 Salk: *Man Unfolding*

CHAPTER 7—CONTROLLED FOLLY

115 Kyōgen Shikan = Hsiang-yen Chih-hsien
116 Horace tr. Charles Stuart Calverly
116 Ruskin: *Crown of Wild Olive*
117 Shiva transcribed by Paul Reps in "Centering" in *Zen Flesh,
Zen Bones*
118 Descartes: *Discourse on Method*, tr. Arthur Wollaston
118 Browne: *Religio Medici*
118 Niffari from *The Book of Spiritual Sayings (Kitab-al-Mawaqif)*
tr. A. J. Arberry
119 Suso: *The Book of Truth*
119 Eckhart tr. C. de B. Evans
121 John of Salisbury's Correspondence: Ep.169, Giles, I, 268
121 Zeno from Plutarch's *Lives*
121–122 Boethius: *The Consolation of Philosophy*, conflation of
translations by Cooper and R. Green
122 Vespucci's *Letter To Pier Soderini*
122 Machiavelli: *The Prince*
122–123 Horace tr. John Conington
124 Gandhi in *Harijan* 21–7–46
124 Zerbolt: *The Spiritual Ascent*
125 *Parzival* tr. Helen Mustard and Charles Passage
126 Horace tr. Hubert Wetmore Wells
126 Seng-ts'an from *Chinese Tipitaka*, tr. Edward Conze
128 Horace tr. Philip Francis
129 Durckheim: *Daily Life as a Spiritual Exercise*
130 Barrett: *Irrational Man*
131 Julian's *Revelation of Divine Love*, ed. Grace Warrack, 1901
131 Mechthild's *Flowing Light of the Godhead*, tr. Lucy Menzies,
1953
131 Saichi cited in D. T. Suzuki's *Mysticism Christian and
Buddhist*
131 Seneca Essay: *On the Happy Life*

SOURCES

SOURCES

SOURCES

CHAPTER 11—CHOOSING THE IMAGE: LIFE/STYLE

SOURCES

CHAPTER 14—VOLUNTARY POVERTY AND THE U.S.A.

INDEX